NEW TESTAMENT CHRISTIANITY

VOL. I.

Edited by
Z. T. SWEENEY

WIPF & STOCK · Eugene, Oregon

Wipf and Stock Publishers
199 W 8th Ave, Suite 3
Eugene, OR 97401

New Testament Christianity, Vol. 1
By Sweeney, Z. T.
ISBN 13: 978-1-5326-4747-5
Publication date 1/18/2018
Previously published by Z. T. Sweeney, 1923

TABLE OF CONTENTS

	PAGE
To the Recipient	5
The Essential, the Important and the Indifferent, J. S. Lamar	7
The Sect Everywhere Spoken Against, Elijah Goodwin	29
Opportunity and Opposition, Isaac Errett	60
Hagar and Sarah—An Allegory, Milton B. Hopkins	86
Unconscious Enemies of Christianity, H. W. Everest	109
The Law of Pardon, J. S. Sweeney	141
The History of Redemption Reproduced in the Redeemed, J. S. Lamar	158
The Church the Body of Christ, Elijah Goodwin	170
The Kingdom of God, Benjamin Franklin	198
Faith and Sight, W. T. Moore	223

Contents

	PAGE
THE MIDDLE WALL, Elijah Goodwin	248
GOD'S PURPOSE IN THE AGES, H. W. Everest	279
SIN AND ITS CURE, Aylette Raines	307
THE NEW BIRTH, Alfred N. Gilbert	340
THE GREAT RENOVATION, James M. Mathes	366
THE WORSHIPING OF JESUS, M. P. Hayden	378
BAPTISM FOR REMISSION OF SINS IS JUSTIFICATION BY FAITH, J. S. Sweeney	391
THE ROYAL PRIESTHOOD, John A. Brooks	402
THE FELLOWSHIP, Isaac Errett	425
THE NAME "CHRISTIAN," Elijah Goodwin	453

TO THE RECIPIENT

THIS book is not for sale. It is for gratuitous distribution among preachers of the Christian Church. Its purpose is twofold:

1. To let our preachers—especially our young preachers—get a clear insight into the aims of the Restoration movement. 2. To arm them for the defense of that movement. When I was a young preacher I had a great horror of plagiarism. This led me to fail to use many a good book's contents, for fear that some of my members should have a copy of it. This book and its contents can be freely drawn upon without any such fear. The articles in this book have, most of them, been out of print for half a century.

There are only a few of this generation that have ever seen them. Besides, they are not private property, but the legacy of us all. I am contemplating the issue of four or five other volumes of a similar character for free circulation. These volumes will make a compendium of Christian Church literature. After reading this book I should be pleased to hear from you regarding its value, and, especially, the propriety of issuing other volumes of a similar character. If you *need and want them, say so.* Sincerely,

COLUMBUS, Ind. Z. T. SWEENEY.

THE ESSENTIAL, THE IMPORTANT AND THE INDIFFERENT

J. S. LAMAR

THE evidences in support of the Christian religion become stronger by the lapse of time and the progress of knowledge. There may be no positive addition to the amount of this evidence, but there is continual increase of its force and effect. The fact that Christianity survives and makes progress, notwithstanding the abuses it encounters from without, makes more and more clear and certain, to the discerning mind, its inherent vitality and essential divinity. It has stood the test of all manner of perversions and counterfeits; it has been forced to carry the burden of superstition and fanaticism; it has been loaded down with unscrupulous and selfish ecclesiasticism; its heavenly spirit and benign doctrine have been covered over with the grossest caricatures; but, in spite of all, it has lived and gone forward, and at last its true features have shone out through the mask of falsehood and delusion in all their pristine symmetry and beauty.

In like manner, the force of the instruments which, from time to time, its enemies have employed against it, has been neutralized, or else they have been captured, and converted into defensive and supporting weapons. This is signally exemplified in the bearing of natural science upon the question of miracles. The universal and uniform reign of law has been accepted as an established fact, and the idea of a supernatural intervention, which should modify the operation of law or act independently of it, has been regarded as absolutely incredible, because contrary to the settled and indisputable conclusions of science. Now, however, as knowledge advances, the thoughtful perceive that the laws of nature can not account for their own existence, nor for the origin of the matter on which they operate. Hence, by an inevitable necessity, science is compelled to base itself upon the miraculous, or else to rest its whole structure of law, of life, and of the matter which underlies them, upon the mist and mystery of the utterly unknown, which is both irrational and unscientific. If, therefore, the material universe rests upon miracle; if life, with its varied forms and characteristics, which modifies in so many ways the matter of the universe, is traced to the same source, there is certainly nothing incredible or unreasonable in saying that a spiritual system, designed to propagate and develop spiritual life, should also rest upon miracle.

The Essential, the Important, the Indifferent

To be sure, this does not prove the miracles of Scripture, but it does take away the presumption which science was supposed to have raised against them, and by so much adds to the force of the positive testimony in their support.

It is deeply to be regretted that, while Christianity in its essence is thus coming forth with more and more strength as the years roll away, it should still be exhibited to the world as a thing of conflicting creeds and discordant sects. Perhaps it is not possible, in the present condition of society, to correct this injurious state of things, but certainly there ought to be wisdom enough among the professors and advocates of this religion to determine and agree upon its absolute essentials. Hitherto this has not been done.

It is of comparatively little moment that there should be discussion on questions which, though they may be highly important, are still not vital. The proper understanding, classification and location of such matters in the system, exhibit Christianity as the purer, the better, the more consistent. Error on these points is an evil, it may be a great evil, but still not necessarily a fatal evil. We do well to combat it with earnest force, and to substitute for it, when possible, the wholesome and beneficent truth which it has displaced. But there should be no controversy respecting those things which enter into the very constitution and life of Christianity; those which are the differentia of the system, which being present, Christianity is present, and being absent, Christianity is absent. I say there should be no controversy among Christians on these points, because the fact of their being in controversy tends to cast doubt upon the whole institution, and thus to weaken and impair its strength as an aggressive power. These things ought to be equally dear to every heart, and set forth and supported by the combined force of all Christian intelligence and affection.

And yet, while it is obviously true that there are and must be elements and parts of Christianity which are absolutely and universally essential in it—elements without which it could not and would not be—it is still the misfortune and the reproach of Christians that they have not been able to agree as to what these essentials are. Some would place in the list matters which are simple, though it may be very highly important; others would elevate to this place matters which, in themselves, are indifferent; while some, on the other hand, would take out of this class elements which obviously belong to it.

The churches have devoted a great deal of earnest thought to the subordinate questions. They are learned in matters of government, and can render reasons for Episcopal, for Presbyterial, and for Congregational forms; the *pros* and *cons* of ritual and non-ritual worship they have at their fingers' ends; and not only in matters of govern-

The Essential, the Important, the Indifferent

ment and worship, but also in those of doctrine, particularly speculative doctrine, they are intelligent and ready. On these points, and such as these, they read and write and meditate. But the question that takes precedence of all others, that gives to them all their importance, be it much or little, that should demand consequently the first consideration, and be settled with gravest and most solemn care, this is dismissed with but slight notice, remanded as it were to some obscure corner, while the great partisan peculiarities and denominational differences are brought forward into the chief places, and honored with most respectful attention. Who gives any earnest thought or devotes any serious attention to the question, What constitutes a Christian? How a Christian should live, how he should worship, how he should be governed, how he may best promote the interest of his church, are practically of no consequence until it has first been determined how *he is to be a Christian at all*. And this, the leading, the all-important, the absolutely essential question, is still awaiting solution and settlement.

Believing that the Scriptural answer to this question, and the universal agreement of Christians in that answer, is the one thing most urgently needed to promote the triumph of Christianity, the writer proposes to contribute something which he hopes will tend to lead the thoughts of earnest minds in the direction of the result. He does not for a moment flatter himself that his own conclusions will be accepted by all, or even by many, as satisfactory and final, but he does hope that the momentous interests involved will induce the reader to weigh with candor what may be written, and to reject only where, in good conscience and fidelity to God and man, he feels that he must.

In prosecuting this purpose, the sacred Scriptures are to be regarded as the only source of authority. Preconceptions, preferences, traditional influences, and all reference to consequences, both personal and associational, are as much as possible to be laid aside, and the mind in perfect freedom is to approach the divine source of information with a hearty willingness to receive and adopt its communication. In the next place, it should be noted that the inquiry will be greatly simplified and abbreviated by considering that the *absolute essentials* of objective Christianity are those the reception of which *makes a man a Christian*. This is necessarily true, because he can not become a Christian, in any worthy sense of the term, without accepting Christianity in every part and element essential to its being, nor can he thus accept it without thereby becoming a Christian. Hence, putting these two preliminary points together, our inquiry is simply this: What, according to the Scriptures, must a man accept—that is, believe and do—in order that he may become a Christian?

The Essential, the Important, the Indifferent

THE ESSENTIAL.

The Protestant motto, "The Bible, the whole Bible, and nothing but the Bible, is the religion of Protestantism," is to be understood as indicating, not what *is* the true religion, but what is the source from which it is to be learned. The Bible reveals it, but the thing revealed is not the thing revealing. It supports, upholds, elaborates and develops it, but still the religion is one thing, and the teacher and defender of that religion, another. The Philippian jailor had never seen a Bible—the few words of the Lord which he heard and received on that memorable night made him a Christian. It is possible to conceive that he never enjoyed the benefit and blessing of additional instruction. And yet, if faithful to the light originally imparted to him, and the covenant into which he then entered, it is evident that he lived and died a Christian. Imperfect he certainly would have been in knowledge, graces, virtues— needing the nurture of the sacred lessons, and the comfort and strength of brotherly communion— but still a Christian. He had received Jesus Christ the Lord. His heart had bowed in loving allegiance to Him, and his life had been devoted in voluntary and unqualified submission to His authority. This was all. But this embraced everything that was absolutely essential. Christ is the embodiment of His own redeeming system, the fountain of all its light and love, the source of all its messages of grace, and all its beneficent institutions and ordinances. To accept Him, therefore, in the fullness of His nature and offices, as presented in the gospel, is the one thing needful. It establishes a vital connection between the sinner and the Saviour, the helpless and the Helper, the dying and Him who has the power over death, and, hence, Christianity, in its essence, can not necessarily be anything more, nor possibly anything less, than this.

If the matter could be left in the form of the above general statement, there would be no room for controversy. Every one would accept it as the obvious truth. That the man who sincerely and heartily embraces Christ, and gives himself to Him, is a Christian; and that he who fails or refuses to do this, whatever else he may do, is not, is a proposition that admits of no question. But the matter can not be left here. The responsibilities of the church to the world, lying in darkness, requires her, not only to preach the necessity of the acceptance of Christ, but also to tell men *how* He is to be accepted, and, especially, what is absolutely essential to such acceptance.

I suppose that no one would hesitate to say promptly, and without qualification or reserve, that Christ is to be accepted by faith. This is not only clearly taught in Scripture, it also follows of necessity from the nature of the case. If

The Essential, the Important, the Indifferent

Christianity were a mere abstract system of precepts and doctrines, it might be different, because these could be received and complied with, regardless of the authority of him who propounds them. But as it is in its essence the allegiance of the heart and the devotion of the life to a person, such allegiance and devotion can not be given without sincere and heartfelt faith in that person. A man may be relatively good or bad without this faith—as good as Cornelius, as bad as Saul of Tarsus—but in neither case is he a Christian. Christianity is not piety, nor alms-giving; not prayer and worship; all these, in various degrees of purity and impurity, may be found in every quarter of the world, and in every kind of religion—Jewish, Mohammedan, Pagan, Christian. Hence, when the gospel feast was spread, the servants were to bring in all that they found, both good and bad. The "good" still needed the atoning blood of Christ, the inspiration of His spotless life, the support and guidance of His divine authority, and the bad needed no more. In a word, they both alike needed to become Christians by accepting the Christ and enthroning Him in their hearts. And this they could only do by faith. It is needless to quote Scripture in support of this. It is the leading practical thought of the New Testament. We are justified by faith, sanctified by it, connected by it to the source of forgiveness, of life and salvation; so that he that believeth on the Son hath everlasting life, and he that believeth not shall not see life—"shall be damned."

One would have supposed that an element so essentially and transcendently important as this would have been studied with most scrupulous and anxious care, so as to be perfectly sure of including in the term "faith" all that necessarily and Scripturally belongs to it. Instead of which, men have sometimes played upon the word; contracted it to the smallest possible dimensions; emptied it of much of its necessary meaning, and actually substituted the term in place of its own contents and significance. The *word* faith is accepted instead of the *thing*—as if a trick of logic could save a soul.

Now, the Scriptural faith, through which such great and eternal blessings are promised, is not merely a blind trust that Christ will bestow these things upon us; but we are taught precisely *what* we are to believe concerning Christ, and in what character He is to be received. This is matter of revelation. It is taught by the Father in heaven. It is the subject of the Gospels, and to establish and confirm it was the object for which they were written. What we are to believe, therefore, is that Jesus is "the Christ, the Son of the living God." And we are to receive Him *as* such, or we do not have faith. A mere intellectual assent to this proposition, a concession, or even a feeling that it is true, is not sufficient. Our convictions

The Essential, the Important, the Indifferent

must be so deep and earnest and heartfelt that it leads to an actual and practical acceptance of the Lord Jesus *in* the character and offices which make Him the Christ. Wordy and windy *professions* of faith have no saving virtue. "Why call ye me Lord, Lord, and do not the things which I say?" Those who reject His authority practically deny, and, therefore, in their hearts deny, the Christhood of the Saviour, the very thing which is essential in the Christian faith. Hence, the Protestant dogma of "justification by faith *alone*" should be more carefully stated (and, indeed, it were better that the unscriptural phrase were entirely abandoned), lest it lead, as very often it does, to the false expectation of justification *by the mere act of believing*. For if men understand "faith alone" to exclude, not simply the works of the law and of human merit, but also the practical recognition of the authority of Christ, manifested by a voluntary and unreserved submission to that authority, such is not faith in the Scriptural sense, and if men are justified by this, they are justified, not *by* faith, but *without* faith.

In a word, the faith of the gospel, the faith so essential to the acceptance of Christ and the blessings offered in Him and through Him, includes obedience to Him as a part of itself. This truth not only follows necessarily from the nature of the formula of the faith, quoted above, but is also clearly taught by the apostle. For example, in

Rom. 10:16: "But they have not all obeyed the gospel. For Esaias saith, Lord, who hath believed our report?" The "report" is evidently the good news, or gospel of Christ. Isaiah foretold that many would not *believe* it, and, in proof that this was fulfilled, the apostle points to the many who have not *obeyed* it. The necessary conclusion is, that true belief of the gospel involves obedience to it. Otherwise we should have the absurdity of Christ accepted by faith, enthroned in the heart, welcomed, honored, loved, trusted, adored, at the same moment that He is repudiated and rejected.

But obedience is a life-work, a daily submission to the Master and consecration to His service. At what point in this obedient course may one claim to have accepted Christ, or to have become a Christian? Obedience being essential to the change, and obedience in its amplest meaning being the service of the whole life, we should expect that something would be, therefore, prescribed, as an approved and acceptable *entrance* upon the life service.

Previous to the introduction into the church of infant baptism, there was no confusion, hesitation nor doubt upon this point. The plain and explicit declaration of the Saviour, illustrated by the teaching and practice of the apostles, requiring believers to be baptized as the consummating and consecrating act of their conversion, as the act of obedience which tested their faith in the Saviour

The Essential, the Important, the Indifferent

as the Christ and brought them into covenant relations with Him, these declarations were gladly and gratefully received as the answer of the Lord Himself to man's most solemn question, "What must I do to be saved?"

No disaster which has overtaken the church has been fraught with greater evil than that which substituted, for the divine ordinance of baptizing believers for the remission of sins, the human institution of infant baptism. It has confused the whole scheme, deprived believers of the test which the Master Himself provided, and of the settled and certain assurance of acceptance and salvation which He was graciously pleased to append to that test, thus leaving men in the agony of doubt and uncertainty, or else forcing them, as it were, to rely upon excited feelings and fanatical transports instead of the word of God.

As a natural consequence, distrust of the word of the Lord has been the painful result, and men will gravely argue against the plainest, the most positive and explicit declaration of the Saviour, while claiming to be justified by faith in Him—as if they could believe in Him, in any proper sense, while disbelieving His truth.

Under the most solemn circumstances, on an occasion forever hallowed and dear, when He was sending out His apostles on the express mission of propagating His religion by making men Christians, He distinctly, plainly and formally tells them how this is to be done: "Preach the gospel to every creature; he that believeth and is baptized shall be saved." If this commission can be rejected, if its terms can be varied, if its provisions, either in whole or in part, can be set aside as nonessential, then Christianity is not an authoritative system, and faith in its Founder is mere emptiness and vanity. If we can repudiate this, we can repudiate all; and if we can repudiate all, we can repudiate Him.

If, then, the Scriptures, and the great source of light and love and life, brought to view in the Scriptures, are to be regarded as authority, and trusted as the only competent teachers on the subject before us, we must conclude that

1. There is no Christianity where Christ is not accepted.

2. He is not accepted where there is no Scriptural faith in Him.

3. There is no Scriptural faith in Him without obedience.

4. The first overt act of obedience, after the preparation of mind and heart, the command which stands in the forefront of the system, and which, resting alone upon Christ's authority, is the test of faith and submission, is baptism into the name of the Father, and of the Son, and of the Holy Spirit.

It is clear, from the practice of the apostles, that they so understood the Christian religion.

The Essential, the Important, the Indifferent

They preached Christ, led men by evidence to believe that He was the Christ, and then they immediately baptized them. Under their administration men became Christians, not by faith alone, but, like the Corinthians, they heard, believed, and were baptized. It was so in the beginning of the gospel, it continued so to the end of the period of inspiration, and, hence, if the question is to be settled by the only authority which Protestants can recognize—the Scriptures of truth—there can be no doubt that we have found the essentials of the Christian religion. *With* these, men were regarded as Christians; *without* them, they were not.

THE IMPORTANT.

It will require but a brief space in which to exhibit what is necessary to be shown under this head. Having seen that the whole Bible, and even the whole of the New Testament, is not involved in the process of *becoming* a Christian, we now reach the point where all of it has place. The larger part of the Bible serves to support, to illustrate and to elaborate its absolutely essential truths. In some sense, therefore, everything connected with Christianity is essential to it—if not to its being, to its well-being. But while some truths are designed to impart life, others are for nourishing and developing that life: some make us Christians; others make us better, wiser, stronger Christians. The former are absolutely, the latter are relatively, essential. The former build us *on* the foundation, the latter build us *up* on it. These latter, therefore, to avoid confusion, are classed here as important. Hence, we say that "all scripture given by inspiration of God is," not absolutely essential to individual salvation, but "*profitable* for doctrine, for reproof, for correction, for instruction in righteousness, that the man of God may be *perfect*, thoroughly furnished for all good works." Hence the gradual process of growth in knowledge, and the infinitely varied adaptations of the Scriptures to the different classes and states of men. Surely, it can not be necessary to do more than enunciate the general proposition. It is so obviously correct that no one will call it in question, while all will appreciate the importance of studying and learning the sacred Scriptures for the sake of their confirmatory facts, their helpful precepts, their stimulating examples, their encouragements, warnings, admonitions, and for the hopes and prospects which they set before the faithful, and for the light which they cast upon the darkness of present trials, and the solution they furnish of the problems of mysterious providences.

We may also include, under the present head, the numerous subordinate questions which, from time to time, agitate and divide religious society. Most of them are worthy of consideration, even

The Essential, the Important, the Indifferent

when viewed in the abstract, and a Christian will find comfort and satisfaction in reaching clear and trustworthy conclusions respecting them. The speculative doctrines of theologians, and their views and positions respecting recondite and obscure passages of Scripture, are of this class. The origin of evil, the effect of Adam's sin, the doctrine of election and predestination, of final perseverance or of possible lapse, the *modus* of spiritual operation, and the like, are questions which, positively speaking, it may not be very important to understand. When such speculative dogmas become the postulates of a system, and mold and color the institutions of Christ so as to affect and change the meaning of the gospel, we are obliged, if they are pressed upon our consideration at all, either to reverse the process of their propounders and bring these speculations to the test of the gospel, or else incur the danger of perverting and misunderstanding the very truth as it is in Jesus.

It is not necessary, for example, that we hold any philosophy of regeneration. The teaching of the Saviour and the apostles sets forth the whole subject with perfect explicitness, so that we know definitely and precisely what regeneration means, and how it is to be effected. But when we see the entire orthodox community wedded to a theory of regeneration which sets aside this authoritative teaching, and actually trusting in this theory, preaching it, practicing it, relying upon it, and with indefatigable zeal propagating it, notwithstanding its direct antagonism to some of the vital essentials of Christianity, the importance of the question is at once apparent.

But this field is too extensive to be traversed in detail. I, therefore, leave it for the final subject of this paper.

THE INDIFFERENT.

In the associated life and work of Christians, or in the exhibition and perpetuation of Christianity as a living institution, questions arise about matters in themselves essentially indifferent, but which, nevertheless, may have a relative importance. These often grow into living issues, and, if not wisely handled, may become the nuclei of parties. They are easily understood and appreciated when viewed in the distance, as matters of history, but when present, with all the passing preferences and antagonisms to which they give birth, the greatest circumspection and wisdom are required in dealing with them. One party will always be inclined to attach to them the high class of essentials, while the opposite, recognizing their abstract indifference, will be in danger of *treating* them with indifference. But, however trivial a matter may be, it acquires a sort of importance, and becomes sometimes practically momentous, by reason of the feelings and prejudices which are engendered by it.

The Essential, the Important, the Indifferent

There is nothing in which such a state of things is more likely to arise than in matters of public worship. These are left largely to the discretion, taste and sense of propriety of the worshipers; and tastes and judgments are likely to be forever, as they have always been, various. One man will think an organ the best thing possible to improve and perfect the singing of a congregation. Another, disgusted with the time and tune of untaught singers, will oppose congregational singing altogether, and insist that the choir and organist should alone participate in the service. Another still regards the organ itself as an abomination, and insists that it must be ruled out or it will rule him out. His sense of propriety is averse to it, his feelings are aroused against it, and ten chances to one if he does not come to fancy that his conscience is involved in the matter, and that the introduction of an organ is a sin as of witchcraft. All parties search the Scriptures for authority, *pro* and *con*, and finding none, as, of course, they do not, the matter not being the subject of Scripture teaching at all, they strain and force different texts into a sort of simulated support of their respective positions, while heart-burnings, uncharitable speeches, and all manner of evil thoughts, grow and multiply, until they die at last a natural death, and some other folly springs up to be nourished by the same passions, and pass through the same stages.

New Testament Christianity

What is needed on this whole class of questions is the hearty recognition, without reserve or qualification, of the liberties and rights of others.

No man, who has looked with philosophic care upon the present state of denominationalism, can have failed to notice that parties aggregate largely upon the single point of taste. Nine-tenths of those who are Presbyterians are so, not because they appreciate the distinctive doctrines of that sect, or really care anything about them, but because they like the Presbyterian way of doing things. Others, whose tastes, feelings, habits and preferences are different, go to the Methodists, for a similar reason. Others of a different type still become Episcopalians. And so, through the whole round. It is only the few who are actuated by consideration of doctrine and creed; for, whether true or false, it is beyond doubt that the prevailing opinion is that in these respects one church is about as good as another. But, aside from these, every man has his preference, and takes position as it leads him.

There is a profound philosophy underlying all this that the successful, the predominant, the true, catholic church of the future will be sure to recognize and act upon. It is the philosophy of not only tolerating, but of providing for, the various tastes and peculiar preferences of the respective classes of men on all these matters of indifference. Hold firmly, teach faithfully, and without

The Essential, the Important, the Indifferent

any wavering or compromise, the essential truth. Make men Christians according to Christ's law, and develop and perfect their moral and spiritual nature by His word and ordinances. Make them one in Him, one in their deference to His authority and their honor for His word, and in all things else leave them free. If they want an organ, let them have it. If they are averse to it, respect their preference. If they wish to conduct their worship like the Presbyterians, the Methodists, the Episcopalians, the Lutherans, let them do so, not only without censure, but with approbation.

But, alas! such is the weakness of human nature, and such the intolerance of the human heart, that we must have uniformity respecting all these secondary matters, even if it hazards the success of vital truth. Men must accept our tastes, be governed by our preference, worship in our mode, or have no place and no recognition among us.

For myself, I should prefer this spontaneous variety, on all these non-essential matters, to a stale, dry, dead uniformity. We seldom need two churches just alike in the same town. And it would be a positive blessing if, when there are several, each should be composed of those who find there their own peculiar tastes provided for, and their innocent preferences gratified. Thus without sects or denominations, with perfect concord and agreement in faith and doctrine, we should be able to reach all classes, and gather in and save from all quarters. Without this we shall address only a small fraction, and the multitudes will find among the diversities of denominations the satisfaction and comfort which we refused to afford them.

In cases where, from the sparseness of population or other causes, it is not possible to provide for all, the hearty recognition of the *principle* will lead in every instance to such compromises and adjustments as will be acceptable, because seen to be, under the circumstances, the best that can be done. The main point is to establish and honor the principle that unity of faith is consistent with diversity of opinion; and, moreover, that the freedom proclaimed for diversity of opinions is meaningless and delusive, unless it extends to the practices dictated by those opinions.

THE SECT EVERYWHERE SPOKEN AGAINST

ELIJAH GOODWIN

"But we desire to hear of thee what thou thinkest: for as concerning this sect, we know that everywhere it is spoken against."—Acts 28: 22.

IN the last chapters of the Acts of the Apostles, we have an account of Paul's perilous voyage to Rome, where he was taken as a prisoner for his devotion to, and his labors in, the cause of Christ. When he was brought into Rome, it is said: "Paul was suffered to dwell by himself, with a soldier that kept him. And it came to pass after three days, that Paul called the chief of the Jews together: and when they were come together, he said unto them, Men and brethren, though I have committed nothing against the people or customs of our fathers, yet was I delivered prisoner from Jerusalem, into the hands of the Romans; who, when they had examined me, would have let me go, because there was no cause of death in me. But when the Jews spake against it, I was constrained to appeal unto Cæsar; not that I had aught to accuse my nation of. For this cause, therefore,

New Testament Christianity

I called for you, to see you, and to speak with you, because for the hope of Israel I am bound with this chain.

"And they said unto him, We neither received letters out of Judæa concerning thee, neither any of the brethren that came shewed or spake any harm of you.

"*But we desire to hear of thee what thou thinkest: for as concerning this sect, we know that everywhere it is spoken against.*"

The course pursued by these persons is somewhat different from that which is pursued by many in our day. Now it is often made a reason why persons should not be heard, because the religious party to which they belong is everywhere spoken against. They now say, we *do not* desire to hear you, for, as for this sect, it is everywhere spoken against.

These persons, however, acted on a different principle. They seem to say, Now, Paul, we know that the sect to which you belong is spoken against all over the country; we know that all parties oppose you, but we are not willing to form our opinion of you or your party, by what others say. Your enemies may not fairly represent you; therefore, we desire to hear you on the subject. We want to hear an exposition of your views from one of the advocates of the system, from one of the leaders of this sect. Reader, was not that the more honorable course? Surely it was.

The Sect Everywhere Spoken Against

The term "sect" was not always as popular as it now is. It is used in the Scriptures, as well as in ecclesiastical history, in a bad sense. The Greek word translated "sect," in the Common Version, is *hairesis,* which occurs, in all its inflections, but nine times in the New Testament, and is translated in the Common Version "heresy" four times, and "sect" five times, which shows that the translators used the words "sect" and "heresy" interchangeably, as both signifying the same thing, and no one uses the term "heresy" in a favorable sense.

Greenfield defines the word thus: "Strictly, a choice, or opinion; hence, a faction; by impl., discord, contention." Hence, Paul numbers sects among the works of the flesh. In Gal. 5:20, he says: "Now the works of the flesh are manifest, which are these: Adultery, fornication, uncleanness, lasciviousness, idolatry, hatred, variance, emulations, wrath, strife, seditions, *heresies* [*hairesis*], envyings, murders, drunkenness, revellings, and such like." Thus the apostle classes *sects,* or *heresies,* with the blackest crimes ever committed by fallen humanity, and even goes so far as to say that "they who do such things shall not inherit the kingdom of God."

Webster defines the word "sect" thus: "1. A body, or number of persons, united in tenets, chiefly in philosophy or religion, but constituting a distinct party, by holding sentiments different

from other men. 2. A cutting scion (*obs.*)."
Though this mighty lexicographer marks this last meaning of the word "sect" as obsolete, he does not tell us how long it has been so. This was doubtless its primary meaning. It seems to have come from the same root from which we have the word "section," which means a part separated or cut off from the rest. Hence, Paul used the term which is rendered "sect" in our text, to represent a party cut off or separated from the true church of Christ. The church of Christ is not, then, properly speaking, a sect; it is the body, the true church of God; while a sect would be a section, a fragment, cut off from the true church of Christ. This is our reason for opposing sectarianism. We believe that the mystical body of Christ is "one body," and that in this body there should be no schism, and that no man has any divine right to draw away a party from the original organism and form a sect of it. This is heresy, the heresy so often condemned by the inspired writers. No doubt these persons used the word in this sense in our text. They were Jews, and doubtless they regarded Paul, and those with him who had embraced Christianity from among the Jews, as a *sect*, a party cut off from the great body of the Jewish nation.

But, in the further discussion of the subject, we will use the term merely to designate the body to which Paul belonged, and not to sanction its use.

The Sect Everywhere Spoken Against

I wish now to present a few plain propositions, in reference to the body of believers with which Paul stood identified. And, in doing this, I do not intend to make one leading statement that will not be received as true by all who may read this discourse:

1. *This sect was everywhere spoken against.* It seems that all parties—Jews and Gentiles, all, all—united in opposing this religious body. Though they could agree in nothing else, though they were at swords' points on every other subject, yet, when this sect was to be opposed, they dropped every other question for the time being, and made one common cause of this, one united effort to poison public opinion in reference to this people. And this is not the only people that have acted thus, nor is this the last time that such temporary unions have been formed, for the purpose of opposing the same cause.

Many hard things were said of these people. Let us notice some of them.

(1) *They were charged with worshiping God contrary to the laws of the fathers* (Acts 18:13). Now, this was a very serious charge. This, in our own day, would, in the estimation of many persons, destroy a man's religious reputation. Let it be said of a man that he is introducing forms of worship contrary to the old-established usages of the church, and how soon would he be cried down. The cry of "Innovation! Innovation!" would

stop all ears against him, and his standing would be ruined. But this was said of Paul and his party; this was one of the things that was spoken against this sect.

(2) *They were charged with heresy.* And this itself was enough to spoil Paul's influence with many persons. You know, gentle reader, that this charge would ruin a man's Christian standing and character, in many communities, even in our own day. Just point at a preacher, now, and cry *"Heresy! heresy!"* and you ruin his Christian influence with many. That Paul and his party were charged with heresy, we have already seen, from the meaning of the word translated "sect" in our text. On another occasion, when Paul made his defense before the Roman governor, after referring to their unfounded charges, and stating that they could not prove one of them, he said: "But this I confess, that after the way which *they call* heresy, so worship I the God of my fathers" (Acts 24:14). He does not acknowledge that he is guilty of heresy, but says that he worships in the way that they call heresy. This proves that they had charged him with heresy, and he admits that, if they are permitted to determine what is heresy, he would be condemned. And who would not be, even in this day of Bible light and Bible liberty, if the accusing party is permitted to prefer the charge, explain in what it consists, and apply the law?

The Sect Everywhere Spoken Against

(3) *They were charged with teaching customs which were not lawful for others to observe.* (See Acts 16:21.) Now, this was no small matter. For this charge, Paul and Silas were beaten with many stripes, and then confined in the dark, damp dungeon. And even in our own day this charge would ruin a man's Christian standing with some of the stricter sects. The rules and customs of many of these bodies are stereotyped, and their forms have become fixed. Now, let any one introduce new religious customs in such a community, and the popular cry of "New customs! Customs not lawful for us to observe!" would soon destroy his influence. But this was said of Paul and his party.

(4) *They were charged with turning the world upside down* (Acts 17:6). And this might have been necessary, for the world may have been down side up a long time. Still, it was a very severe charge, one that was well calculated to destroy the influence of this party. By this they meant that this sect was a set of *"disorganizers;* breaking up old ecclesiastical organisms, disturbing the quiet of society, unsettling everything, and settling nothing." There are men now living against whom these same things have been said, and they know something about the influence that such a charge has in stopping the ears of the people against a public teacher of religion. But all this, and much more that we can not now men-

New Testament Christianity

tion, was said of the religious party spoken of in our text.

2. My second general proposition in reference to this sect is *that, in the sight of God, this was the only true party, the only right church in the world.* Yes, notwithstanding all parties opposed this religious body, yet God acknowledged it, and it was the only church upon which He looked with approbation. To this proposition I am sure no one objects. All say it is true. And should not this fact teach us to be very sparing of our condemnatory denunciations against any people claiming to be the disciples of Christ, lest haply we be found to fight against God? Thus, it often happens that things that are highly esteemed of men are very lightly esteemed of God, while things that men disapprove and unite in condemning are very precious in the sight of God.

3. My third proposition is that God *never authorized the existence of any other sect or religious party.* Are you ready to say that this is one proposition that you can not receive? But when I tell you what I mean by divine authority, you will not object even to this statement. By divine authority I mean Bible authority. All the divine authority that we now have for the performance of any religious act is found in that blessed Book.

Now, I ask, where, in all the writings of the inspired apostles of Jesus Christ, do we find any command for forming any other sect than the one that was at this time everywhere spoken against? Where do we find even a clear license, or divine permit, to do such a thing? Every Bible student is ready to answer, Just nowhere at all.

Now, if all this is true, and true it is, how important is it that we understand all the distinguishing peculiarities of that party. If it was the only right party at that time, and if God has never authorized the formation of any other religious party, we should surely be anxious to learn all the leading features of that sect. I speak after the manner of men. Feeling the importance of this subject, we will attempt to define that party, that old sect. And, while engaged in this investigation, I wish every other sect to be left out of view; let us draw a veil over every other religious party, and especially the various sects that exist at the present time; let us leave all these behind the curtain, while we attempt a description of that party that was everywhere spoken against, some eighteen hundred years ago.

1. THEIR CREED.—When we attempt a description of any religious party in our day, the first thing we inquire for is their creed. And when we have found that, we have made a pretty fair start towards learning the distinguishing features of the party. We inquire, then, for the creed of this ancient sect. And by their creed I mean their book of religious faith and religious practice.

New Testament Christianity

Was it the Nicene Creed? You answer "No," because that creed was not formed for some 350 years after this sect had become so numerous as to be everywhere spoken against. If, then, we unanimously decide that the Nicene Creed was not the creed of that party, because of its youth, what shall we say of all church creeds which have been formed since? Not one of these can be the creed of that ancient sect; they are all too young, by many long centuries.

Speaking on this subject, one who spoke by inspiration said: "All scripture is given by inspiration of God, and is profitable for doctrine, for reproof, for correction, and for instruction in righteousness: that the man of God may be perfect, thoroughly furnished unto all good works" (2 Tim. 3:16, 17). This is said more in honor of their creed than to describe it; still, it points pretty clearly to the rule by which they regulated their religious practice.

He who is addressed in our text as one well acquainted with all the usages of this old sect, said of its members: "Now therefore ye are no more strangers and foreigners, but fellow-citizens with the saints, and of the household of God; and are built upon the foundation of the apostles and prophets, Jesus Christ himself being the chief corner stone" (Eph. 2:19, 20). Now, as observed in a former discourse, the constitution of a church is its foundation. Well, as Christianity is a system of faith as well as practice, all church constitutions express the faith of the church organized upon them. This expression of faith is called the creed of the church. Now, as this church was built upon the foundation of apostles and prophets, it was organized upon and governed by the teaching of these inspired men of God, and by that alone. Thus, we have found their creed; namely, the Holy Scriptures, given by divine inspiration.

Now, to this position I believe there is not one dissenting voice in all the land. All, both Catholic and Protestant, agree that the church had no creed, no rules of faith or practice, at the beginning, nor for many long years after, but the writings or teachings of the apostles and prophets of God. No controversy here.

2. THEIR NAME.—In describing a religious sect, it is very necessary to learn its name. Two churches sometimes adopt the same creed, and yet differ in name. I believe there are some five or six different sects that adopt the Westminster Confession of Faith. Hence, if you wish to know to which party a man belongs, it would not be enough to be told that his sect takes the above-named creed. You could not tell from that whether he was a Covenanter, Seceder, or Old or New School Presbyterian. Hence, we must, in such cases, inquire for the name of the sect. So, in pursuing our description of this ancient sect, we ask for its name.

New Testament Christianity

I learn from their creed, the Holy Scriptures, that they were called in their collective capacity the church of God, the church of the Lord, the church of Christ. (See 1 Cor. 1:1; Acts 20:28; 1 Tim. 3:5; Rom. 16:16; 1 Cor. 11:16.) In their individual capacity they were called saints, brethren, disciples of Christ, Christians. (See Eph. 1:1; Gal. 6:1; Acts 20:7; Acts 11:26.) Now, to any of these titles they would answer. Call them saints, and they would respond, "Here am I;" call them disciples of Christ, and they would say, "Speak, for thy servant heareth;" call them Methodist, Presbyterian, Campbellite, and they would be as silent as the grave; but call them *Christians,* and they would respond, "Here I am; for though I suffer as. a Christian, I am not ashamed." Or should you speak to one of this old sect in reference to his church, he would say he belonged to *"the church of God at Corinth"* (1 Cor. 1:2), or the church of the Lord at some other place.

Now, this was name enough; these titles, or any of them, showed precisely where those who wore it belonged. Having, then, found the name of this old party, let us consider:

3. THEIR OFFICERS AND CHURCH POLITY.—This is a very essential part, always, in giving a description of any religious body, for churches differ more in *polity,* or religious *politics,* than in anything else. Hence, you have never fully defined

any church until you have pointed out the officers and polity of the church.

Let us, then, inquire into the officers of that sect that was everywhere spoken against. To learn the truth on this subject, we must go to their creed, the New Testament. From a careful examination of this Book, we have discovered that in that ancient church there were bishops, deacons and evangelists.

(1) The term "elder," among them, meant older, or persons advanced in years, persons of age and experience, but as their bishops were all such men, this term is sometimes used in their book of faith and manners interchangeably with the term "bishop." Hence, Paul "sent to Ephesus and called the elders of the church," to whom he delivered a very touching address, near the close of which he said: "Take heed, therefore, unto yourselves, and to all the flock, over which the Holy Ghost hath made you overseers" (Acts 27:17-28).

Now, the word which is here rendered "overseers" is *episkopos*, which is the same that is rendered "bishop," wherever the term "bishop" occurs in the New Testament. We have a very similar expression in 1 Pet. 5:2: "Feed the flock of God which is among you, taking the *oversight* thereof." Here we have the word *episkopee*, which is defined in Liddell and Scott's English and Greek Lexicon thus: "An overseeing, charge; the office of an *episkopos*." Literally, feed the flock of God, exercising the bishop's office. Here, then, are two instances in which the *elders* are commanded to do the work of bishops, which shows that when the teachers in that old religious party used the term "elder" as an official title, they always applied it to the bishops or overseers of the church.

In further evidence of this position, read Tit. 1:5-7: "For this cause left I thee in Crete, that thou shouldst set in order the things that are wanting, and ordain elders in every city as I had appointed thee. If any be blameless, the husband of one wife, having faithful children, not accused of riot, or unruly; for a bishop must be blameless," etc. Why must the elders be of the character here described? Because a bishop must be blameless. Thus are the terms "elder" (*presbuteros*) and "bishop" (*episkopos*) employed to express the same office or work.

The work which pertained to this office, according to the creed of this *sect*, was to oversee and feed the church, to provide for the spiritual wants of the flock of God, to rule well, to keep things in order, and thus exercise a general oversight over the church, watching for the good of their souls, as they that must give account. And to them, or to their decisions and counsel, the members of the congregation were commanded to submit. (See Acts 20:28; 1 Pet. 5:2; 1 Thess. 5:12; 1 Tim. 5:17; Heb. 13:7, 17.)

The Sect Everywhere Spoken Against

In every individual congregation belonging to the body of which we now speak, where the proper character could be found, they had a plurality of these bishops or overseers. 'Tis true, congregations existed for a time without such ordained rulers. Hence, Titus was left in Crete, to ordain elders in every city, which shows that there were churches in those cities, but there was something wanting; they lacked the proper overseer, and, therefore, Titus is left with them, for the purpose of supplying this lack, by ordaining elders in every city. The same fact appears in the fourteenth chapter of Acts. Here we have an account of a general tour made by Paul and Barnabas, on which tour they visited many congregations, and it is said: "When they had ordained them elders in every church, and had prayed with fasting, they commended them to the Lord, on whom they believed" (Acts 14:23). I have quoted this Scripture to show that churches existed for awhile, among the sect which was so generally spoken against, without elders, but it also proves that when the proper character could be found, they had a plurality of ordained elders in every church or individual congregation. Here we have the church in the singular, and the elders in the plural. The same form of expression is found in Acts 20:17: Paul "sent to Ephesus, and called the elders of the church"—"church," singular; "elders," plural.

Some of these official elders seem to have labored in word and doctrine, or preached the gospel publicly, while others did not. Hence, the apostle says: "Let the elders that rule well be counted worthy of double honor, especially they who labor in word and doctrine" (1 Tim. 5:17). Those who thus labored seem to have been particularly regarded as the pastors of the church; hence, they were to have double honor. The word which is here rendered "honor" is *timee,* which occurs forty-one times in the New Testament, and is translated, in the Common Version, "precious," once; "sum," once; "honor," thirty-one times, and "price," eight times. Greenfield defines it: "A price, value, a price paid, money, honor; *i. e.,* state of honor, dignity, honor conferred, token of respect, etc." Most commentators think it means "price" or "reward" in 1 Tim. 5:17. The reason why such elders were to have double pay was because they rendered double service; they spent much time, labor and means in their devotion to the church, and, therefore, it was but just that they should be well sustained in the work, that they might give themselves wholly to it.

One other remark, in reference to these bishops. Their official power or work seems to have been confined to the individual congregation to which they belonged. We never read in their creed, or in their writings, of the *bishop* of the *churches,* but *bishops* of the *church.* (See Phil. 1:1.) Not one bishop to many churches, but many bishops to one church. Reader, don't begin to look behind the curtain, behind which we concealed all modern sects a short time ago. Let them remain out of view as much as possible, until we have completed our description of that ancient sect which is named in our text.

(2) *The deacons,* in this religious body, seem to have had the charge of all the temporal affairs of the congregations. In every organized body composed of flesh and blood and breath, there must necessarily be financial concerns. So, in the church of which we speak. The places where the congregations assembled had to be lighted, warmed, and kept in order; this required money. Then, the poor were to be provided for, and the Lord's table was to be furnished. All this, and many other contingencies, required funds; and this required men whose special business it should be to take charge of and oversee these matters. Such men were appointed in that old body, and they are, by common consent, called deacons. The word translated "deacon," in the Common Version, is *diakonos,* which means "a minister; one who renders service to another; an attendant; servant" (*Gre. Lex.*). According to the "Englishman's Greek Concordance," this word occurs thirty times in the New Testament. It is translated, in the King's Version, "minister," twenty times; "servant" seven times, and "deacon," three

times. But it is worthy of remark that they never applied this word to the bishops or elders of the church, notwithstanding they were servants of the church. Thus, it would seem that they intended, by this word, to express a particular class of servants. Such as served the church in reference to her temporal affairs were especially called deacons, though they may have also ministered the Word of life to the people. The first account we have of setting persons apart, to serve the church in this capacity, is recorded in Acts 6:2-6. These men were set apart, by prayer and the laying on of hands, to serve the congregation in raising, holding and distributing the funds which were raised for the support of the poor, and, especially, poor widows.

(3) *Evangelists.*—The term "evangelist" comes from the Greek word *unangelistees,* which means "one who announces glad tidings." To do the work of an evangelist, therefore, is to preach the gospel, or announce to the world the good news concerning Christ. Such were Timothy, Titus, and many others who, in the days of the apostles, went forth to proclaim salvation to the people, to convert sinners to God, and to plant Christian congregations.

Now, what a beautiful arrangement this was. In every individual congregation were the bishops, overseeing the church, laboring for their spiritual welfare, settling their difficulties, instructing the ignorant, strengthening the weak, encouraging the fearful, seeking out and restoring the wandering, and building up all upon their most holy faith. Then, there were the deacons, superintending all the temporal affairs of the congregation, seeing that the poor, the widows and orphans were provided for, and that all the contributions of the brethren were properly and judiciously applied. And then there were the evangelists, going like swift-winged messengers of light, bearing the news of salvation to a dying world, turning them from darkness to light, and from the power of Satan to God, planting new congregations, and thus enlarging the borders of Zion.

Thus we see something of the offices and order of that sect which was everywhere spoken against.

(4) *Their Ordinances.*—In order to give a full description of any religious denomination, we must always inquire into their ordinances. Some parties agree in almost everything but their ordinances. Some sprinkle water upon their members, while others immerse their members in water. Now, this constitutes a very striking difference, which would distinguish these parties from each other, if they were alike in everything else.

Well, the church that we are endeavoring to describe had its ordinances also. They observed one leading and important ordinance, which was sufficient of itself to distinguish this party from every other sect upon earth. I think I may safely say that among all the various religious sects that then existed, or that ever had existed, human or divine, no such ordinance as this ever had existed. I ask, Where was it ever known that a religious sect observed a public ordinance in memory of the death of the founder of the party? The birthdays of kings, and of the founders of kingdoms and empires, have often been celebrated by public festivals, but did ever a nation thus celebrate the day on which a benefactor died?

Such, however, is the nature of that distinguishing ordinance to which I now refer. It is sometimes called, in their book of faith and manners, *the Lord's Supper;* sometimes it is simply called *the breaking of bread,* and sometimes, *the communion of the Lord's body, and of the Lord's blood.* (See 1 Cor. 11:20; Acts 20:7; 1 Cor. 10:16.)

This ordinance was very simple in its form, but very powerful in its import. It consisted, simply, in giving thanks, breaking and eating of bread, and drinking from the cup the fruit of the vine, in memory of the broken body and shed blood of Jesus the Christ. There is one fact connected with the founder of this body of people which accounts for this most unusual ordinance, and that is that, though "he was put to death in the flesh, he was quickened by the Spirit." Yes, He rose from the dead on the third glorious morn, and thus brought to light, life and immortality.

The Sect Everywhere Spoken Against

Well, then, may His followers commemorate His death, since by His death and resurrection He has secured salvation from sin, and eternal life to all who believe in Him and obey His holy commands.

Am I asked on what day they attended to this significant ordinance? They "came together on the first day of the week to break bread" (Acts 20:7). But do you ask, "On what first day"? I answer, "On *the* first day." I can not learn, from all the records they have left us of their customs, that they made any difference in Lord's Days. The record does not say that they came together on *a* first day, or on *some* first day, but on *the* first day. As often, then, as the first day of the week came, they came together to observe this ordinance, and thus they commemorated two of the most interesting events that have ever transpired since time commenced her march, conjointly: the death of Christ for our sins, and His resurrection for our justification. This, of itself, was enough to distinguish the sect from all others.

This people practiced another ordinance, which was not so much an ordinance *in the church* as an initiatory rite into the church. This ordinance is called *baptism*. All the members of this sect were baptized. While defining this religious body, it may not be amiss to state that, with them, baptism was a burial. Hence, the apostle said:

"You are buried with him by baptism" (Rom. 6:4; Col. 2, 12).

(5) *Their manner of converting sinners, and adding them to the church,* or, to use a modern phrase, their manner of making Christians. Their practice in this matter was quite different from most of the other religious bodies around them. The apostle Paul speaks of their practice, in the fourth chapter of 2 Corinthians, first *negatively,* and then *affirmatively.* He first tells what they did not do, and then what they did do. He says they "renounced the hidden things of dishonesty." They used no unfair means to make proselytes; they did not "walk in craftiness"; they used no cunning trickery to seduce men into their party; they renounced all the secret tricks and cunning craftiness and hidden mysteries, by means of which the leaders of other parties deceived the people. (See Eph. 4:14.) They pursued an open, aboveboard, straightforward course. They did not *"handle the word of God deceitfully."*

How may a man do this? What is meant by "handling the word of God deceitfully"? I answer, by making it speak a language that the author did not intend, or convey a different idea from what the Lord intended to convey. This may be done by taking parts of sentences from different portions of the Book, and putting them together under another arrangement. In this way a man can prove anything he pleases from the

The Sect Everywhere Spoken Against

Bible. The Scripture says that Judas "went and hanged himself"; and Jesus says: "Go thou and do likewise." Now, this is all Scripture, and what does it prove? Why, that a man should hang himself. Now, this is handling the word of God deceitfully.

The same may be done by suppressing a part of a sentence. Example: "Let him that stole, steal" (Eph. 4:28). Now, that is every word Scripture, and it proves that it is right to steal. But the apostle finishes the sentence with the words *"no more"*—"Let him that stole, steal no more." Now, the preachers in that old sect never handled the word of the Lord in this way. They did not disconnect and scrap the word of God; they did not handle it deceitfully, for the purpose of making proselytes. They gave God's word fair play. By "manifestation of the truth, they commended themselves to every man's conscience in the sight of God." They proclaimed the plain, unvarnished truth, the whole truth, and nothing but the truth, and thus, by "warning every man, and teaching every man," they reached the hearts and consciences of the people.

But when they thus reached their consciences, until they were pierced in heart, and asked what they must do, what course did these teachers pursue? What did they tell the poor, trembling, heart-smitten, anxious, inquiring, mourning seeker to do? Reader, don't call from behind the curtain any sect now living, until we hear the direction of one of the leaders and teachers in the sect whose distinguishing features we are now endeavoring to set before you, given to persons in this very distressing state of mind. Hear it, reader; hear it with an honest heart: *"Repent, and be baptized every one of you in the name of Jesus Christ for the remission of sins; and you shall receive the gift of the Holy Ghost"* (Acts 2:38).

Now, what did these mourning souls do? Did they begin to object, and argue the case with the apostle? Did they begin to inquire what good there was in *water baptism?* No, verily. They were in good earnest; they were honest before God. Hence, it is said: "Then they that gladly received his word were baptized: and the same day there were added unto them about three thousand souls" (v. 41). Here, then, is a practical illustration of their whole process of making Christians and adding them to the church.

Now we are prepared to contemplate this ancient sect in all its parts. It now stands out before us in bold relief. We have found its creed, its name, its officers and polity, its ordinances, and its manner of converting sinners and adding them to the church. We have seen that all who became members of this religious body heard the Word until it was commended to their hearts, and that they then repented of their sins, and were baptized. Mark this well. They were all obedient believers.

Now, I feel very confident that no man who professes faith in Christ, or in His word, will dispute one proposition that we have made, or one of the distinguishing features that we have pointed out in the religious party that we have been describing, unless it be the very last sentence which I penned in the description. But if any doubt the truth of that statement, we must leave them to their own musing, only requesting them to examine that proposition very carefully, before making a final decision.

We now have one important question to answer, after which we shall close this discourse. Does that ancient sect now exist? Is it still standing, or has it waxed old, like a garment, and vanished away? Have the desolating ravages of ambitious men, which have uprooted kingdoms, desolated countries, blotted from existence churches, and changed times and seasons, slain that old party of which we have been speaking? Has the ever-rolling wave of time swept it away forever, or does it still maintain a visible existence among the myriads of ecclesiastical organisms of the present day? These, gentle reader, are important questions. If, as you have admitted, that old sect was the only right party at that time, and if there is no Bible authority for the existence of any other religious party or body, then it is important to know whether that party is dead or alive. We then repeat the question, Does that party now exist?

"Yes," says the Roman Catholic, "it still exists. Here it is; we are that same old sect, come down in regular succession from the apostles. We have the regular apostolic succession, and, therefore, are the same body of people, and all who desire to be members of the real, genuine, old mother church, should join us."

But I hear an objection—a deep-toned, thundering voice, like the sound of many waters—crying out, "*No, no!* we are the true party. We are the same old sect that was everywhere spoken against; we have the true and regular apostolic succession." This voice comes of the Protestant Episcopalian Church, or the *high church* of England. But, if this is true, she must have changed her position since our text was written, for then it was the *low* church spoken against all over the country. But it is not my object to settle the question as to which is, or which is not, the true church. I only make this suggestion in passing.

I suppose, however, that it is a well-known fact that there is a controversy now going on between the Roman Catholics and Episcopalians, on the subject of the succession. Each seems to admit that if they can not trace their church organization and their ministerial ordination through an unbroken chain back to the apostles, their church fails to be the church of Christ; that it is an unauthorized sect; a figment broken off from the true church or body of Christ.

The Protestant Episcopal Church reasons thus: They say that the church is no more a new church after the efforts of Henry the VIII., than a man is a new man when he falls into a mud puddle and then washes himself clean. He may look very different, but still he is the same man. So, they say, it was with the church. They admit that the church had become very corrupt, that it was much defiled by sin; but that Henry VIII., of England, cleansed the church, washing off its impurities, and that these excrescences gathered themselves together, and by some unholy principle of adhesion formed the Roman Catholic Church! This, however, is denied by the Church of Rome. She contends that she is the only holy and apostolic church, and that Henry was excommunicated for his worldly ambition and fleshly lusts, and his want of fidelity to his legal wife.

But, while these two great religious bodies are contending for the apostolic succession, each endeavoring to defend its title to primitive ground, I hear the muttering sound of voices, as of a mighty multitude all in confusion, crying out and saying: "You are both wrong; we are the old sect; we have come down in a regular line from apostolic times." But, when pressed at this point, I find most of them denying the succession as claimed by the churches of Rome and England,

New Testament Christianity

and contending that every man has a right to make his own church, and found his own church polity!

Reader, are you a Protestant? Then I know your course of reasoning, when you are examining the claims of the Church of Rome to being the sect spoken of in our text. You first ascertain all the leading features of that old party, and then you compare these with the leading peculiarities of the church as it now exists; and if these do not correspond, you say the churches are not the same. Suppose, for illustration, that some leading member of the Methodist Church should assume that the Methodist Church is the real old Baptist Church, that had come down in regular succession from the days of Roger Williams. You would reply: "This can not be; as a church, you have a different creed, a different name, different officers, different ordinances, and you have a different mode of receiving members; therefore, being different from the Baptists in all these points, it can not be the same church."

Just so you reason the case with the Romish Church. You bring up before your mind all the leading, distinguishing features of that old church that was so generally spoken against in the beginning, just as I have done in this discourse, and then you compare these items with the corresponding items in the Romish Church, and, finding such a great difference, you decide that that is not

The Sect Everywhere Spoken Against

the same church. You say the Romish Church has a very different creed and system of church polity from that old sect; that it is different in name, and, as to officers, it has swarms of these that were unknown in that old church, and as to ordinances, you say that there is no resemblance between them at all. Now, you say, with all these differences, it can not be the same church.

In all this, my dear reader, you are correct. Your reasonings are logical and fair, and your conclusions just and true.

Now, all that we ask of one who may be desirous to know the truth on this subject, is for him to adopt the same course of reasoning in every case, when attempting to ascertain which is the sect that is named in our text. Bring up all these leading features, and compare them with those of any denomination now claiming succession from that old religious body, and I will be satisfied with the result. Whenever you find a religious body, or church, organized upon and governed by the same creed and church laws, and by them alone, called by the same name, having the same officers, with the same powers—practicing the same ordinances and using the same means for the conversion of sinners—telling the penitent believer to do the same things for remission, and receiving members into the church in the same way that that old party did, you have then found the same sect, the same religious body. Yes, this is the true succession.

It is not a succession of ordination, or of ordained ministers, but a succession of faith and practice, that makes the true, holy, apostolic succession.

Should a company of persons who never saw a Bible or a priest be shipwrecked, and cast upon some uninhabited island; should they there find a Bible containing both Testaments, and, by reading it, they all become firm believers in Christ, the Son of God, and the divine Saviour—suppose, then, that one of the company baptizes one of the number, and he, in turn, baptizes the rest; suppose, then, that they adopt that holy Book, containing the teaching of the apostles and prophets of God, as their only rule of faith and practice; they appoint their bishops and deacons according to that Book, and proceed to keep the ordinances as they were delivered by the apostles—that would be, to all intents and purposes, the same body of people—not the same persons, but the same religious organism. It would be the regular, pure and holy apostolic church.

Now, I am not going to make the application. My object has been to prepare the reader of this discourse to make the application himself. I have endeavored to develop great, important principles—principles the truth of which is uncontroverted—hoping that the reader will have interest enough in the subject of church standing to give the subject careful examination, and honesty of heart and nobility of soul sufficient to enable him to act

The Sect Everywhere Spoken Against

according to the honest convictions of his own mind, enlightened by truth divine, on the great subject of Christianity.

Reader, this is no ordinary subject. The importance of this theme overreaches the cold boundaries of time, and lays hold on things eternal and invisible. Your interests in two worlds depend upon your action in the premises. Oh, then, be honest with yourself, your conscience, your Bible, your God, and act for eternity while you may,

OPPORTUNITY AND OPPOSITION

An Address Delivered by ISAAC ERRETT, May 23, 1871

"For a great and effectual door is opened unto me; and there are many adversaries."—1 Cor. 16: 9.

IN Scripture style, and indeed in classic style, "door," in its metaphorical use, often signifies *an opportunity*. Thus (Acts 14: 27) Paul and Barnabas, on returning from their first missionary tour, related to the church in Antioch "what things God did by them, and that he had opened a door of faith for the Gentiles." This does not mean, as many have supposed, that faith was the door through which the Gentiles entered into the church, but simply that God had given them an opportunity to believe, through the preaching of Paul and Barnabas. Again: "When I came to Troas to preach Christ's gospel, and a door was opened unto me of the Lord" (2 Cor. 2: 12)—that is, a good opportunity was offered to preach the gospel. And to the Colossians he says: "Pray for us that God would open to us a door of utterance to speak the mystery of Christ'' (Col. 4:3)—that is, an opportunity to utter the Word. And to the church in Philadelphia, He "who opens and none can shut, and shuts and none can open," says: "I have set before thee an open door, which no one is able to shut" (Rev. 3:7, 8). I have made an opportunity of deliverance from thine adversaries, and an occasion to do good in my service.

According to our text, an unusual opportunity was afforded at Ephesus for preaching the gospel; it is called a *great* opportunity in reference to its *extent*, and *effectual* in regard to the effectiveness of the labor bestowed

We learn from all these texts that, in preaching the gospel, success depends much on the *providential openings* that are granted. While the means divinely ordained for the world's salvation are always the same, and the gospel is as much the power of God at one time as at another, so far as its essential efficacy is concerned, yet it does not always produce the same results, because the means of access to the hearts of men are not all times equal. It is not the gospel in a book or in the mind of the preacher that is the power of God to salvation, but the gospel in the sinner's heart, understood, believed and accepted. But the means of access to the individual heart, and to the hearts of a whole community, are no part of the gospel. They furnish a channel through which that power flows. Power, even to almightiness, may be locked

New Testament Christianity

up in the gospel, but it is just equal to no power at all until it is brought to bear upon the sinner for whose salvation it is intended. It must, in some way, be transferred to his mind and heart and conscience; and, in effecting this transfer, much depends upon the door of opportunity that may be opened. The state of the individual mind; the state of the public mind; the influences that may hold up or cast down ancient prejudices—that may carnalize the tastes of a population so as to destroy all desire after spiritual things, or blast that carnality by terrible experiences that set all hearts to hungering and thirsting after righteousness—that may lead a political power to prohibit the preaching of the gospel, or to allow the liberty of speech—that hold up a system of error or imposture in a particular juncture, reveal its untrustworthiness and hideousness, so as to cause a decay of public sentiment: these have much to do with the matter of the gospel's success. Hence, the success of the gospel is dependent on Divine Providence, and its success is, therefore, a subject of prayer. God raises up and casts down men and nations, grants prosperity to blind and harden men, and sends adversity to open their eyes and soften their hearts. The winds and waves, the treasures of rain and hail and thunder and lightning, the caterpillar, the palmer-worm and the locusts, war, famine, pestilence, commercial prosperity and disaster, and all other agencies and instrumentalities that affect the condition of society, and move on the hearts of men for salvation or destruction, are at His command. He opens, and none can shut; He shuts, and none can open.

This suggests to us a truth of the greatest possible moment. The success of the gospel is not simply a question of ways and means of our creation or at our disposal. The gospel may have in it, as it has, all the saving power necessary for its object; we may have all the means necessary for its promulgation, eloquent preachers, learned advocates, powerful writers, men and money, numbers, social position, and all else that wise policy or worldly prudence could suggest, and yet, if the door is not opened, if God open not the way of access to the hearts of men, vain are wealth and learning and skill and system, and social influence, and vain, too, is gospel truth and grace. I apprehend that much of the controversy on spiritual influence would cease if parties understood each other. I am inclined to think that what others call, in the one phase of the subject, the work of the *Holy Ghost,* we call *Divine Providence,* and the difference is about the *name* rather than the *thing.* Certain it is we all admit that, while Paul may plant and Apollos water, it is God, and God alone, that gives the increase. We all pray for the conversion of sinners. We all feel, though none of us as deeply as we should, that if anything is done in the conversion of sinners, the utmost that man can say is, "Behold what God has done by me." With others, this is called the immediate work of the Spirit; with us, it is called the gracious providence of God. Call it what you will, there must be the door opened, and it is God who opens the door. It is ours to pray for the opening, to watch for the opening, and, when it comes, to enter in and work with God and for Him.

But our text places in juxtaposition with the thought of great opportunity providentially afforded, another thought, not in itself startling, but startling from the place it occupies, and the relation it bears; that is, *great opposition*. Great opportunity and great opposition. A great and effectual door is opened, *and there are many adversaries*. Strangely as this sounds, the association is not unnatural. The same soil that produces a luxuriant yield of corn produces also a corresponding abundance of weeds and noxious plants. The same sun and rain that make the grass to spring, start also the poisonous vine, and the slimy serpent is warmed into life by the beams of the same sun that speeds the flight of the lark and wakes his morning song. If the press gives us Bibles, it gives us also infidel books as readily. If free speech enables us to preach the gospel without restraint, it equally removes restraint from the enemy of the gospel. If the influences of the age quicken intellect and promote education, this fur-

Opportunity and Opposition

nishes power as well to the foe as to the friend of Christ. If steam speeds the movements of the herald of truth, it equally speeds the movements of his adversary. And if the hearts of good men are stirred to attempt great things for God, it is to be expected that the hearts of bad men will be stirred to attempt great things in opposition. Moreover, there is a law in the moral universe corresponding to that which prevails in the material system, by virtue of which harmony and equipoise are developed by the play of antagonistic forces. The centripetal and centrifugal forces belong to both systems, and far beyond what we can comprehend in our greatest grasp of thought, the purposes of God in behalf of ultimate order, peace and blessedness are developed in the fierce antagonisms of good and evil, truth and falsehood, life and death. We need not wonder, therefore, at the juxtaposition in our text of great opportunities with great oppositions. Inattention to the inevitable association of these is what gives rise to the entirely opposite estimates made of the age we live in. To some it is an age of great progress and of great glory. Slavery is dying; liberty is triumphant; thrones of despotism are tottering; Church and State are dissolving their accursed partnership; light is spreading; the public conscience is becoming more sensitive; science is winning marvelous triumphs; war is losing its horrors; sectarianism is being shorn of its prestige;

nations are coming into closer relations; barbarous empires are opening their gates to Christian influences, and the millennium is surely coming! On the other hand, we have a most lugubrious outlook and most dolorous vaticinations. Wars are more terrible than ever; crime is rampant; vice is shameless; pride and fashion are swallowing up all manly virtue and womanly goodness; stock gambling and drunkenness have utterly debauched the public conscience; marriage has lost its sacredness, and the foundations of society are crumbling; liberty is but a name; imperial despotism and red republicanism are but different phases of the same utter godlessness that blots out all virtue; the Pope of Rome is supplanted by the more hateful and reckless king of Italy; crime is increasing, even in the lands where it was supposed it had reached its maximum; the world is godless, the church is Christless, and there is no hope left for truth and virtue but for Christ to come and put an end to the controversy by the terrors of omnipotence.

These parties have each but half a picture. They are both right and both wrong, like the knights who fought over the shield which was gold on one side and silver on the other, but of which they each had seen but one side. Our text affords a solution of the difficulty: a great and effectual door is opened, and there are many adversaries.

Opportunity and Opposition

This leads into the heart of our discourse—the encouragements and discouragements that belong to the work in which we are engaged. It is wise to look at both.

I. Let us look at the great and effectual door that is opened to us in our missionary work. Going back half a century to the beginning of this reformatory movement, let us look at the errors and wrongs which the reformers complained of as justifying their plea for reformation.

1. Numerous, ever-increasing and hostile sects, filled with strife and bitterness, "hateful and hating one another."

2. Human creeds, some of them of large dimensions, embodying much more philosophy than faith, and substituting metaphysical speculations for the simplicity of the gospel of Christ; and these erected into standards of orthodoxy and tests of fellowship, so that believers who ought to have been one in Christ were alienated and divided by rival systems of theology, and ruled by party watchwords, such as the Bible knows nothing of, to the great scandal of the cause of Christ.

3. Religious mysticism, the simple faith and obedience to which the gospel calls us, being supplanted by mystical conceptions of spiritual influence, so that dreams, visions, strange sights and sounds, and unusual emotions were of more authority in the matter of regeneration and conversion than the plainest declarations of the word

of God, and a text of Scripture, springing into the memory under strong excitement of the mind, was more the voice of God than the severest deductions resulting from the most careful and enlightened exegesis of the holy Scriptures.

4. Hierarchical arrogance, the uplifting of clerical and priestly claims to expound the Scriptures and rule the church of God, so that merely human inventions and pretensions were making void the commandments of God, and defacing, if not destroying, the character of the church of Christ as a spiritual brotherhood. Along with this were formalism and ritualism, the other extreme from that blind emotionalism mentioned in the last item, reducing religion to a stereotyped set of doctrines and round of ceremonies almost wholly unknown to the primitive church.

5. A superstitious reverence for King James' Version of the Scriptures, so that even its errors and absurdities were regarded as inspired, and all attempts to remove them by faithful and learned criticism as sacrilege.

The results of all this were deplorable. Religion was to myriads a matter of awful uncertainty; there was no telling whether one was a Christian or not. Men vibrated between exultant hope and blank despair, all lifelong robbed of settled peace in believing. Myriads more were driven into doubt as to the truth of religion itself. Party animosities not only divided and distracted the forces which ought to have been moving on in harmony for the conquest of the world, but presented so hateful an aspect of religious life to the world as to rob it of converting power. The clangor and clashings of the theological warfares did not sound like that sweet singing of the angels when Christ was born: "Glory to God in the highest, peace on earth and good will to man." Moreover, the rivalries of the sects gave rise to every sort of effort, on the part of each, to gain or to maintain the ascendency, so that the church was largely secularized, and the power of primitive unity, spirituality and singleness of purpose almost utterly lost. This is a sad picture, but it is very feebly and dimly drawn, and does injustice to the truth in its too limited and too feeble statements.

In opposition to all this, the plea for reformation was sent forth, marked by the following distinctive features:

1. The essential unity of the followers of Christ. Sects are unscriptural, mischievous and wicked, and the people of God should abandon them and return to the original teaching of one Lord, one faith, one baptism, one body, one Spirit, one hope, one God and Father of all.

2. The alone-sufficiency and the all-sufficiency of the holy Scriptures as a rule of faith and practice. Authoritative human creeds should be abandoned, and nothing be required as a term of membership in the church, or as a bond of fellowship, for

which there can not be produced a "Thus saith the Lord," in express precept or approved precedent.

3. The gospel, the power of God to salvation, in opposition to all professed revelations of the Spirit in dreams, visions, voices and impressions. The gospel consists of (1) * facts—facts replete with the wisdom, grace and power of God; facts to be believed, and which, when believed, will shatter skepticism, destroy pride, root out sinful desires, and bring the soul in repentance to bow humbly to the will of God; (2) of commandments—commandments to be obeyed; commandments in cheerfully accepting which we may test our change of heart, and learn how far we are genuinely converted; (3) of promises—promises of pardon, adoption, of the Holy Spirit, of fatherly guidance, priestly intercession, and spiritual fellowship, and of the joys of an endless life; promises to be appropriated and enjoyed as the result of hearty obedience to the gospel. So that when we believe the facts, obey the commandments and enjoy the promises of the gospel, we are Christians, and may know it and rejoice in it as surely as we may know the existence of God and of Christ. And all this is in the gospel always, everywhere, day and night, year in and year out, for every one who will accept it, and for all on precisely the same conditions.

4. The equal brotherhood of all Christians—all children of God, all kings and priests to God. No

popes, no cardinals, no archbishops, no clergy, no hierarchy; "for ye are all one in Christ Jesus." Fatherly teachers and guides, brotherly helpers, and genuine brotherly co-operation in all good works, these may be and must be, but no lords over the heritage of God, none to have dominion over our faith.

5. The *pure* word of God as our light and our food, and fellowship in keeping the commandments of our Lord Jesus Christ. Every one bound to honor Jesus and to obey Him—no one bound in aught outside of this. Every soul answerable to God for its convictions and doings in all else—answerable to its brethren only for integrity in the faith of Christ and faithful obedience to His laws. Hence, it became a matter of first importance to possess the pure word of God, and to cast out all interpolations and corruptions of the text. The careful and critical study of the original text, and a faithful translation of the text, that all men might know the truth and walk in its light, became an essential demand from the principles already adopted. In a word, the church of the New Testament in opposition to sects; Christ in opposition to all human leaderships; faith in Christ and obedience to Christ, as terms of fellowship in opposition to all doctrinal and ecclesiastical tests; the New Testament in opposition to all human creeds, as the standard of truth in the church,

New Testament Christianity

and gospel facts, conditions and promises in opposition to all imaginative, arbitrary or mystical evidences of pardon or adoption. These are the prominent items of the reformation we have been pleading, which in fifty years has gathered half a million of communicants in this land, and thirty thousand in this State.*

The conflict has been a severe one—not always wisely waged, it may be; not without some mixture of error and extravagance, but, in the main, it has been manfully and ably waged, and bravely sustained against tremendous opposition. But to-day we are enabled to say, with Paul, in reference to this plea: "A great and effectual door is opened unto us." These fifty years have witnessed a gradual, but wonderful, revolution in the religious sentiments of the people. The hyper-Calvinism and Antinomianism often so prevalent, and so fruitful a source of protest and revolt, are scarcely heard of. Many of the fierce controversies of that time have entirely ceased. The theological speculations of that period have given place to matters of more solid, practical import. The theologians and mystics of that time regarded us as little better than infidels, because we fixed the sinner's attention on Christ, and received him to baptism on his simple avowal of faith in Jesus as the Christ, the Son of God, but rationalism has forced this issue upon the Christian world, so that to-day the great

*Fifty years ago.

Opportunity and Opposition

question in theology is the Christological question, and everything distinctive between the believing and unbelieving world hinges on the answer to this question: "Is Jesus the Christ, the Son of God, or not?" Creed authority is on the wane; has, in fact, largely departed. Even in good old Scotland, where metaphysics and stubbornness find their sacredness, their wise men confess that a new departure must be made. In this country, no one dreams longer of holding the members of the churches to the church standards; and they are fast learning that they can not hold the clergy either. More and more, men are learning everywhere to value faith in Christ and obedience to Christ as the true test of Christian fellowship, and to reduce all else to the plea of expediency. Sect dominion is also rapidly waning. The demand for the union of Christians is increasing every day, and the charms of denominationalism are not half so prominent in the public eye as its evils and mischiefs. The science of Biblical criticism may be said to have been reconstructed during these fifty years, so that the necessity for a more faithful translation of the Scriptures is no longer debatable.

Add to this the general revolution in the public mind as to investigating all these questions. There is no longer trouble to obtain a hearing. No apology is needed these days for overhauling these questions and pointing out the need of reformation. It is rather demanded. A man needs but to be manly, honorable, respectful and competent, and everywhere his plea will be listened to with interest.

In all this it will be seen that a great and effectual door is opened to us. I need allude to but one additional fact of this nature. The last year has brought us into more friendly and favorable relation with our Baptist brethren, in so far, at least, as to prepare the way to exchange the hostilities of the past for friendly and candid inquiry. What may come of this, no one can foresee, but it must be good and not evil. Essentially we are one people. There are not more serious differences between us than they find among themselves or than we find among ourselves. In all that is cardinal in Christian faith and practice—standing on the authority of the same New Testament, pleading for the same Lord, the same faith and the same baptism—we are, I repeat, essentially one people, and ought to be able erelong to enter into friendly intercourse and hearty co-operation. Our differences belong largely to the past. Those which remain are not sufficiently serious to warrant a hostile array of forces. We have no desire to attempt to force a union; nor have we, indeed, any great anxiety as to the issue of the attempt we have made to overcome the alienations of the past. We have only followed the leadings of Providence, and we have confidence that if union is the best thing, a great and effectual door will be opened.

II. But now we must look at the other side. "And there are many adversaries." It is idle to attempt to disguise the fact that, while the opportunity for speaking the truth is great, the opposition is correspondingly great.

1. Look at Roman Catholicism, with its shameless avowal of the despotic spirit and doctrines of the darkest of the Dark Ages, and its impious claim to Papal infallibility; its open hostility to freedom of speech, free school and state education. And look at her progress in spite of all this, in our own land—her immense purchases of real estate, her control of politics and of the public funds, and the fear and dread of offending her that is manifested by our politicians generally; and you have one style of opposition formidable in its dimensions and in the practiced skill by which it is conducted.

2. Look at rationalism in its varied phases—undeifying Christ and pantheistically defying human reason, plying the inquisitive minds of the age with the follies and discords of the Protestant world, and paralyzing the faith of myriads in the word of God and the divinity of our Lord Jesus. Not so much in the converts openly made as in the indifferentism everywhere engendered, is its power to be dreaded. It is a fearful reaction from the creed bondage of the past. In rejecting human

authority, they reject also the divine, and the inspired creed is swept with the uninspired into a common condemnation.

3. Far more widespread is the mischief arising from the *intensely secular spirit of the age.* The second mentioned evil is one that is realized by thinkers and students; but the mass of people do not think or study closely on these subjects. Without much thought or study they drink in the spirit of the age, which is grossly material and worldly. It is an age of material interests. Even science is subsidized by materialism, and has its chief value in ministering to the advancement of material interests. Education no longer proposes intellectual and moral enlargement and elevation as an end. Its end now is to fit us for the successful pursuit of wealth. Money is more than intellect, and intellect more than heart, these days. We are willing to wear the long ears of Midas, if only everything we touch may turn to gold. This insane thirst for riches, and the absorbing interest in the worldly pursuits which it necessarily engenders, puts every spiritual interest in peril. Not only are the devotees of wealth impervious to all attacks made by the gospel on heart and conscience, but the church is unnerved for the attack that ought to be made. This secular spirit is eating out the piety of heart and home and church. The closet is forsaken; the family altar crumbles. The Bible is no longer the book of the household. The daily

papers, saturated with worldliness and reeking with vice and crime, and the weekly or monthly journal of literature and fashion, utterly Christless, if not positively infidel in its tendencies, form the reading of the family. Beyond this, if books are reached, they are apt to be frothy fictions, written to minister to sentimentalism, and leaving the reader with hot blood and prurient desires. Our children go from these almost godless homes to secular schools, from which everything moral and religious is being most diligently rooted out, in obedience to the atheistic demands of a foreign population, who are not content to enjoy in this land the liberty which Christianity has given them, but seek to establish in our country the same atheistic principles that have already sapped the foundations of morals in Europe, and made France the helpless, pitiable spectacle she is to-day. And our churches are invaded by the same secular spirit. The simplicity and spirituality of the church of God are sacrificed to pride and fashion. The crashing thunders of truth against all sin and wrong are exchanged for dulcet notes of rhetorical elegance, or for the sky-rockets of a sensational oratory. A false and hollow liberalism succeeds to the stern old bigotry that used to reign in the pulpit. Very short prayers and ten-minute sermons are the rage now. For the rest, the house of God must be made a place of refined amusement, so as to draw. Either delicious music or startling oratory must be had to *draw*. And when our children go from such homes into such schools, and from such schools into such churches, what sort of a generation are we training for the work of God? I tremble when I think of it. I am no foe to refinement or to oratory, and certainly no advocate of boorishness or of Ishmaelitish aggressiveness in the pulpit; but I would a thousand times rather see our pulpits filled with hairy Elijahs that could call down fire from heaven and send terror and slaughter among the foes of Israel, than with the most accomplished trimmers and slaves of the hour.

It is this worldliness, so widespread and so insinuating, that more than anything else paralyzes our missionary efforts. We are so intoxicated with the spirit of the times that we can not be brought to sympathize with a world that is rushing down to death. And we grow so selfish and ambitious in the midst of our earthly prosperities that we have no heart to give as we ought to give to the missionary work. There is ever an increasing selfishness, attending our growth in wealth, which very few escape. We have less sympathy with the world, and more anxiety for our own interests. And this operates in regard to our religious giving as in all other things. We lose our sympathy with the world of mankind. We learn to sneer at Foreign Missions, and figure on it to ascertain how much it costs to convert a soul in

Opportunity and Opposition

Africa or in India. Nor does it stop there. We soon lose all interest in benevolent enterprise in our own land, outside of our own neighborhood. Nothing can open our purse, unless it is something in our own neighborhood for *our* church, and for the benefit of *our* community. Nor will it stop there. For this mean selfishness is ordained to curse its possessor until it withers and blights every generous and noble impulse of the nature, and will eat him up at last with carking care and nervous fear lest even he himself should desire some benefit from his possessions and make some needless drain on his own resources. "There is that scattereth and yet increaseth; and there is that witholdeth more than is meet, and it tendeth to poverty."

When I look to-day on the gates that God has opened in Italy and Spain and Austria and Mexico, that His people may enter in, and think of the demands for Bibles and colporteurs and preachers, to give the bread and water of life to famishing multitudes, and remember that we have not one man offering for the work, nor one dollar to give to such an one were he to offer, I bow myself in the dust for very shame. When I look at our own broad land, and listen to the cry coming up from all quarters—from men of every country who have come hither for refuge and rest—and look at the millions of degraded freedmen ready to sink back into the lowest superstitions, and think how little we are doing for them, I begin to ask whether we believe what we preach. But when I look into our own State, and see the demands at our very doors, and the openings that God has made for us, and see how slow we are to enter, and how little there is of spontaneity in our benevolence, I am staggered at the spectacle, and know not what to say.

If we had no other motive than ordinary patriotism, it should inspire us to greater effort than we are making. I have alluded to the secular character of our public-school education, and to the fact that it is becoming less and less moral and religious. It is, to my mind, clearly evident that such an education can never subserve the interests of the State, and that the church must do for the State what the State can not do for itself—infuse into society the moral and spiritual potencies which alone can conserve the interests of freedom, and impart the soul culture without which a merely intellectual education may be more of a curse than a blessing. In Binghamton, N. Y., on Tuesday last, a criminal received his doom as a murderer, whose intellectual attainments have caused our best scholars to marvel. As a linguist, he was a prodigy. His profound and varied acquirements were such that an appeal was made for his life in the interests of literature and science. Yet he was a murderer, thief, and an ingrate of the blackest dye. His sublime recklessness threw a spell about his history until the last moment. Obscenities and blasphemies filled the hours until the last, and without a tear or a prayer, or a penitential sigh, he sported on the very brink, and carried his audacity and recklessness with him into the world beyond. Such brilliant intellect, with such moral recklessness, looks like a personification of Satan himself— for the Satan of the Bible is a piercing intellect joined to a thoroughly bad heart—and pity 'tis that we should seek to conform to such a model in our educational systems. We can not keep this country for God and for freedom unless moral and spiritual culture shall keep pace with intellectual culture and material enterprise. "Righteousness exalteth a nation." The fear of God is the beginning of wisdom. And this culture the church alone can give. From the very nature of our free institutions, the Government can do but little in this line. He is the truest patriot, then, who most effectually promotes moral and religious interests in the community, and wins most hearts to virtue and righteousness.

But this is putting our plea on low, utilitarian ground, and is itself, perhaps, an appeal to selfishness. We must look higher. I said, in the outset, that the gospel is only the power of God when it comes in contact with the heart and conscience; and that we must rely on Providence to open the door of access to individuals and to communities.

But that is not the whole truth. There is not only room here for divine agency, but for human agency as well. If God opens the door, we must enter in and bear the gospel with us. Between the printed page of the glorious gospel of the grace of God and the human heart in which it is to plant the power of God, there is room for a great variety of ministries. The parent, the Sunday-school teacher, the preacher, the colporteur, the editor, the tract distributor, the Bible reader, all have work here. And here is our sphere of operations as a missionary society. When we look on the deep and dark idolatries of men, the mad devotion of the human heart to sinful pleasure and selfish gratification, the terrible enslavement of men to every form of sin until they hug their chains and bless their bondage, we can not but feel our impotence in attempting the regeneration of society. No human power can effect it. But the power of God is made available for this end. It comes to us in the gospel. It is a living and powerful Word. It penetrates, it smites, it breaks in pieces; it wounds and heals; it kills and makes alive; it reaches the very fountain of life with the energy of omnipotence; its thunders boom over the conscience with crashing terror, and its tempest force sweeps like a hurricane over the soul, and pride and stubbornness and the idols of the heart are swept away in crushed fragments like a leaf in the storm. It sheds light and peace when

Opportunity and Opposition

the storm is over, and in its light a new creation rises, over whose regenerate beauties and glories the morning stars sing a sweet anthem and all the sons of God shout for joy. *But this power must be applied.* That is *our part.* God grants the power, God opens the way for it. But we must apply it. We can not create good men ourselves. But we can let in the creative power of God upon the souls of men, that they may be created anew in Jesus Christ. We are honored with this august position as coworkers with God; shall we be so base as to sell this birthright for a mess of pottage—so ignoble as to refuse, through indolence or indifference, to sway this godlike power for the salvation of the world?

But I said, We must pray—pray to Him who alone opens the door, who alone gives the increase; and I greatly fear that our lack of work grows largely out of our lack of prayer. Think you we have ever yet learned to pray? I know some who think the Lord's Prayer a thing of the past, but I doubt if we have ever yet learned to breathe that prayer aright. I doubt if we have yet learned the true spirit of its first petitions. Let us see. What is the first petition in that prayer? Grant me life? No. Grant me health? No. Grant me wealth? No. Bless me and mine with all good things, and keep me from all harm and suffering, and let not adversity come nigh us, and let us have our own sweet will to do as we please? Oh, no! no! no! The first petition is, *"Thy kingdom come."* And the second is like unto it; namely, "Thy will be done in earth as it is done in heaven." And how much does He teach us to pray for of worldly good? *Just one day's supply of food*—that is all. "Give us this day our daily bread." Christ would thus teach us to subordinate the earthly to the heavenly, the material to the spiritual. We have never learned *that prayer,* then, unless we have learned to make the spiritual *first* in our affections, and the interest of the kingdom of God the *first* and dearest desire and aim of our lives; and unless we have subjugated our will to the will of God, until we can say, "Thy will, not mine—Thy will be done, as in heaven, so on earth." Oh! it is this, dear brethren, that we need to make us what we ought to be. We are too much devoted to our *theories* of the world's conversion, and too little given to the work of converting the world. We are too little humbled before God in view of our weakness and inefficiency, our selfishness and sinfulness. We know far too little of that absorbing, enthusiastic desire for the spread of the kingdom of God which would lead us to pray always first, "Thy kingdom come, thy will be done." It was the first and the last struggle of the tempter with Jesus to persuade Him to supplant the will of God with some other will—any other, no matter what; it was the first and last victory of Jesus

Opportunity and Opposition

over the tempter, though it cost bloody sweat and bitter cryings and tears, to cling to the will of God, and say in the darkest hour, "Thy will be done." Would that we might all be brought, through whatever humiliation and agony, to the point of entire submission—how mightily would God enable us to move forward the triumphs of His kingdom! We have the men, we have the money, we have the open door; we want supreme devotion to the will of God—a devotion that shall conquer the lusts of the world and our carnal natures.

HAGAR AND SARAH—AN ALLEGORY

By Elder M. B. HOPKINS

TEXT.—"Tell me, ye that desire to be under the law, do ye not hear the law? For it is written, that Abraham had two sons, the one by a bondmaid, the other by a freewoman. But he who was of the bondwoman was born after the flesh; but he of the freewoman was by promise. Which things are an allegory: for these are the two covenants; the one from mount Sinai, which gendereth to bondage, which is Agar. For this Agar is mount Sinai in Arabia, and answereth to Jerusalem which now is, and is in bondage with her children. But Jerusalem which is above is free, which is the mother of us all. For it is written, Rejoice, thou barren that bearest not; break forth and cry, thou that travailest not: for the desolate hath many more children than she which hath an husband. Now we, brethren, as Isaac was, are the children of promise. But as then he that was born after the flesh persecuted him that was born after the Spirit, even so it is now. Nevertheless what saith the scripture? Cast out the bondwoman and her son: for the son of the bondwoman shall not be heir with the son of the freewoman. So then, brethren, we are not children of the bondwoman, but of the free. Stand fast therefore in the liberty wherewith Christ hath made us free, and be not entangled again with the yoke of bondage."—Gal. 4: 21—5: 1.

Hagar and Sarah

MY respected auditors, I ask your careful and prayerful attention to the consideration of the foregoing Scripture, from the pen of the great apostle to the Gentiles—one whose whole life and energies were spent in an effort to bind with Christian bonds, in one fraternal society, both Jew and Gentile.

The topic, you perceive, before the mind of Paul is the covenants—the two covenants considered, illustrated and traced out under the beautiful, striking and impressive figure of an allegory, drawn from certain allegorical personages in the early family of Abraham. A correct and comprehensive knowledge of the two convenants here brought to view is of the utmost importance to the Bible student. No one can have an enlarged horizon of Bible information without it. As we explore the principles, promises, incidents and attributes of these covenants, we explore the Jewish and the Christian dispensations, the Old Testament and the New, the law and the gospel; and by their aid we are enabled to make the grand survey between the territories of Judaism and Christianity, and bound the authority of Moses and Jesus Christ. Ignorant of these covenants, and the Bible is in chaos—Judaism is Christianity, and Christianity is Judaism; a Jew is a Christian, and a Christian is a Jew. Darkness covers the Bible, and gross darkness hovers over the understanding. It knows no order. A stranger to all arrangement, it bids defiance to all efforts at classification. We would as likely look into the Book of Chronicles for the way, the truth, the life, as into the Book of Acts of Apostles; but with this knowledge the sun rises in the heart, the veil is stripped from the understanding, and we behold, as in a glass, the glory of the Lord, and, while with admiration and rapture we gaze upon His transcendent glory, are changed into the same image, from one degree of glory to another, by the Spirit of the Lord.

It is of the utmost importance that we have a clear and accurate definition of the word "covenant," in this investigation. The liberal acceptation is "agreement." In its legal and technical sense it applies only to such agreements as are under seal, the making of which is accompanied with great solemnity. No circumstances of greater solemnity can be imagined than those that accompanied the making of the Sinaitic covenant. Jehovah descended upon the pinnacle of Sinai. The pealing thunder announced his awful presence. Darkness and blackness enshrouded the mountain. It smoked as a furnace. The tempest howled to the storm. And the voice of the trumpet, exceeding loud, struck terror to the heart of Israel. God called Moses to the top of the mount, and in the midst of this terrific scene delivered to him the words of the covenant. He sketched before him what he had done for Abraham, Isaac and Jacob, and for the present generation of their descendants.

Hagar and Sarah

He further informed him of all that He purposed to do for that nation, and also what He should require of them. Moses, having received these words, descended from the mount, and came and told the people of all the words of the Lord, and all the judgments, and all the people answered with one voice and said: "All the words which the Lord hath said, will we do." Here is the agreement—the mutuality of agreement—but no covenant. It must be reduced to writing, and sealed. Moses reascends to God, and writes in a book all the words of the Lord. And after its reduction to writing, he took the book of the covenant, and read it in the audience of the people. Both parties, the covenantor and the covenantees, hear this written agreement, with all its propositions, stipulations, conditions, etc. And after the careful reading by Moses the people signify a second time their acceptance. But still the covenant is not perfected. It must be sealed. Moses, killing the proper animal, caught the blood in a basin, and, dipping the hyssop in the blood, sprinkled both the book of the covenant and the people, accompanying it with the repetition of this solemn formula of words: "This is the blood of the covenant which God hath enjoined upon you." The covenant is made. God and Israel stand in covenant relation to each other. He is no longer known as the God of Abraham, Isaac and Jacob only, but as the God of the Hebrews also.

New Testament Christianity

Solemn, impressive and melting were the circumstances attendant upon the making of the new and better covenant. The covenantor descended upon our earth in the person of Jesus, the Mediator, clothed in our nature, and made the pilgrimage of human life, from the womb to the grave, that he, *experimentally*, might know us, in all our infirmities, ignorance, trials, temptations, sufferings and death, that thus perfected, fully qualified, he is a faithful High Priest, and is able to have a right share of compassion on the ignorant, and them that are out of the way, *seeing He Himself was encompassed with infirmity*—enveloped in humanity—baptized beneath the mighty wave of human suffering, and in the presence of a blushing sun, and bursting rocks, He sealed with His own blood the new covenant with the house of Israel and the house of Judah.

The two covenants embody within them all preceding covenants and promises made with the Jewish people. The covenant conveying the land of Canaan to Abraham, as an estate of inheritance forever, was merged into the legal dispensation. Gal. 3, 18, 19: "For if the inheritance be of the law, it is no more of promise; but God gave it to Abraham by promise. Wherefore, then, serveth the law? It was added because of transgressions, till the seed should come to whom the promise was made." The law was added. Added to what? To the promise of the inheritance. The inheri-

Hagar and Sarah

tance of Canaan, till the seed should come. The covenant of circumcision passed from the hand of Abraham to that of Moses, and became part and parcel of the Mosaic institution. John 7:23: "If a man on the sabbath day receive circumcision, that the law of Moses should not be broken." Acts 15: "Except ye be circumcised, after the *manner of Moses, ye cannot be saved.*"

The covenant concerning the Christ, made 430 years before the date of the law, maintained a separate and distinct existence, forming no part of the Sinaitic covenant. Hence, in all the legislation of Moses, there is not one word of reference to this spiritual promise. The new covenant is but a development of this promise. The oak from the acorn. The great tree, in the branches of which all the fowls of heaven may lodge, from the mustard seed. Thus there arise before us the two great institutions, covenants or testaments, in all their grandeur and glory. The old and the new— the Sinaitic and Jerusalem—the temporal, and the spiritual and eternal, all these covenants are thus contrasted in the sacred Scriptures, but never *identified*. A distinct agent was employed by the covenantor in the making of these covenants, called mediators, or middle persons. Moses stood as a middle person between God and Israel. Ex. 20:21: "And the people stood afar off, and Moses drew near to the thick darkness where God was." Gal. 3:19: The law "was ordained by angels in the hand of a mediator." The man Christ Jesus is the Mediator of the new covenant. Heb. 9:15: "He is the mediator of the new testament, that by means of death, for the redemption of the transgressions that were under the first testament, they which are called might receive the promise of eternal inheritance."

But, my auditors, while we have thus clearly before us these two covenants, and their respective mediators, I am about to propound that the Bible also reveals, describes and defines two churches, standing each upon one of these two covenants: a church upon the old covenant; another, not the same church, upon the new covenant. Here is the battlefield. Here I must break a lance with my pedobaptist brother. For pedobaptism, or infant baptism, as the word *pedo* indicates, stands upon four *glass* legs. They are as follows: *First*, the church before Christ and after Christ, one and the same, *identical*. *Second*, circumcision the door into the Jewish church. *Third*, circumcision done away under Christ. *Fourth*, baptism substituted for it. Upon these four pillars rests all the weight of the pedobaptist temple. Shall I break one of them? I will try first the identity of the churches. The identity of the Jewish commonwealth with the church of Jesus Christ. It ought only to be necessary to state it, to disprove it. What can be the logic of this proposition of identity? Let us hear it. Well, here it is. Both

Hagar and Sarah

are called by the name "church." Both are called the people of God. Both had ordinances of divine service. Both had the gospel preached. Both were under obligations to live a holy life, etc.; therefore, they are identical. What a conclusion! Shall I expose the fallacy? Men are called animals; so are the beasts. Both are called the creatures of God. Both live by eating. Both are subject to pain. Both are mortal, etc., therefore they are identical!! *They argue from resemblances to identity.* There is the breadth of the heavens' difference between similarity and identity. But let us hear Paul on the question of identity. Eph. 2:14, 15: "For he is our peace who hath made both [Jew and Gentile] one, and hath broken down the middle wall of partition between us; having abolished in his flesh the enmity, even the law of commandments contained in ordinances, for to make in himself of twain *one new man,* so making peace." The term "new man" is equivalent to "new body," "new society," or *"new church."* Mark, a new church; but the expression "new church" associates with *old church.* Here we have it, then, an old church and a new one. The old church was the church in the wilderness: "This is he that was in the church in the wilderness with the angel." The Jewish church stood upon the old covenant. The new church is the Christian church, standing upon the new covenant.

New Testament Christianity

Let us hear Jesus upon the same topic. Matthew 16: "Who do you say that I am?" Peter replies: "Thou art the Christ, the Son of the living God." Jesus replies: "Upon *this rock* I *will build* my church." Not, I have built, but, I will build it. There is a vast difference between *building* a house and *remodeling* it.

Connected with all bodies, societies and churches is the idea of a constitution. Without a constitution they are in chaos—with, there are shape, proportion and strength. But may I inquire, What is a constitution? The constitution of a state is but the definition of the supreme authority of that state. If it be an absolute monarchy, the constitution is very short. The Czar is supreme—is the constitution of Russia. The constitution of the Jewish church is: "Hear, O Israel, the Lord your God is one Lord." Jehovah was the center and source of all power. Just before the ascension of Jesus into heaven, He informed His apostles that the scepter had changed hands: "That all authority, in heaven and in earth," was given to Him. He ascends to heaven, above all principalities, powers, might and dominion, and every name which is named.

The apostles, assembled in constitutional convention at Jerusalem, promulgated the constitution of the kingdom of heaven in the following words: "Therefore, let all the house of Israel know assuredly, that God hath made that same Jesus whom ye crucified, both Lord and Christ." Thus, while we have one God and Father, we have also one Lord Jesus Christ.

It is a common saying—indeed, it is the outburst of common sense—that every church must have a law to govern it—a creed-book, church ritual, or whatever name you may see proper to give. No sooner, therefore, had Moses organized the Jewish church than a divine volume issued from the press, appropriately called the Old Testament. It is appropriately so called, because it was for the government of the old church, standing upon the *old covenant*. This was the *creed-book* of the church for fifteen hundred years—the only authoritative book. Upon the organization of the new church, in Jerusalem, a new volume made its appearance, appropriately called the New Testament—a creed-book—the only creed-book of the new church.

But who can think or speak of the church without associating with it in his mind the proclamation of the gospel? The proclamation of the gospel is as essential to spiritual life as oxygen to animal. While, therefore, the church was in its pilgrim state, in the wilderness, Moses, Aaron, Joshua, Caleb, and other elders, preached the gospel to them. Heb. 4:9: "For unto us was the gospel preached, as well as *unto them*, but the word preached did not profit them, not being mixed with faith in them that heard it." Here, you perceive, Paul affirms the gospel was preached to them as well as to us, but surely not the same gospel. McKnight says it was the gospel of the earthly inheritance—the earthly Canaan promised, four centuries before, to Abraham. And so says the context: whereas the gospel preached to us is the glad tidings of the heavenly inheritance which is incorruptible, undefiled, and that fadeth not away.

Into every church there is an initiatory process, or rite, mechanically called a door. Into both these churches there are doors of ingress and egress—a door in and a door out. What was the door into the Jewish church? Ah! this is a most important question. Here I must break the second glass leg of infant membership. Was circumcision the door into the Jewish church?—the only door into said church? Then, was the Jewish church composed of males only? "Every man child among you shall be circumcised." This is no pettifogging. It is a fair conclusion from the premises. It is inclusive and exclusive—including males and excluding females.

That circumcision was not the door into the Jewish church is proven by another fact. It is impossible to pass from the outside of a building through the door of the building, and not enter the house. If we pass through the door, we must enter the building; but whole tribes entered through this so-called door of the Jewish church,

Hagar and Sarah

but never entered the church. There were the tribes of Ishmael (Esau), as well as the six nations descended from the six sons of Abraham by his second wife, Keturah; all were circumcised, and observed it in their generations for many years; but were they members of the church? The very law of circumcision shows most conclusively that that rite did not change the ecclesiastical relations of the recipient of it. "God said unto Abraham, Thou shalt keep my covenants, therefore, thou and thy seed after thee, in their generations. This is my covenant, which ye shall keep, between me and thee and thy seed after thee; Every man child among you shall be circumcised. And ye shall circumcise the flesh of your foreskin; and it shall be a token of the covenant betwixt me and you. And he that is eight days old shall be circumcised among you, every man child in your generation, he that is born in thy house, or bought with money of any stranger, which is not of thy seed. He that is born in thy house, and he that is bought with thy money, must needs be circumcised: and my covenant shall be in your flesh for an everlasting covenant. And the *uncircumcised man child* whose flesh of his foreskin is not circumcised, that soul shall be *cut off* from his people; he hath *broken* my *covenant*" (Gen. 17: 9-14).

The uncircumcised man child, you perceive, was to be *cut off* from his people. The branch can not be cut off from the trunk unless it first be united with the trunk. No one can be cut off from the church unless first a member of the same. The uncircumcised Jew was to be cut off from his church for his neglect. He was a member of the church before his circumcision; circumcision, therefore, did not make him a member. It was no door. It constituted no new relationship between the individual subject of it and the Jewish people. Let us, then, return to our former inquiry, What was the door into the Jewish church? I answer, *Birth* and *purchase.* "He that is born in thy house, and bought with thy money, must needs be circumcised." All born of Abraham's flesh, and bought with Abraham's purse, were, by virtue of said birth or purchase, members of the Jewish church, and were circumcised, not to make them members, but because they were already members.

The ligament that bound the Jew to his church was a fleshy one. The Jewish church was the Jewish nation, and *vice versa.* A man entered the Jewish church as and when he entered the nation; yea, as he entered the world. Membership in the church was hereditary. All the sacred offices in the church descended from father to son, on hereditary principles. The crown floated down the channel of David's flesh and blood—the sacerdotal robes, that of Aaron. Into the church of Jesus Christ, as the kingdom of heaven, there is also a door. What is that door? How do the

Hagar and Sarah

sinner and the humble enter the church of God? I answer by *birth*. Ah! that is only part of the truth—by a second birth; not by being born, but by being *born again;* not a birth of flesh and blood, but of the Spirit of God. The Lord for the first time laid the great naturalization law of the kingdom of heaven before Nicodemus: "Verily, verily, I say unto thee, Except a man be born of water and the Spirit, he cannot enter into the kingdom of heaven." The ligament of union to this church is not Abraham's flesh, but Abraham's faith. "They that are of faith are blessed with faithful Abraham." The preaching of John the Baptist was: "Say not among yourselves that we have Abraham to our father, but bring forth fruits meet for repentance."

Thus, my respected auditors, we have before your minds two covenants—the *old* and the *new;* two mediators—Moses and Messiah; two churches—the church in the wilderness, and the church of Jesus Christ; two gospels—two inheritances; two books—the Old Testament and the New; and two births—the one of flesh, the other of Spirit—all and singular of which is beautifully, clearly and forcibly taught by Paul in the allegory before us. Let us hear him with care and candor. "For it is written that Abraham had *two* sons, the one by a bondmaid, the other by a freewoman; but he who was of the bondwoman was born after the flesh, but he of the freewoman was by promise:

which things are an *allegory.*" What is an allegory? It is not a metaphor or simile, but a number of metaphors. It sustains the same relation to a single metaphor that a cluster of grapes does to a single grape. This allegory is a cluster of four metaphors—the two women and their two sons. The two women represent the two covenants. "These are the two covenants: the one from mount Sinai, which gendereth to bondage, which is Hagar; the other from Jerusalem, which is Sarah." Sarah, the wife proper, represents the spiritual covenant made at Jerusalem; Hagar, the bondwoman, represents the covenant made at Sinai. The two sons, Ishmael and Isaac, represent the children or churches of the covenants. Ishmael represents the Jewish church; Isaac, the Christian church. Let us, therefore, examine the distinctive features of these two churches, as they were typified and adumbrated in the early family of Abraham, in confirmation of all that I have before said concerning them.

These two sons, although both the sons of Abraham, are so upon very distinct principles. Ishmael, the son of the bondwoman, was born on principles perfectly natural. "He who was of the bondwoman was born after the flesh;" but Isaac, the son of the freewoman, was born on supernatural principles: "He of the freewoman was by promise." Isaac was the offspring of faith: "Through faith, also, Sarah herself received strength to conceive seed, and was delivered of a child when she was past age, because she judged him faithful who had promised; therefore sprang there even of one, and him as good as dead, so many as the stars of the sky in multitude, and sands of the seashore innumerable." "And being not weak in faith, he considered not his own body, now dead, when he was about an hundred years old, neither yet the deadness of Sarah's womb. He staggered not at the promise of God through unbelief, but was strong in the faith, giving glory to God." Thus have we stereotyped, in this patriarchal family, the radical distinction between Jewish and Christian churches, in the very nature of the births of these two sons. The Jewish church is the church of the flesh. Its members, like Ishmael, are born of the flesh, and according to the flesh. The principle of growth and increase is natural generation. The Christian church is the church of the Spirit, because born of the Spirit, and filled with the Spirit. *Its* principle of increase is supernatural regeneration. "Verily, verily, I say unto thee, Except a man be born again, he cannot see the kingdom of God."

The second point of difference in these two sons, illustrative of the difference of the two churches, is in their *condition*, considered in reference to the institution under which they lived. The one was a slave; the other was free. In all slave countries the offspring takes the character and condition of the mother. If she be slave, the descendant is slave; if free, the descendant is free. Ishmael, therefore, was a slave; Isaac a son, a free son. They appropriately shadowed forth the difference in the moral and spiritual condition of these two churches. The Sinaitic covenant "generates to bondage." The Jewish church wore a yoke, a slavish yoke, that "neither they nor their fathers were able to bear." "They were entangled in the yoke of bondage," "all their lifetime subject to bondage through fear of death." The Jerusalem covenant is free; she regenerates to freedom. "Stand fast therefore in the liberty wherewith Christ hath made us free." We, brethren, as Isaac was, are the children of promise. "If the Son make us free, we shall be free indeed." The church of God is freed from condemnation by justification, strengthened against temptation by the Spirit of God, and has overcome death by faith in the resurrection. "Blessed be God, who giveth us the victory through our Lord Jesus Christ."

A third and most important difference between these two sons was in their relations to Abraham's property. Ishmael, because a slave, was not the heir; he was entitled only to a slave's portion—"a bottle of water and a loaf of bread." Food and raiment was a slave's right. Isaac was the heir apparent to all the estate of Abraham, which was by no means inconsiderable. Isaac was a

Hagar and Sarah

wealthy prince. How strikingly illustrative this of the comparative wealth and blessing of the two churches—the one limited to the earthly Canaan, its bread and water, its milk and honey; while the other, as a joint-heir with Jesus, anticipates a heavenly Canaan, an incorruptible, undefiled and unfading inheritance at God's right hand. Paul's schedule of their property is as follows: "Whether Paul, or Apollos, or Cephas, or the world, or life, or death, or things present, or things to come, all are yours." They wait "for a far more exceeding and eternal weight of glory."

But the fourth and last difference between these sons of Abraham, typical of a most important difference in these prospective churches, was in their *spirit*. There is a spirit homogeneous with the condition of man. The slave Ishmael possessed a slavish, low, mean and persecuting spirit, whereas the free Isaac was docile, humble, pious and a suffering man, elevated above the flesh—a spiritual man. This difference in their spirit is developed most strikingly at an early period of their lives, while both resident in their father's family, Isaac having reached the age of five years, a period at which patriarchal mothers removed their children from the breast. "Abraham made a great feast the day Isaac was weaned." Large numbers of happy guests surrounded the table laden with patriarchal simplicity; joy and hilarity covered the board. The young prince was the topic of conversation. Mother Sarah received many an honest compliment on account of her son. Many a heart breathed silently a sincere prayer to God for blessings upon a son of faith and old age; joy and gratitude filled each heart, with one exception—a feeling of jealousy and hatred raged in the bosom of Ishmael. Ishmael mocked and persecuted Isaac. But what does this persecution mean? Would to God it had no *meaning*. Paul gives a solemn interpretation to this short piece of history (twenty-ninth verse of text): "But as *then* he that was born after the flesh persecuted him that was born after the Spirit, even so it is *now.*" These sons, in their spirit, and in the fruit of their spirit, represent the two churches—the one filled "with the spirit of bondage to fear," the other "with the spirit of adoption, whereby they cry Abba, Father." Ishmael stands for a persecuting church, Isaac for a persecuted one. No sooner were these two churches together in Jerusalem than the church of the flesh opened the fires of persecution against the church of the Spirit. The fire broke forth first in Jerusalem, spread to the cities around, and to all the Roman provinces wherever a synagogue was to be found. Here is the beginning of the cruel sufferings of the people of God, for conscience' sake; while Jerusalem has its tens of thousands of hallowed associations, it has at the same time many unpleasant reminiscences. From thence bloody and cruel edict after edict was issued against the disciples. There the first martyrs sealed their testimony with their own blood: while the Jewish church had power, blood ran from every vein of the church of Jesus Christ; but "the blood of the martyrs became the seed of the church." The arm of this Ishmaelitish church was at length broken by the Roman power. Peace and gratitude ensued for a season. About this time infant membership had its rise; a wicked hand was laid upon the only naturalization law of the kingdom of heaven. "The birth of the Spirit," "ye must be born again," and flesh was substituted for it. Flesh and blood, and not faith and a holy life, became the passport to citizenship in the kingdom of God. The effect was that tribes and nations moved right into the church of God, not by operation of the Spirit of God, but by operation of the touch of a moistened finger in the name of the Trinity to the babe of hereditary flesh and blood. The church swallowed the world, or the world the church, it is difficult to determine exactly which. The law of the Spirit being, if not stricken from the statute of the kingdom of heaven, at least a dead letter, corruption now poured into the church. Whole nations of unregenerate men and women now crowded the gates of the kingdom, filled with pride, ambition, and a love of power. Modern Italy, Spain and Portugal, and I might say Mexico, are lamentable illustrations of the corrupt workings of the flesh rather than the spirit. In these countries all belong to the church, from the self-denying monk to the plundering guerrilla party. Give to such a church as that civil power—and civil power they will have—and you may confidently look for the desolating scenes that disgrace the pages of sacred history. I solemnly look upon this plea of flesh rather than the spirit as the cause of the persecutions in the past. What else could be looked for from a church composed of flesh and blood, superstition and ignorance—a church without spirituality and even sound morality? History confirms my position here; all the persecuting churches have been those who received far many more accessions on account of their flesh than on account of their faith. It is justly the boast of Baptists that they never persecuted—they never drew the sword from the scabbard. They chose to suffer with the Lord themselves, rather than cause suffering to others.

But, my auditors, I must take you once more with me to Abraham's family, at the weaning of Isaac and feast of Abraham. We are there informed that the mocking of Ishmael was observed by Sarah. Displeased with the treatment of her son by her servant, she requested Abraham *"to cast out this bondwoman and her son, for the son of the bondwoman shall not inherit with my son, even with Isaac."* Abraham was grieved. He *loved* his son tenderly, and, whilst he stood re-

Hagar and Sarah

flecting, God spoke and said: "Abraham, hearken to the voice of thy wife; *cast out the bondwoman and her son.*" But this woman and her son are typical personages—typical of Jewish covenant and church. To cast out the bondwoman and her son is but a precept *to cast out the Jewish covenant and the Jewish church.* But mark the reason of this repudiation of the bondwoman and her son. "The son of the bondwoman"—the son of the flesh—shall not inherit with the "son of the freewoman"—the son of the spirit. Here is a repudiation of the *fleshly principle,* and an indorsement of the *spiritual*—the children of the flesh are not heirs. It is, therefore, no matter of surprise that the Baptist said, "The ax is laid unto the root of the tree." The tree that brings the *good* fruit shall stand; the unfruitful tree shall be hewn down and cast into the fire. Flesh was about to give way for spirit; blood, for piety and a holy life. Wonderful revolutions in divine things are clearly taught by this allegory: the *old covenant* has given way for the *new;* the mediator Moses for the *mediator* Messias; *the Jewish church for the Christian church;* the *gospel* of the earthly inheritance for the *gospel* of the heavenly.; the *earthly Canaan* for the *heavenly;* the *old testament* for the *new;* the *birth* of the *flesh* for the *birth* of the *spirit.*

That which now stands between the individual, whether Jew, Greek, barbarian, male or female, bond or free, and the kingdom of heaven with all the fullness of its blessings, is the *birth of the spirit*. This is God's own naturalization law, made for the benefit of oppressed foreigners and strangers. Let no ruthless hand touch it, but let it stand from age to age as the door of the kingdom of heaven; and blessed is he that hastens to enter through this gate into the city. Amen.

UNCONSCIOUS ENEMIES OF CHRISTIANITY

H. W. EVEREST

IT is Christianity or nothing. All false religions go down before the march of modern civilization. No enlightened man can worship either Isis or Osiris, Jupiter or Woden, Brahma or Vishnu. The world is saved from the superstitions and cruelties of idolatry. Excepting Christianity, there remains only what science may do. But science, whether we consider its adaptation to such a work, or the irreligious bias of its devotees, gives little promise of anything reliable. If soul and body rot together in the grave, there is nothing to be said, and science is dumb; if the soul is immortal, science can not demonstrate it, much less declare the duties we owe to this immortality. Had science any tendencies in this direction, yet would it be inadequate; its progress is slow, retrograde at times, and its results uncertain. Æons would pass away before this coral reef could rise above the ocean of ignorance and superstition; æons more, before it would be habitable by a majority of our race. Just now, God and eternity are declared to be needless hypotheses; or, if realized at all, they are to be classed with the unknowable. Men who have thought their way through this subject will tell you calmly, perhaps sadly, that this one alternative at last confronts them—Christianity or nothing. Said the writer to a skeptical lawyer: "Since you reject Christianity, what other trust have you?" "None, absolutely none!" was the reply. This, at least, is severely logical; for when one has condemned all the evidence for Christ as utterly worthless— history, prophecy, reason, nature and experience— he has thrown down the pillars of all religious faith whatsoever. There is nothing left whereon nor wherewith to build a new faith. In proportion as other systems disappear in the receding darkness, Christianity rises into the clear light of day. If the war slackens about heathen altars, it is growing fiercer about the cross. Christianity is discussed by the fireside and the wayside. It is the theme of the pulpit, the rostrum and the press. The cross hangs in every sky, and the nations can but gaze. Momentous questions these! Have we light, or is it the midnight of eternal darkness? Is the coffin the only house prepared for the soul, or is there a life beyond? Is it divine forgiveness or everlasting guilt?

The world-wide conflict thus introduced to us is an intellectual and a moral one. It can not be decided by sacrificing the wealth of Christendom, nor by the meeting of infidel and Christian armies. We expect no great discoveries nor decisive experiments. We await no angel's coming to trouble the waters. We ask not for sign and miracle. We sleep, not hoping for dreams and revelations. The prophets are in their sepulchres, and the heavens have received the ascending Christ. On the field we now occupy, and with the weapons now in our hands, we must fight this battle. It is a contest between the intelligence and moral power of the church on the one side, and the intelligence and skill of all the world besides on the other. Shall Christian logicians so work out the problem, and so spread before the world the clear solution, as to satisfy every candid mind and silence every objector? or shall the skeptical world show the most learning, research and dialectic skill, and, though we have the truth, shall they have the victory?

If, turning the pages of history, and surveying the present condition and attitude of the hostile forces, we shall ask how this great intellectual conflict is going, we shall find many things to cheer us. The nominal Christian population of the globe is more than four hundred millions, and these comprise the wealth, the learning and the civilization of the age. There is a high degree of missionary zeal. A large percentage of the world's wealth is devoted to intellectual and moral culture. The Sunday-school movement promises much. As the battle sways from the old ground to the new, the issues become fewer and grander. Religion is less a matter of miracle, and more a subject of law and science. The sword of the inquisitor is sheathed, and national barriers are broken down. False religions and philosophies are waxing old and ready to vanish away. Even the concentration of infidel forces and the boldness of their attacks are auguries of good, for we shall find the enemy and know where to strike. Still, with all these evidences of progress, we cry in our impatience, "How long, O Lord, how long!" Why are so many millions unsaved? Why do so many reject this religion? It is from God, and the evidence most abundant and unanswerable. Why, then, can not all conscientious, thinking men be made to see it?

In answer to this question, it is evident that, while much is owing to non-investigation, and more to that moral grossness which makes men unwilling to believe because unwilling to obey, still by far the most prolific source of unbelief is the *misrepresentation* of Christianity. This is the northern hive, whence swarm the Goths and Vandals of infidelity. They do not see Christianity as it is, but only some horrid caricature. The light in which they see even this is subject to double refraction, coming as it does through the dense media of false training and moral prejudice. Is the Roman hierarchy the reign of heaven? Is

Unconscious Enemies of Christianity

Protestantism, mangled and bleeding, the body of Christ? Is a Calvinistic creed the Bible doctrine of liberty? Does a Methodist camp-meeting present Scriptural examples of conversion to Christ? "If this is religion," says the objector, "then I want none of it." We have an example of this reasoning in Draper's "Conflict between Religion and Science." In this work the Roman Catholic Church is "religion," and the better teachings of philosophers, "science." When he has twisted these perversions in opposite directions, of course there is a "conflict." Though this is the old logic of comparing a rough saint with a smooth sinner, yet it illustrates how misrepresentations of Christianity are the chief sources of unbelief.

The unconscious enemies of Christianity are the authors of these perversions. I call them *enemies* because they are not only corrupting the church, but also giving the unbelieving world its most destructive weapons; and *unconscious* enemies because they are doing this in entire ignorance of their hostility to religion, but rather with the pious intention of defending and propagating the faith. There were such in the olden time. When Uzzah, in his overzeal, stayed the tottering ark of God, he delayed its triumphant bringing into Jerusalem by twenty years. When Peter would dissuade Jesus from going up to Jerusalem to be condemned and crucified, he was an unconscious enemy of Christ, and heard the rebuke,

New Testament Christianity

"Get thee behind me, Satan." In all the progress of the church such enemies have existed, and they are exceedingly numerous and dangerous in modern times. It is a sad fact that one may be dangerous to a cause for the triumph of which he would gladly lay down his life. How frequent and fervent should be the prayer, "Cleanse thou me from secret faults!" It is a sad fact that the great source of unbelief is the innocent enmity of the church. Its divisions; its multitudinous and absurd creeds; its mistaken zeal; its feeble arguments; its monkish seclusion; its persecuting spirit; its unholy, because overdrawn, sanctity; its senseless opposition to reason and science—are but too many proofs of this enmity. Our needle-guns are more dangerous to friends than enemies. Our cannon explode more destructively on this side than our shells on that. Not the gates of Hades, but ourselves, we need to fear. Profoundly convinced of this fact, and believing that every Christian desires to be not only the professed, but also the real, friend of Christ, the following pages are devoted to this discussion of the unconscious enemies of Christianity.

I. The first mention shall be of those who pledge the Bible, as a book, to an *unscriptural perfection and comprehensiveness*. Let Christian scholars claim constantly for the Bible an unwarranted perfection, and extend its scepter over provinces of thought where it asserts no jurisdiction; and then let the unbeliever show that these claims are unsupported, and that this extension of authority is a usurpation, and the argument is complete. Unconsciously, the Christian vies with the infidel in destroying his own religion. Now, the great body of the church, and not a few prominent writers, are doing work of this kind. On the one hand, they claim that the Bible is all, and in the highest sense, the word of God; that the holy men of old, through whom it was given, were mere automata, and that the volume thus given has been miraculously preserved in all its original purity. They practically claim for it absolute authority, not only in religion, where it is admitted to be supreme, but also in geography, history, chronology, medicine, literature, social law and natural science. It is set forth not only as a book of principles, but also as one of specific commands, intended to regulate, in all ages of the world, the minutest concerns of individual life. On the other hand, it will be shown that the Bible contains the words of men and angels, good and bad, as well as of God; that the writers drew on their own sources of knowledge, had a style of their own, and wrote in harmony with the then state of human knowledge; that the text of Scripture had come down to us borne by the natural currents of literature, and not without many an interpolation and corruption; and that it was given to men of other times and states of civilization and application to this remote age. It will be shown that, as a treatise on geography, history, medicine, government, and many other human sciences, it is a failure.

Nothing could be more disastrous to Christianity than these false notions among the masses—notions destined to be taken away, and with them the Bible itself. The remedy is not to be found in a dogmatic and blind defense of these pseudo claims. Nothing will serve Christianity but the truth. A true position alone can be defended. Our views of inspiration must harmonize with the facts, and not exclude them. We must show that the extension of the Bible beyond the province of religion is an abuse. Admitting the human transmission of the Scriptures, we must show that various readings and interpolations do not touch any essential fact or doctrine. We need maintain only that the Bible "is able to make us wise unto *salvation.*" We need not barricade the progress of the age with Bibles, unless a sound exegesis shall lay upon us the command.

II. A second class represent Christianity as something *wholly apart from reason and science.* In many a sermon, reason is denounced as weak, corrupt and presumptuous. Reason and faith are held up in contrast; the one to be condemned and scouted, the other to be trusted and extolled. Everything is to be taken on authority. To ask the reason why is an unpardonable sin. Clergymen

Unconscious Enemies of Christianity

are sent to cram their dogmas down our throats, however our moral stomachs may loathe and reject them. Reason must do homage to religious dogmatism. The less reason, the better Christian. The less reasoning in the pulpit, the better preaching. "Reason and Religion" is the subject of any amount of pious and learned nonsense. From the sacred desk and in religious periodicals, science is often the subject of disparagement and ridicule. Much that is false, and some things that are true, are said about the limited vision, the inadequacy, and the hypothetic and shifting nature of science. As in politics and religion, so in science and religion, there is a desire to have them served on separate plates. We tolerate a science of mind and of morals, but what church would hear anything about the science of religion? Here, as before, Christians and unbelievers are working together to build up an argument against religion. It is clear that if Christianity is against reason and science, it is not from God. When the preacher decries reason and science, the infidel says: "So I thought, and so I have been constantly affirming; it is unreasonable, and must go down under the stunning blows of science." These tirades against science are only widening the breach, and causing multitudes of earnest men to turn away in disgust.

Rightly considered, what have reason and science to do with religion? Much every way.

The term "reason" is used in three different senses: to denote the intuitive faculty, when it is called "the reason"; to denote the ratiocinative faculty, or that mental activity by which we deduce conclusions from admitted premises; and to designate man's whole mental nature as distinguished from instinct. Now, in whatever sense used, reason is indispensable in religion. Without reason, in the first sense, there could be no conscience, no idea of right and wrong, no perception of obligation to do right, and no condemnation if we do wrong. Without the reason, man would not be a religious being; for conscience must go with us into all religious duties, and we are to seek constantly to have consciences void of offense toward men and toward God. Without reason in the last two senses, religion is equally impossible. How can one incapable of seeing the relation between proposition and proof believe in Christ? How could he be held accountable? Reason is the faculty to which God appeals. It is the only avenue through which a revelation can reach us. It must decide whether a professed revelation is really such. And how does the preacher reach the conclusion that reason has little to do with religion, except by delivering a sermon on the subject, except by reasoning about it? But if reason is invalid when employed about religion, then his sermon, or reasoning on the subject, is equally invalid.

Unconscious Enemies of Christianity

It is not the province of reason to manufacture premises. "What can we reason but from what we know?" Both nature and revelation furnish us the great facts from which we reason concerning them. Nor can reason reach beyond the premises; it only serves to analyze and bring out what is implied in them. The idea of a revelation, indeed, implies the inability of reason to discover the things revealed. And yet we are not asked to believe anything unreasonable; nor would it be possible if we were. To believe that Jesus raised Lazarus from the dead is reasonable, because the proof is conclusive. It would be most unreasonable to reject such evidence. *How* Jesus performed this miracle we do not understand nor believe, but only the fact. And so, generally, what we believe is always that portion of the matter in hand which we understand. In this respect, religion stands with all other sciences. He who goes beyond reason is walking in darkness. If we obey the commands of Christ, it is not without reason; we do it because He is divine and infallible. Instead of depreciating reason, would it not be better to urge the unbeliever to a more vigorous and well-directed use of reason? It is not very manly, to say the least, to persuade our opponent to meet us unarmed of reason. Let us rather meet and conquer him with all his armor on.

Science, instead of being the enemy, is a co-worker and servant of religion. We should judge beforehand that these two departments would illuminate each other. They have the same author. All truth is harmonious. Separate systems of truth combine to form the one universe of science. The natural and the supernatural are but halves of the same sphere. Science is the methodical statement of God's thoughts, as embodied in natural forms. If Christianity presents the divine thoughts concerning us, it must be in the highest sense scientific. The crystal, the leaf, and the wing of the insect, are constructed under perfect laws. Science exhausts her technicalities and her formulas in explaining even man's physical nature. Mind is also subject to law. Now, if we find science in all the universe besides, and every force and process guided by immaculate law, how can we suppose that in the higher realm of religion the All-wise works fortuitously and without wisdom? Mental, moral and social science is each closely allied to religion. Religion appeals to the intellect, it purifies the moral nature, it regulates the family, and gives laws to the state; it gives direction and impetus to every measure for the civilization of degraded races of men. Does religion seek to do this in contravention of these sciences, or in harmony with them? If the latter, then, certainly, these sciences will justify and explain the methods and requirements of religion.

Nor does physical science refuse this service. It is occupied in discovering the plans, the thoughts and the methods of the divine Worker. If there be thought in nature, then there is an infinite Thinker. However atheistic scientific men and theories may be, they are piling demonstration mountain high relative to the being and attributes of God. Natural science is removing all presumption against the immortality of the soul. Matter is found to be quite as subtile and unknowable in its essence as spirit. The indestructibility of matter; the conservation of force; the infinitude of beings below, as well as above, man, and their immense variety—are all parts of this argument.

We should welcome every sound argument for Christianity, from whatever source it comes; and certainly there is nothing more natural or more worthy of Christianity than that the works of God should corroborate his word. If the preacher can show that nature coincides with revelation relative to the natural attributes of the Deity; if he can illustrate from history, what the Bible declares, that all have sinned; if he shall show that there underlie the atonement the profoundest principles of government; if he shall point out the adaptation of the gospel to change the heart and life; or if he shall show the reasonableness of the awards annexed to the divine commands—who can object, or upon what grounds? This would not underrate nor weaken other proofs. It is not an admission that the older evidences are inadequate. There are also other reasons for this method of treatment. A large and growing class, who are not skilled in weighing historic proofs, are accustomed to this method. Illustrations drawn from science are generally understood. How greatly it expands the horizon to see that Christianity is in perfect accord with every natural and spiritual law! How it exalts our religion to a companionship with the very stars, to show that He who spoke by prophet and apostle, in the olden time, is the same almighty One who spoke worlds into being and flooded them with life and light. Churches are not ruined by this broad, Christian culture, as some suppose. It is rather those who move in narrow, sectarian grooves, who are mainly bent on teaching how to spell or pronounce the party shibboleth, and who are ever acting the religious demagogue, that ruin the churches. If this be the true relation of science and Christianity, what shall we say of those theological schools which are confined to endless genealogies and disputes about words? Of the two, would it not be better for the ministerial candidate to seek first a thorough literary and scientific education, and then trust the pressure and opportunities of his profession for Biblical training? or, rather, would it not be *best* to unite both in a broad and thorough culture of both science and theology?

III. A third class consists of *those who pledge the Bible to false science.* Here the professed friends of Christianity unite with its avowed enemies to build an adverse argument. Who so competent to interpret the Bible as lifelong theologians? and who so worthy of confidence as men eminent in science? Now, if these shall place the Bible and science in diametric antagonism, how can this result otherwise than disastrously to the church? Doctors of divinity, from their pulpits, may decry science, and vigorously apply the Scriptural epithet of "science falsely so called"; but the great world, swayed as it is by an irreligious bias, will desert the theologians and follow the savants. This antagonism, of course, is wholly chargeable to vicious interpretation, since the word and the works of God are in perfect accord. That human science is progressive, and that this progress implies a continual recasting of present theories, scientific men themselves will freely admit; but it is also true that not a few Christian scholars are persistently and blindly pledging the Bible to false science. This was done in former ages, as witness the efforts to array the Bible against the progress of geography, and the opposition of the Roman Church to the Copernican system of astronomy. "Does not," said they, "the Bible speak of the ends of the earth? Did not the sun stand still in the valley of Ajalon, and the shadow go back on the dial of Ahaz? Does not the sun come forth as a bridegroom from his chamber, and rejoice as a strong man to run a race?" It is not only possible, but quite certain, that this folly is being repeated in this enlightened age.

There is a large class who understand the Bible as maintaining the following theses:

1. The universe is not more than six thousand years old.

2. God spoke the world into existence in a sort of magniloquent Miltonic way.

3. God's days are like man's, and only twenty-four hours long.

4. There was no death in the world till Adam sinned.

5. It did not rain till the time of the flood, and there was no rainbow till then.

6. The Deluge was universal to our globe, and the animal kingdom was collected, crowded into the ark, kept alive, and distributed again, all by miracle.

The design and limits of this paper forbid any discussion of the merits of these questions. This, however, may be said: The believer in the Bible who affirms these propositions enters upon a gratuitous work. He is not compelled to their maintenance. He need not pledge the Bible to doubtful, not to say false, science. The sacred writer does not date that "beginning" when God created the heavens and the earth. *How* God made the world, He does not say. Science, without fear of excommunication, may discover this if she can. The word "day," in the first chapter of Genesis, does not of necessity mean twenty-four hours. When it is said this is its plain, literal meaning, we have a bold *petitio principii*. In this chapter and the first of the next, as Professor Dana has shown, Moses uses the word in no less than five different senses. Green, in his excellent Hebrew grammar, shows that this word has great breadth of meaning. The first day, with its long primeval night; the third, when the continents were elevated and the seas formed; the sixth, when man performed so much work and had such varied experiences; and the seventh, lasting till the present time as God's Sabbath relative to this world—were evidently long periods. Very probably the other days were like them. Could the twenty-four-hour interpretation be fixed upon the word, what would be gained? Nothing whatever, and much would be lost. Granting the larger meaning, the order of creation, as given by Moses, is corroborated by every science competent to testify. Why sacrifice, without necessity, so powerful an argument for the inspiration of the first utterances of the Bible? The penalty of death was annexed to human sin, and there is no need to interpret this as being more extensive than the crime. Why so construe the Scriptures, and that without necessity, as to call the ancient generations of plants and animals from their graves to testify against them? The account of the Deluge is susceptible of a better construction than that which makes it universal. Why, then, make it more extensive than the race to be destroyed? Why submerge the entire globe to purge the earth of a few tribes in western Asia? for it is not at all probable that the race spread far over the earth till after the dispersion from the plains of Shinar. If the Scriptures themselves give us searoom, why run into the straits or cling to the rock-bound coast?

Generally, those who dogmatize the most are least entitled to a hearing. The ease and self-assurance with which some preachers declare what the Bible *must* mean, and their off-hand relegation of scientific theories, facts and authorities to the shades of uncertainty, would be simply ridiculous, if it were not so harmful to the cause of Christianity. It is even more pitiful when men who have spent their whole lives in scientific pursuits, who have narrowed their minds down to the study of some particular monad, or who have nearly gone crazy over protoplasm, shall assume to pronounce on historical evidence and religious doctrines. Such charlatanism brings both science and religion into disrepute.

IV. *These who hold unreasonable doctrines and seek to fasten them upon the Bible* constitute a fourth class. By *unreasonable doctrines* is not meant, in this connection, doctrines about which reason says nothing, and which are above reason. Of course, such doctrines can be known only by revelation, and reason has only to say whether the professed revelation is of divine authority or not. This reference is rather to doctrines which are inconsistent with the admitted intuitions and deductions of reason. Infidels endeavor to load down Christianity with the religious wars and persecutions involved in its history; with church quarrels and divisions, and with the weaknesses and immoralities of its advocates. With these infidels many good and great men unite, when to this already crushing burden they add tons of unreasonable and absurd dogmas.

Among illustrative examples, Calvinism is entitled to take the lead. It never saved a soul; for salvation is through faith in Christ and obedience to Him. Myriads have stumbled over it into hell. It is concentrated fatalism. From eternity the unchangeable One elects and reprobates. This election is made sure by a partial atonement, for Christ, according to this doctrine, died only for the elect. To make this fatality doubly fatal, men are totally depraved, and are only capable of doing evil, and that continually. Lest this depravity should, by some mischance, prove ineffectual, Calvinism makes sure that none shall believe and be saved without the "effectual call." Still further, the Almighty's hand is on those who are called, and, however they may wander and resist, they are bound to persevere and be saved. This election was determined by no merit in the saved, nor by any foresight that they would believe in Christ, but solely by the arbitrary will of God. This untrue and degrading view of human nature, this blasphemy against the character of God, this theological system having so much more damnation in it than salvation—these, if any things, are condemned of reason as moral absurdities. The wonder that so many generations should commit the keeping of their souls to such a system is only second to the greater wonder that so many good and learned men can subscribe to a creed which they no longer believe nor preach. And yet there is a true doctrine of election. God, at various times, elected men and nations to carry out His plans, though not to eternal life. , He has elected character rather than persons. It is an election through belief of the truth and sanctification of the Spirit—an election in which the soul itself gives the casting vote. Calvinism is sustained by obscure passages, and far-fetched metaphysical inferences. As a system of human speculations, it is but cobwebs, compared with the universal commands, promises and whosoever-wills of the divine Word.

Equally absurd is that tenet of Arminianism which teaches that a person can not understand and obey the gospel till he has become the subject of miraculous converting power. It makes little difference whether the election and reprobation were an eternity ago, or in this life. In either case the doomed soul has no alternative. In either case God is represented as refusing men the power to believe, and then condemning them for not believing.

Another example is the claim of sanctification, in the sense that one can reach such a state of perfection that he no longer commits sin. If by attending a so-called "Holiness camp-meeting," or by importunate prayer, one could rise to such serene heights, it would be a consummation devoutly to be wished; especially would it be a good thing if some of our public men could graduate in this school before their election to office. That sinlessness is to be approximated by feeling rather than by learning and doing; that this quick and patent method is better than the old-fashioned way; that we can surpass prophets and apostles, or reach such a stage that we shall need no advocate with God—are suppositions sufficiently daring; and we have no need to face the Scripture declaration that "if a man say he has no sin, he is a liar, and the truth is not in him."

Christian learning and piety have often been employed in giving the sanction of Heaven to systems of immorality and oppression. The blessings of God have been invoked on the cruelest tyrannies. Scripture texts have been patched together by ingenious men to hide the deformities of states and institutions. Intemperance continues its ravages by the sufferance of professed Christians.

New Testament Christianity

The church has the power to slay this monster at a single blow. If these unconscious enemies could make Christianity support oppression and crime, this success would be fatal to our religion. The moral purity of Christianity, like the sinlessness of its Founder, is the rock on which it is built. As the sun needs no proof that it hangs in midheaven but its own light and heat, so the moral purity of Bible teaching declares its divine origin.

Again, there are whole nations who maintain that Roman Catholicism is Christianity; and it must be admitted that they are sincere in this. In proportion, however, as they shall succeed, will they undermine the religion they profess to love. Men of reading and thought can never believe that any pope, however wise and good, is God's vicegerent, is infallible in the interpretation of the Bible, or immaculate in the management of the church. The nineteenth century can not brook the Romish confessional, which, in its very nature, is an invasion of the sanctity of home. The sale of indulgences, of masses for the dead, and of prayers for souls in purgatory, are but so many means by which the priest may hold his victim over the pit of hell, and threaten to drop him in, unless he pays handsomely. The horrors of the Inquisition, the impurity of its priests, and its grasping after political power, reveal its true character. History, reason and science impeach it of high crimes and misdemeanors.

Unconscious Enemies of Christianity

It is evident that all these advocates of error are enemies of true religion, however unconscious of this enmity and however pious they may be. And it is evident, furthermore, that Christianity must make slow progress while these things stand in its way.

V. Another class of unconscious enemies is composed of some of the most pious and zealous members of the church—*those whose ideas of conversion, and methods of promoting it, are not in harmony with mental and moral science.* The prevalent and misnamed orthodox teaching concerning conversion is, undoubtedly, the chief obstacle to the propagation of Christianity. In one view, it is a marvel that all do not accept this religion. Its demands are evidently right, for they are simply that we shall do the best for ourselves and our fellow-men. It enjoins the noblest life. In this world it brings us the peace of God, and, in the world to come, life everlasting. It requires the renunciation of no real enjoyment, of no permanent good. The disappointments and sorrows of this life, our consciousness of guilt, and our fear to tread the lonely pathway of the grave, powerfully dissuade us from the rejection of this, our only hope. Against these pleadings within and without, pride of consistency, fear of man, and the love of sinful pleasure could not prevail. If the earth repels and all the stars attract, how shall we not leave this blighted world and soar to

New Testament Christianity

the heavens? So it was in the ancient times. Three thousand accepted the first offer of mercy. Two thousand were the result of a second sermon. In less than three centuries the whole civilized world acknowledged the lordship of the Nazarene. Now, after months of preaching, we rejoice over a few scores or hundreds. The vast multitudes remain unmoved. There are various causes for this difference, but among them all the most potent hindrance is this popular, but unreasonable and unscriptural, view of conversion. A charge so grave as this requires careful statement and proof.

First, conversion is presented, not as a moral change to be brought about by moral means, and as something to be done by the moral agent, but as a spiritual change, to be wrought by divine and superhuman power. The teaching from ten thousand pulpits is that faith, repentance, and a consequent change of life, are no part of conversion, but that above and beyond these we must have what is called a "change of heart," or the "new birth." This inward renewal is secured by an act of special mercy, and made known to the recipient by a special and peculiar experience. This experience is the passport into the church, and often the only hope of heaven. *Secondly,* it is evident that, in order to secure such a conversion, two things must be done. The sinner must be induced to believe in Christ and repent, as necessary conditions; and then the believing penitent must unite with the church in supplication for this divine grace, for this spiritual change. Both God and the sinner must be converted. After the preaching to sinners, there must be the praying to God. The first meeting is for sinners, but the second is for God; and the latter is usually the longest, most earnest and most uncertain. *Thirdly,* the evidence of this conversion is not the certainty of any divine promise, nor the compliance with any divine commands, but this experience rather. This is a brief, but just, statement of popular teaching and practice. There may be minor differences, but these are the prominent features.

The consequences of this teaching are most injurious. There is no reason to doubt the validity of the professed experience. It can not be clearly defined; and, in fact, no two are alike. One sees a light, and another dreams a dream. Some fall as dead, and others shout till they are hoarse. Mental excitement and anguish of soul prevent all calm observation and judgment; and yet upon this change life and death depend. How much of this experience is owing to joy consequent upon submission to God and to sympathy with the joy of our praying friends, and how much to this spiritual change, none can tell. Belief in its reality is exceedingly fluctuating. It depends on mental states. In times of despondency, when most needed, it vanishes away. A large portion of Christian people have a "standing doubt," where there ought to be the utmost certainty. Besides, if this change is real, why is it not relied upon as a continual miracle in proof of Christianity?

It certainly would be miraculous, and as demonstrative as the raising of the dead. Instead of prophet, apostle or argument, call in a score of witnesses, put them under oath, and let them testify. But this is never done, because Christians themselves have so little confidence in it. The overthrow of such a claim has a powerful recoil against religion itself. Another result is, that "getting religion" becomes an experiment, and few men like to subject themselves to such experiments, and that in a public manner. It is a trial, and often a failure. Many a penitent suppliant turns away from the anxious-seat a confirmed infidel. Few like to submit to the manipulations and whisperings of a certain class of revivalists and their fanatical helpers. This is all so different from everything else, and all so foreign to their methods of investigation and self-determination, as to prevent even a trial of this way. Further, this view represents God as being most capricious. Now, He loves the world and gives His Son for it. He sends abroad the gospel proclamation, inviting whosoever will to come and live; and yet He is so unwilling to hear and forgive that all this importunity is needed; nay, is often unavailing.

Unconscious Enemies of Christianity

By this view, churches are restricted and greatly hindered in their efforts to evangelize. Revivals are believed to come as special providences. The rain may fall on one country, but not on another. There may be a work of grace at Pittsburgh, but can not be at Cincinnati, unless God comes down the river. Most churches sit, like Elijah on Mt. Carmel, with their heads bowed upon their knees, waiting till some sign shall appear. There is also, on this view, a wonderful misdirection of effort. If churches would reason and plead with sinners as they do with God, they would soon be converted. Not that it is wrong to pray for things God has promised, but we do not *truly* pray unless we work for the fulfillment of our prayers. This view of conversion leads to the wildest extravagance and fanaticism. Prayers are offered that the Holy Spirit may "just now" touch the hearts of distant friends and convert them; as if these friends would not have been converted long ago, if it depended solely on the divine will. Revivals sweep over society like cyclones from the tropics, leaving only years of religious declension in their path.

The apostles advanced no theory of spiritual influence. They preached not the Holy Spirit, but Christ and Him crucified. They plainly declared the conditions by an honest compliance with which every man might have the divine assurance of pardon. Such preaching now, as then, would commend itself to the reason and conscience of the most gifted and cultivated men, and also be level to the comprehension of the great mass of mankind.

VI. The last class to be considered is composed of *those who are devoted to the maintenance of denominationalism.* It is no more certain that these are unconscious of hostility to Christianity than that religious parties are injurious to the church; both must be granted. The Saviour established but one kingdom, and He prayed that all His followers might be one as He and the Father were one, that the world might believe that God had sent Him. Nothing would so hasten the day of millennial glory as the organic and spiritual union of all believers in Christ. Those who take the opposite position do so in disregard of the prayer of Christ, the purest aspirations of the church for peace and universal fellowship, the results of union in ancient and modern times, and the deep conviction of nearly the whole Christian world. They are only exercising their ingenuity in defense of a bad case. Denominationalism not only distracts and discourages those who are seeking Christ, but it is also a powerful weapon in the hands of infidels.

Multitudes would abandon sectarianism and this unconscious hostility to Christ, if they could see any way out of the labyrinths of Protestant creeds and parties. This is undoubtedly a most difficult problem. It implies not only the opening of the prison doors and the great iron gate, but also unbinding the prisoners and inducing them to escape. It would be to this age what the Reformation under Luther was to the sixteenth century. Without claiming the solution of this problem, which perhaps is possible only to Divine Providence, a few suggestions only are offered:

1. Those who maintain denominationalism mistake the purpose of the church. It was commissioned to publish the gospel and help men in their struggle against sin. It does not receive men to doubtful disputations and the discussion of endless genealogies. It is not a convention for the adoption of a creed. It is not an Inquisition to try and burn heretics. It is not its province to keep an *index expurgatorius* of men as well as of books. But it is a home for those who would break off their sins by righteousness. Its sole business is to *help* those who are ready to perish. How sadly the Christian world has forgotten this! While the day is far spent, and uncounted millions are ready to perish, we are settling dogmas, measuring one another's relative soundness, and arranging the etiquette of worship! A man may be very ignorant, and consequently very unsound, and yet be a child of God. If we must all be "sound" in order to be saved, God have mercy on those who *think* they are sound.

2. Again, it may help us to consider that all truth is not equally important. There are truths

which were all-important to men of ancient times, but which have little to do with us. There are other truths which will be important when we come to them. How evil came into existence is an interesting question, and also whether the soul is conscious or not between death and the resurrection; but they have little to do with the present time. Men *are* sinners, and it *is* appointed unto men once to die. The present truth is essential. How shall dying men be saved, is the great practical question. It is an ever-present truth that we should add to our faith courage, knowledge, temperance, patience, godliness, brotherly kindness and charity. If we should erase from our creeds all dead and all unborn truths, they would become wonderfully short and simple. Passing over a thousand questions whose discussion only serves to divide, weaken and delay, let us hasten to the rescue of the shipwrecked multitudes.

3. How far should we hold ourselves responsible for the religious views of other people? Before we set about the task of making all men see alike on every subject, it might be well to ask if this would be pleasing to the Lord. Has any man a right to thrust himself between another man's soul and his God? Is it not the right and the duty of every man to study the Bible for himself, as he must answer for himself before the judgment-seat of Christ? Who would assume the responsibility of another man's soundness in

religious matters? Who, even if he had the power, would make all men believe as he does? It is our duty, indeed, to give all the light we can, and also to receive it from whatever source, but, further than this, how can we be responsible? And yet the great object of the struggling sects is the questionable privilege of regulating the beliefs of all others. In their over-self-confidence, they would make all others like themselves. Shall we disfellowship whole parties because they differ from us in matters not essential to salvation? Would such a course make matters better? Would it not be our duty, rather, to mingle with them and afford them light? Besides, our own eyes might be opened. If Baptists have light which Methodists need, and *vice versa,* how are they to illumine one another in total isolation? Difference of religious views is generally a reason for association, and not for Pharisaic separation.

4. Again, it might be useful to inquire what association with religious people implies an indorsement of their heresies. Do we indorse their errors when we go along the street with them, when we trade with them, when they become business partners, when we read their books, when we hear their preaching, when we pray with them, when we work with them in helping on benevolent enterprises? If any or all of these acts imply an indorsement of all the views of associated persons, then who can be saved? We must needs go out of

the world. All this demonstrates that the basis of union must be simple, and composed only of saving truth.

5. Finally, in our search for a plan of union, it would be well to ask if there is a Scriptural, a divine plan. What was the one truth to be believed in ancient times? What degree and kind of union prevailed then, and how was it secured? Particularly, how were Jews and Gentiles made one in Christ? This divine plan might be worth ten thousand of human invention.

Incomplete as this enumeration of the unconscious enemies of Christianity may be, it suffices to show two things: *First,* that the greatest hindrance to the progress of Christianity comes from the church itself. Historical criticism, false science and infidel ridicule are nothing compared with this. These unconscious enemies are all the more to be dreaded because they are sincere and pious. Their complete removal requires ages of religious progress. It should lead to prayerful searchings of heart and life, to find and bring into judgment any lurking and unconscious enmity to Christ that may be there. *Secondly,* it shows the inherent power of Christianity. It can endure the mistakes of its friends as well as the attacks of its enemies. Notwithstanding both, it is marching on from conquering unto conquest.

THE LAW OF PARDON

J. S. SWEENEY

TO ascertain the terms of pardon offered to the alien under the gospel dispensation is the object of this sermon. And as to the importance of the subject, not a sentence is deemed necessary. But a few definitive remarks shall constitute the preliminary.

1. *The inquiry is for the terms on which an alien can obtain pardon.* That an offending citizen of Christ's kingdom can obtain pardon—and must, if at all—by repentance and prayer, is very generally conceded by Christians; but that these simply are the terms on which the gospel offers pardon to an *alien* is denied.

2. *Pardon under the gospel dispensation* is treated of, and not pardon under former dispensations. And the gospel dispensation can be dated no further back than to the time our Lord gave commission to His apostles to "go into all the world, and preach the gospel to every creature." Touching this point, Richard Watson, the great

Methodist theologian, in his "Institutes," says, after citing the commission as recorded by Mark:

"To understand the force of these words of our Lord, it must be observed that the gate of the common salvation was only now for the first time going to be opened to the Gentile nations. He Himself had declared that in His personal ministry He was not sent but to the lost sheep of the house of Israel; and He had restricted His disciples in like manner, not only from ministering to the Gentiles, but from entering any city of the Samaritans" (p. 630).

Again, the same writer, same book, after speaking of the baptism of John and that practiced by the disciples of our Lord previous to His resurrection, says:

"For since the new covenant was not then fully perfected, it could not be proposed in any other way than to prepare them that believed in Christ, by its partial, but increasing, manifestation in the discourses of our Lord, for the full declaration both of its benefits and obligations, which declaration was not made until after his resurrection" (p. 632).

But *divine* authority for this definition will appear as we proceed with the investigation.

3. The terms "pardoned," "saved," "forgiven," and the phrase "remission of sins," will be used as expressive of the same idea—*will be used interchangeably.*

The Law of Pardon

4. *Pardon and conversion, in their popular acceptation, are two distinct things.* Conversion is generally understood to refer solely to an internal change; and that it does refer to such a change, when not used in its most extended sense, is not denied. But pardon never indicates such a change, except that it may imply that such a change has passed. Conversion, in the sense generally assigned it, passes in the mind and heart of the person converted; while pardon passes in the mind of the Lord, and is something done *for* the person pardoned. Pardon comes after conversion, and is dependent upon it. This will appear from one or two Scriptures:

"Lest at any time they should see with their eyes, and hear with their ears, and should understand with their heart, and should be converted, and I should heal them" (Matt. 13:15).

"*Heal*," here, evidently means *pardon*, and, it will be observed, comes after conversion, and is something the Lord does *for* the converted person.

"Repent ye, therefore, and be converted, that your sins may be blotted out" (Acts 3:19).

Evidently the phrase, "that your sins may be blotted out," simply means that your sins may be *remitted*. And here, also, we see that remission of sins, or pardon, comes after conversion, and depends upon it. Let it be constantly borne in mind, then, that, by pardon, conversion is not meant.

New Testament Christianity

These definitions understood, and we are prepared to proceed with the proposed investigation.

All who are laboring for the salvation of sinners must, on a final reference, refer to our Lord's last commission for all the divine authority they have for so laboring. From what other source has any man living derived any sufficient authority for *offering pardon to a sinner on any terms?* To think of this question but for a single moment brings us to the answer.

As, therefore, all our authority for offering pardon to sinners, for preaching repentance and remission of sins in the name of the Lord, is derived from this commission, it follows irresistibly that we are only authorized to propound pardon *on the terms therein stipulated.* And this view of the matter should, were it possible to do so, swell the importance of this great commission in our estimation, in the investigation of this subject. To this important document, then, we are now ready to give attention:

"Go ye therefore and teach all nations, baptizing them in the name of the Father, and of the Son, and of the Holy Ghost" (Matt. 28:19).

"Go ye into all the world, and preach the gospel to every creature. He that believes and is baptized shall be saved; but he that believes not shall be damned" (Mark 16:15, 16).

"Thus it is written, and thus it behooved Christ to suffer and to rise from the dead the

The Law of Pardon

third day, and that repentance and remission of sins should be preached in his name among all nations, beginning at Jerusalem'' (Luke 24: 46, 47).

"As my Father hath sent me, even so send I you. And when he had said this, he breathed on them, and said, Receive ye the Holy Ghost: Whosesoever sins ye remit, they are remitted unto them, and whosesoever sins ye retain, they are retained" (John 20: 21-23).

Here we have before us our Lord's great commission, given for the Christianization of the world, as recorded by four inspired writers; and *from these records we are to eliminate the terms of pardon.* And it is noticeable that these records are not given in the same words, yet there is the utter absence of anything like contradiction. For where the same facts are touched by any two or more of them, they perfectly accord. Yet, in their testimony, they do not seem to notice the same points, and narrate them in the same order. But, so far from throwing any doubt over their testimony, as has been claimed, this circumstance strengthens it, and to thinking persons displays the wisdom of God. As illustrative of this, let us suppose an analogous case: A. is accused of the murder of B. and is brought to trial for the crime. Four witnesses are introduced to prove his guilt. They testify each to facts not noticed by the others, but, wherein they touch the same facts, there is perfect harmony. In all their testimony there is no contradiction, and, taken as a whole, it establishes the guilt of A. Now, because these witnesses do not all testify to precisely the same facts in the same words, shall their testimony be ruled out of court? Certainly not. And again, must not the jurors, in making out a verdict, consider all the testimony of these four witnesses? Certainly. Precisely of such character is, and so must be treated, the testimony God has given concerning His Son. If we would have the whole truth concerning any fact connected with the life, death or resurrection of our Lord, or concerning anything taught by Him, this rule must be observed: *Consider all that is said touching it by the four inspired witnesses.* This rule must be strictly observed if we would understand the commission. And for this reason attention is called to the commission as it is given in all the inspired records. This rule has not been generally observed. For when the advocate of infant sprinkling would find authority for it in the commission, he has use only for what he calls "Matthew's commission." It says nothing about faith or repentance as antecedents to baptism. He reads it simply, "*disciple* the nations, baptizing them," etc. But were he to read this great commission as recorded by all the inspired penmen, it would simply ruin his argument. But to return: Let us now carefully examine these records of the commission, and gather all its specifications.

The Law of Pardon

From Matthew we get simply *"teaching"* and *"baptizing."* Mark has it, instead of "teach all nations," *"preach the gospel* to every creature." What, therefore, Matthew means by *"teach,"* Mark expresses by *"preach the gospel."* Preaching is teaching; that is, sensible preaching—such as the Lord contemplated—is. But Mark adds: "He that *believes* [here is an additional item] and is baptized [here he touches one of the items given by Matthew, and harmonizes with him] shall be saved; but he that believes not shall be condemned." All this last is more than was mentioned by Matthew, but not contradictory of anything he said. Putting their testimonies together, we have *teaching, faith, baptism, salvation* and *damnation* to the person that believes not. But, by examining Luke's testimony, we get the additional item of *repentance,* and learn what Mark means by "saves"; for Luke calls it "remission of sins." He also informs us that this great work among "all nations" was to have its "beginning at Jerusalem." John is more general in the terms of his record than any of them, and from him we get nothing additional.

Summing all up, then, we have as follows: *Teaching, faith, repentance, baptism, remission of sins,* and *damnation* to him who believes not. We also learn from the testimony before us that this commission is universal in its character: it sends the preacher to "all nations"—in this respect unlike any commission previously given by Heaven to man.

Now, that all the items before enumerated are in this commission, is agreed to by all the parties of the day. They all contend for them, preach and practice them in some order in discipling persons. The difference between us, therefore, is not so much in *fact* as it is in *order*. The *order* in which these items stand is the matter about which we differ so widely and contend so strenuously. In what order does a person come to teaching, faith, repentance, baptism and pardon? Here we differ widely, and hence we differ about the antecedents and conditions of pardon. Let us look this difference full in the face; for there is no use to cover it up. We are all agreed that the commission, under which we profess to operate, authorizes us to *teach*, to require *faith, repentance* and *baptism*, and to promise *pardon*. But in what order do these matters stand in the divine arrangement? This is the question! Now, there are *three orders* advocated by the professing Christians of the day. There are the pedobaptist, the Baptist and the Christian *orders;* and they are as follows:

1. *Pedobaptist:* (1) Baptism, (2) teaching, (3) repentance, (4) faith and (5) pardon.

2. *Baptist:* (1) Teaching, (2) repentance, (3) faith, (4) salvation and (5) baptism.

3. *Christian:* (1) Teaching, (2) faith, (3) repentance, (4) baptism and (5) pardon.

The Law of Pardon

Are all fairly represented here? It may be said that the pedobaptists are not—that they do not put baptism first in order, as they are here represented. But still it is contended that the order here given them is correct; that is, that it is their order. It will not be denied that this is their order in the case of infants—that baptism is the first thing in the commission they give to them. Well, it is submitted that this is their rule, and anything else they may practice in case of adults is merely exceptional. It is granted that they do sometimes baptize persons who have been previously taught and who believe, but it is done in every such case simply because they *could not baptize such persons before they were taught*. Their rule is to baptize in infancy, and before teaching, and that they may baptize after they have been taught and believe are merely exceptions to the regular pedobaptist order. This is obvious. Notwithstanding this, it is freely granted that pedobaptists are in the habit of complaining that others get their subjects to the water too soon! Now let every one be held responsible for his own consistency. Pedobaptists are the first people to the water!

It is difficult to see how they can find in the commission one order for an infant, and another different one for an adult. For who can not see that to whom any part of the commission applies, it all applies; and that the order in which it applies to one is the order in which it applies to all? The Lord makes no such distinctions and variations as appear in their practice. But now we are ready for the most important question of all, and the one that bears directly upon the subject of this discourse. Is any one of these orders correct, and, if so, which one? Here we have a question of order to which there are three parties claiming respectively as follows:

1. *Pedobaptists:* (1) Baptism, (2) teaching, (3) repentance, (4) faith and (5) pardon.

2. *Baptists:* (1) Teaching, (2) repentance, (3) faith, (4) pardon and (5) baptism.

3. *Christians:* (1) Teaching, (2) faith, (3) repentance, (4) baptism and (5) pardon.

To whom shall we refer this question? To Father Wesley? We are not agreed. To Dr. D. R. Campbell? Still we are not agreed. To A. Campbell? No! no! Then, to whom shall we refer it? It is proposed that it shall be decided by the Spirit of God—the Spirit of unerring wisdom. Who objects? Surely none can.

Immediately following Luke's record of the commission we have this promise and instruction given by our Lord to His disciples: "And behold, I send the promise of my Father upon you; but tarry ye in the city of Jerusalem till ye be endued with power from on high."

And in another place He promises them the Spirit in these words: "But the Comforter, the Holy Ghost, whom the Father will send in my

The Law of Pardon

name, he shall teach you all things, and bring all things to your remembrance, whatsoever I have said unto you.''

From these Scriptures, and others that might be cited here, it appears that the apostles, before entering upon the work assigned them in this commission, were to tarry in the city of Jerusalem till they received the Holy Spirit; and that by it they were to be guided into all the truth. We learn also from Acts (first and second chapters) that they did go, as instructed, to Jerusalem, and there awaited the coming of the Spirit; that the Spirit came as promised by the Saviour: ''And they were all filled with the Holy Spirit, and began to speak with other tongues, as the Spirit gave them utterance.'' There and then they began the work assigned them in the commission, guided by the Spirit of God into all the truth. Then, and ever afterward, when proclaiming the gospel, they were directed by the Spirit that never errs. It is proposed, then, that we take our stand here and see the *order* of the commission set forth infallibly right. For whatever order is set forth here manifestly bears the divine sanction, for it is the work of the Spirit of the living God.

After explaining the miraculous phenomena of the occasion, for these attracted the attention of the people, the apostle Peter preached the gospel to the multitude; or, in other words, *taught* the people concerning Jesus. After a profound and convincing argument, he concluded: "Therefore let all the house of Israel know assuredly, that God hath made that same Jesus, whom ye have crucified, both Lord and Christ."

Evidently the first in order here is *teaching*. This can not be disputed. And we are informed that when the people "heard this they were pierced in the heart, and said unto Peter and the rest of the apostles, Men and brethren, what shall we do?" Here we have, in the second place, unmistakable evidence of *faith*. When these persons are "pierced in the heart" with what they had before supposed to be false, and call on the apostles, whose mouths they had before stopped, to know *what they must do,* do they not *believe?* It would be too great a compromise of common sense to argue such a question. The question now to be answered by the direction of the Holy Spirit is, What must such persons do?—persons who have been *taught* concerning Christ and who *believe*. Hear the answer: "Repent [this settles the order of faith and repentance, for here *believers* are told to repent], and be baptized every one of you in the name of Jesus Christ for the remission of sins." Here, then, we have all the items contained in the commission set forth in the following order: (1) Teaching, (2) faith, (3) repentance, (4) baptism, (5) remission of sins. This settles the question of *order*. Here we find the *place* in the divine arrangement, and consequently

The Law of Pardon

the conditions of pardon. A man must be *taught,* he must *believe, repent,* and be *baptized,* and then he comes to pardon, as it stands in the gospel plan.

This order of the great commission is not so fully and clearly set forth in any subsequent case of salvation that occurred under apostolic preaching; nor was it necessary that it should be. Yet not a single instance in which a person came to pardon in any different way can be shown in the entire history of the preaching of the apostles. There are cases, it is true, where persons came to pardon, in which all these items are not named in their order, but they are clearly understood. With the case we have examined, which was the *beginning* of the work, fully before our minds, we will readily see the same simple order throughout the entire Acts of the Apostles. Nor is there anything contrary to this—as it has been claimed—in any of the apostolic Epistles. On the contrary, it is there corroborated. It is true that, as against this order, such passages as predicate our justification, of salvation, of faith, or of grace, or of something else without naming all the condition, are often cited. But for the power of prejudice over the mind on which it has hold, this objection need not be noticed; but, on that account, a brief notice is deemed necessary. It is not held that we are saved *by* the conditions before set forth—nor *on* those conditions—independently of the grace of God, the blood of Christ, the resurrection of Christ, or the work of the Holy Spirit. We are saved by the grace of God, by the blood of Jesus, by the resurrection of Christ, by the Spirit of God, *and yet* we must be *taught*, must *believe, repent,* and be *baptized* for the remission of sins. But for the grace of God, Jesus would never have died for sinners; but for His death, there would have been no gospel; but for the Spirit of God, the gospel would never have been preached to men; but for the preaching of the gospel, men would never have been *taught*, could not have *believed*, would not have *repented* and been *baptized;* and, consequently, there would have been none saved. When, therefore, the Scriptures predicate our salvation of grace, it is right; and so of the blood of Christ, of the Spirit of God, of the name of Jesus Christ, of knowledge, of faith, of repentance and of baptism. When grace is the subject of which the *inspired* writer treats, he predicates our justification of it, without there naming any other cause or condition. So of the blood of Christ. So of faith. So of any cause or condition of our salvation.

The passage, "Therefore being justified by faith," only teaches that we are *justified by faith.* That's all. The language does not exclude the grace of God, the blood of Christ, repentance or baptism—in one word, *it excludes nothing.*

Again, the expression, "Baptism doth also now save us," only predicates our salvation of bap-

The Law of Pardon

tism—not of baptism *alone*—because the apostle is there *speaking of baptism*. It is submitted, therefore, as a rule, *that where in the Scriptures our salvation is predicated of a named cause or condition, every other cause and condition named elsewhere in the Scriptures must be understood.* Otherwise, the Scriptures will be made self-contradictory.

Perhaps the only objection that will ever be raised to this discourse will be that it makes baptism a condition going before pardon. True, it does, and simply because the word of God does. And so have taught the most eminent men in all the denominations that now denounce the doctrine as terribly heretical. It may not be out of place, therefore, to conclude this discourse with a few quotations from some of those eminent men:

1. John Wesley: "It is true, the second Adam has found a remedy for the disease which came upon all by the offence of the first. But the benefit of this is to be received through the means which He hath appointed; through baptism in particular, which is the ordinary means He hath appointed for that purpose; and to which God hath tied us, though He may not have tied Himself" ("Treatise on Baptism, Doctrinal Tracts," p. 251). This doctrine was published for several years, and up to 1864, by the General Conference of the Methodist Episcopal Church. True, in 1864, the Conference laid this treatise by Mr.

Wesley aside, substituting therefor one by a committee appointed by Conference for the special purpose of revising Methodist doctrine on that subject—in which new tract we have as follows:

2. "Baptism, therefore, is a sacred rite, without which no man can be initiated into the visible church of Christ. See Rom. 4:11, etc., where baptism is clearly connected with the promise of God respecting our salvation. And also Mark 16:16, where the promise of salvation is secured to the baptized believer; namely, 'He that believeth and is baptized shall be saved' " (pp. 244-5).

In Richard Watson's "Theological Institutes"—a book that the Methodist Discipline recommends him who would be a Methodist preacher, to study *four years*—we have this language, after some extended and sensible remarks on 1 Pet. 3:21:

"It is thus that we see how St. Peter preserves the correspondence between the act of Noah in preparing the ark as an act of faith by which he was justified, and the act of submitting to Christian baptism, which is also obviously an act of faith, *in order to the remission of sins*, or the obtaining a good conscience before God" (p. 630).

This language is as strong as it can be, and so plain that all can understand it without difficulty.

Next we will hear Dr. Gale, than whom we have no superior scholar or writer among the Baptists. In his "Reflections on Wall's 'History of

The Law of Pardon

Infant Baptism'" (Letter II., p. 83), we have as follows:

4. "Baptism, I grant, is of great necessity; and though I dare fix no limits to the infinite goodness and mercy of God, which I am confident He will give mighty proofs of, in great instances of kindness toward all sincere, though mistaken, men; however, the gospel rule is, according to the doctrine of the apostle, *to repent and be baptized for the remission of sins.* We should be very cautious, therefore, of making any change in these things, lest we deprive ourselves, through our presumption, of that title to pardon without which there is no salvation."

The concluding *caution* of this eminent Baptist is most affectionately urged upon his brethren, who, of late, it seems, for the sake of being orthodox, as well as the pedobaptists, have agreed with them to call baptism a *non-essential.*

May God help all who strive for the truth! Amen.

THE HISTORY OF REDEMPTION REPRODUCED IN THE REDEEMED

J. S. LAMAR

"How shall we, that are dead to sin, live any longer therein? Know ye not that so many of us as were baptized into Jesus Christ were baptized into his death? Therefore we are buried with him by baptism into death: that like as Christ was raised up from the dead by the glory of the Father, even so we also should walk in newness of life. For if we have been planted together in the likeness of his death, we shall be also in the likeness of his resurrection: knowing this, that our old man is crucified with him, that the body of sin might be destroyed, that henceforth we should not serve sin. For he that is dead is freed from sin."—Rom. 6: 2-7.

THE leading doctrine taught in this Scripture, and which it shall be my object, in the present discourse, to prove and illustrate, may be summed up in a single proposition; namely, *that what the Lord did and suffered in order to enter into His glory must, in some sense, be done and suffered by every one who is to participate in that glory.*

Before entering upon the argument and elucidation of this proposition, it may be well to remark that it embraces the whole of duty and salvation.

Redemption Reproduced

There is nothing for us to do or bear that is not exemplified in the history of our great Captain and Leader. At the same time, it is important to remember that, in seeking to follow His example, we are not to commence with His birth, or baptism, or temptation, or any of the labors of His active life. All these we pass by, and begin with the *last* scenes *first*. And it is not until after we have followed Him through all these, and been made thus the sons of God; not until we can say, "Christ liveth in us"—that we can begin to live the life of Christ, or hope to imitate the example of that life. Hence the Scripture from which we shall draw our discourse points us to the last events of His earthly career as the first for our imitation, thus teaching us that if we would be "glorified together" with Him, we must, first of all, *re-enact the history out of which His glory sprang*. A part of this history is implied, and a part is expressed, in the text. Let us refer to it in its regular order, and make the application as we proceed.

It was just after Judas had gone out to betray Him, that He exclaimed, with triumphant exultation, "Now is the Son of man glorified;" by which He doubtless meant that He was now about to enter upon those sufferings for which He was to be crowned with glory and honor. But so completely was His heart enraptured by the blessedness beyond, that He overlooked or disregarded the intervening sorrows of the Garden, the pains of Calvary, and the darkness of the tomb. And yet it was *out* of these the glory was to arise, and *for* these the crown was to be conferred. And is it not true of every man that, when heaven is, first of all, appreciated, and its holiness perceived to be the chief good; and when the freeness and fullness of gospel promises give assurance that all may be his—he forgets the crucifixion and burial, which must necessarily antedate his resurrection to life and bliss, and learns, not till afterward, that no man can reach the crown without first coming to the cross; and that no man will come to the cross who has not first passed through the garden?

It is the teaching of revelation, confirmed by every Christian's experience, that he who comes to Christ has previously felt "weary and heavy laden"; has realized the agony of sin; his soul has been made exceeding sorrowful—the "godly sorrow for sin which worketh repentance." And how often has such a man retired into the darkness, to struggle with his burden, and to pray all alone; and so, "pierced to the heart," weeping and in anguish, and doubtless strengthened in his weakness by some messenger of God, he comes at last to say, nay, to desire, "Thy will, O God, be done." Thus he "learns obedience by the things which he suffers." He realizes the *necessity* for it. His own misery teaches him the consequences of sin, and he determines henceforth to obey; and from his heart he cries, "Lord, what wilt thou have me to do?" It is then, in the hour of darkness and tears and agony, that he gives the first solemn pledge to God to be, to do and to suffer all that He wills.

When such a man hears the command, "Follow the Lord Jesus," he will not be careful to analyze it into its external and internal elements, nor to test it by some alchemy of human philosophy, to see whether it be essential or non-essential; enough for him that it is the voice of God. Hence, he goes boldly forward. It may be in the presence of scoffers and infidels; he cares not. He has a settled purpose that he will identify himself with Jesus Christ, and confess with his mouth the confidence he has in Him; and he does it, rejoicing that he is permitted, even in this, to imitate Him "who, before Pontius Pilate, witnessed a good confession."

But it should not be forgotten that, though this is "the good confession," and though "with the mouth confession is made unto salvation," it can only result in this blessing when the subsequent conduct is consistent with it. If he pause with the bare profession with the mouth, it is but lip service; and hence, while the Saviour has graciously promised to confess those before His Father who confess Him before men, He does not fail to warn us that many *call* Him Lord who *do* not *obey* Him *as* Lord; by which He would teach us that the confession which secures salvation is one which ultimates in obedience. All would be willing to be Christians in name, doubtless, if they might be allowed to live on in the lusts of the flesh and the pride of life; but the plain intimation of the text, and which perfectly accords with the example of the Saviour, is that this confession necessitates *death;* and just here is, for most men, "the stone of stumbling and rock of offense." They are willing to pronounce eloquent, and, it may be, heartfelt, panegyrics upon the cross of Christ. They can speak in melting tones of Calvary, and point to the "marred visage" of the Crucified with evident emotion. They can tell us, too, in well-selected phrase, of the infinite merits of the whole world; but they are slow to learn that, as a matter of fact, it really *does* take away the sins of those only, not who *admire* Him, but who are *"crucified with him."*

"Take up *thy cross,"* says the Saviour, "and follow me." How prone we are to explain away this "cross," by making it no more than some public confession, some speaking or praying before men, or the performance of some other duty that is simply disagreeable, as though it were the symbol of mere embarrassment, or as though Christianity held modesty as sin, and self-distrust at discount. No, the word means *death,* as is explained by the passage which says: "**Whosoever** will *save his life,* shall lose it; and whosoever will *lose his life* for my sake, shall find it." And certainly this means that *only* he who loses his life shall find it; or that the old life *must* be destroyed before the new *can* be superinduced.

A point so important and so practical deserves a fuller illustration. Let me quote, then, some passages from the Epistles, which will settle the matter, as I think, beyond question: "Our old man is *crucified with him,* that henceforth we should not serve sin; for *he that is dead* is freed from sin." But suppose he is *not* dead! "If Christ be in you, *the body is dead* because of sin." "I am *crucified with Christ;* nevertheless I live; yet not I, but Christ liveth in me."

How this illustrates the words of the Saviour! The apostle took his cross, was crucified, "lost his life," and, according to the promise, "found it." But he does not hold his case as peculiar, for he says: "They that are Christ's"—*i. e.,* all that are Christ's—"have crucified the flesh with the passions and lusts." Certainly, then, they that have not done so are not Christ's. It is, therefore, "a faithful saying; for, *if we be dead with him,* we shall also live with him."

I presume, of course, that no one will understand these Scriptures to refer to a strictly literal "death" and "crucifixion." But let us beware. Because they are not *literal,* it does not follow that they are not *real.* We have no right to set aside the included, veritable *truth,* because it happens to be presented enveloped in a figurative expression. Hence, it is certain that "he that *lives* in pleasure"; he that is *alive to the world,* to the *lusts* of his flesh, to his *carnal passions*—can not be said to be *dead* or *crucified* with Christ, or to have "put off the old man with his deeds."

But even this "crucifixion"—this "death to sin"—to the flesh, and to the world, is not all. That would indeed be a very inadequate exhibition of Christianity which should leave us with a *dead Saviour,* and ourselves merely as *dead to sin,* but not *alive unto God.* We can not pause with the crucifixion, therefore, without losing the very blessing for which it was endured. It is a part of the gospel of salvation, not only that "he died for our sins," but that *"he was buried."* In this, too, as in all things, it is our exalted privilege to follow Him, to be *"buried with him."* But what can this mean? How are we buried with Him? On this question, there might have been room for doubt and perplexity, if the Scriptures had not been so explicit in furnishing a solution. As the death to sin is not strictly a literal death, it might have been thought—if we had been left to our own reasonings—that the "burial" is not a *literal* burial, but may be some monkish retirement from the world, a "burial" in the caves or dens of the earth; or that, possibly, it has some "spiritual," and, of course, indefinite, sense, such as fanaticism has dictated for so many other requirements of the Scripture. Happily, however, we are not left in doubt. A word is added which relieves the matter of all uncertainty, *and forbids us giving any other explanation:* "We are buried with him *by baptism.*" This is, then, the only way in which we *can* be buried with Him, and any explanation which leaves out this act of burial is sheer infidelity. God has spoken in the premises: let all the earth keep silent before Him.

Another question, however, may arise here, and that is: The meaning being settled, is it *necessary* that we should be thus buried with Him? To which we simply respond: *The new life emerges from the tomb!* The Saviour did not rise from the *cross,* but from the *grave!* These are facts which no logic can ratiocinate out of existence. They constitute a living demonstration that Christianity contemplates, not simply life from the dead, but life from the tomb; and, at the same time, they confirm the assurance that those who have been crucified and buried with Him shall rise *from their burial,* to walk in newness of life with Him.

Again, let us see what the Scriptures say upon the subject: "*Therefore,* we are buried with him by baptism into death; that like as Christ was raised up from the dead by the glory of the Father, even so we also should walk in newness of life." If, now, the question be; *why* the burial,

the answer is given, *"therefore* we are buried"—
for this very reason, with this identical object in
view—that we may walk in newness of life. The
one is the natural antecedent of the other; nay,
the one is clearly *conditional* on the other. Once
more: "Buried with him by baptism, *wherein* also
ye are risen with him." The apostle immediately
proceeds to address these parties as those that are
"risen with Christ," and tells them, *"Ye* have
put off the old man with his deeds, and have put
on the *new* man." As much as to say (what, indeed, he did say in other places): "As many of
you as have been baptized into Christ have put on
Christ;" and, "If any man be in Christ, he is a
new creature." With what clearness and force do
these passages illustrate and confirm the doctrine
of the text; viz., that "our old man is crucified"—
"dead with Christ"—"dead unto sin;" that, as
such, it is "buried with him by baptism"—
"planted in the likeness of his death;" and that
from this baptismal burial we are "raised up" to
"walk in newness of life"; the "old man," still
"dead, indeed, unto sin," but the "new man"
evermore "alive unto God through Jesus Christ
our Lord." And hence the appositeness of the
conclusion, "Yield yourselves unto God as those
that are *alive from the dead.*"

We have now followed the great Captain of
our salvation through death and burial and resurrection—coming, thus, into the enjoyment and

manifestation of a new spiritual life. "I live, yet not I, but Christ liveth in me; and the life which I now live, I live by the faith of the Son of God." "If Christ be in us, the body is dead because of sin, but the *spirit is life*, because of righteousness." If we, then, be risen with Christ, if He is our life, while our old dead body may remain upon the earth, the spirit, the heart, the affections, must *ascend with Him*. In this sense, "we *have come* to the heavenly Jerusalem, to an innumerable company of angels, to the spirits of just men made perfect, and to God, the Judge of all." "Our citizenship is in heaven;" we are no longer of the world; our heart and life and home and treasures are all above, laid up secure, beyond the reach of corruption or danger.

And, finally, we are *glorified with Him*. This is the *terminus ad quem* of all the past. Yes, we *are glorified*, though still encompassed with infirmity, and walking through great tribulation, subjects of toil and sorrow and pain and tears; for "whom he justified, them he also *glorified*." In one sense, certainly, this glory is still future. And, in this view, we joyfully "suffer with him that we *may be* also glorified together." We are, in this respect, like the Saviour in His humiliation—*our glory is not manifested*. We are living His divine life, we partake of His divine nature, we are filled with His divine Spirit; but "the world knoweth us not, even as it knew him not."

It is "the *manifestation* of the sons of God," for which the "earnest expectation of the creature waiteth"; and this is not the *impartation* of glory, but "the *revelation* of the glory that is *in* us." Consequently, the Christian, having *reproduced the great facts of redemption* in his conversion to Christ, is now remanded to the *example of Christ's life upon the earth*, to reproduce *that*, in order to his final glorification. In other words, being made *a son of God*, he is now to lead the life of *the* Son of God upon the earth.

It will be observed that this is not, as in the former case, to be done in *particulars*, but in *generals*. Ours is to be, like His, a life of love and mercy; of gentleness and forgiveness; of prayer and humility; of labor for the good of others; and, in one word, of *self-sacrifice for the salvation of the world*. Such a life will be continually blessed by the presence and grace of God; and, in closing such a career, we shall, like our glorious Leader, simply "lay down" the divine "life" which is in us, to be taken again. We shall, of course, go with Him once more to the tomb, but we can now look forward to that *broken prison* without a fear, knowing that "if the Spirit of him that raised up Christ Jesus from the dead dwell in us, he that raised up Christ from the dead shall also quicken our mortal bodies by his Spirit that dwelleth in us." And after this—beyond the resurrection—"it doth not yet appear what we shall be, but we know that we shall be *like him;" "*we shall be glorified together"—"manifested" to the universe as the "sons of God"; and if sons, then heirs, "heirs of God and joint-heirs with Christ."

Such, in brief, is the wonderful scheme of salvation. It is simply being *with Christ,* from first to last, from the darkness to the glory. But, oh! it must needs be, if we are *with him,* that *He also is with us;* with us in our exceeding sorrow for sin; with us in the good confession, the shame and derision, the crucifixion and burial; with us, aye, *in* us, in the resurrection; and with us and in us evermore, in all our toils and temptations and sufferings and tears. Yea, though we walk through the valley of the shadow of death, we will fear no evil, for still He is with us. And beyond the grave, in the glorious world of immortal life, where the Saviour reigns the exalted Lord and Christ, the prayer which He breathed in the days of His humiliation is still heard and answered: "Father, I will that they also whom thou hast given me *be with me where I am."* O blessed consummation! This is the fruition of all hope, the reward of all labor, the satisfaction of all desire, the very fullness of the blessing of the gospel of Christ—*"ever with the Lord!"*

THE CHURCH THE BODY OF CHRIST

ELIJAH GOODWIN

"And he is the head of the body, the church."—Col. 1: 18.

VARIOUS are the figures employed by the inspired writers for the purpose of illustrating that religious organism which is called "the church of God, the ground and support of the truth"; and in every such figure Christ is spoken of as supreme. Are the members of the church represented as the branches of a living vine? Then, He is the vine. Is the church represented as a flock of sheep? Then, He is the good shepherd, who even gives His life for the sheep. Is the church spoken of as a kingdom? Then, He is the King who reigns over that kingdom. Is the church represented under the figure of a body, as in our text? Then, He is the head of that body. In all things, therefore, He should have the pre-eminence.

This is not the only Scripture in which Christ is represented as the head of the church. To the

The Church the Body of Christ

Corinthians, Paul says: "I would have you know that the head of every man is Christ" (1 Cor. 11:3). To the church at Ephesus, he says: "The husband is the head of the wife, even as Christ is the head of the church, and he is the Saviour of the body" (Eph. 5:23). Again: God "hath given him to be head over all things to the church, which is his body" (Eph. 1:22).

My design in this discourse is to speak of the church as the body of Christ, and of Christ as the head of this body, in doing which I propose the following order:

I. Speak of the character of Christ, the head of the church.

II. Speak of the church under the figure of a body—our physical organization.

III. Notice the union that exists between the head and the body.

IV. Close with practical conclusions, drawn from the premises which will, by that time, be before our minds.

I. According to this order, we are first to notice the character of Him who is the head of the church.

1. The dignity of His divine character is clearly indicated by the works which are ascribed to Him. In the context it is said: "By him were all things created, that are in heaven and that are in earth, visible and invisible, whether they be thrones, or dominions, or principalities, or powers;

all things were created by him and for him" (v. 16). Again: "All things were made by him, and without him was not anything made that was made" (John 1:3).

Surely, no power short of the power of God could perform such stupendous works. Indeed, finite minds can not comprehend this mighty creation; how, then, could a finite mind contrive it, or a finite mind execute it? Contemplate, gentle reader, the vastness of creation. What a world is this which we inhabit!—with all its mighty mountains; its roaring and muttering volcanoes, ever and anon belching forth rolling torrents of burning lava. Behold its widespread plains, its deep-rolling rivers, and its mighty oceans, whose mountain waves are ever lashing the shore at the feet of the awe-stricken beholder. Then contemplate the innumerable tribes of living beings, formed to inhabit every part of this mighty world of ours; the beasts of the field, the fowls of the air, and the fishes of the sea; but, above all, contemplate man, made in the image of God; and then remember that all, *all*, were created by Him who is the head of the church, and we may form some faint idea of His glorious character.

But our little world is but a speck in creation; as but a grain of sand on the seashore, compared with the immensity of the created universe. The sun, moon and stars are the works of His fingers; He "in the beginning laid the foundation of the earth, and the heavens are the works of his hands" (Heb. 1:10). Imagine every fixed star—even those that can only be seen by the aid of our largest and most powerful telescopes—to be a sun, placed in the center of a system of worlds, all performing their annual revolutions around their respective suns; then imagine all these worlds, with their innumerable hosts of living inhabitants, to be a very small portion of the workmanship of His almighty power; and then think how glorious must He be who is the head of the church and the Saviour of the body.

2. But the Scriptures teach that He not only made all things, but that He upholds all things. In connection with our text, Paul says: "He is before all things, and by him all things consist" (v. 17). Again the same apostle says: "God, who at sundry times and in divers manners spake in time past unto the fathers by the prophets, hath in these last days spoken unto us by his Son, whom he hath appointed heir of all things, by whom also he made the worlds; who being the brightness of his glory, and the express image of his person, and *upholding all things* by the word of his power," etc. (Heb. 1:1-3). The apostle here seems to represent the power of Christ as a mighty arch, reaching from eternity past to eternity to come, or spanning that broken-off fragment of eternity which we call time; upon which arch is suspended the universe, all borne up or upheld by

Him "whom God hath given to be head over all things to the church." He who created all things, and who upholds all things, must be divine.

3. But the very term which expresses divine nature is applied to Jesus, the Christ.

John says: "In the beginning was the Word, and the Word was with God, and the *Word was God*. . . . And the Word was made flesh, and dwelt among us, and we beheld his glory, the glory as of the only begotten of the Father, full of grace and truth" (John 1:1, 14). Now, it can not be that this title "God" is applied to our Lord Jesus merely on account of any delegated power or authority which He may have received from the Father, nor on account of any office that may have been conferred upon Him. In such cases it might be said that He was *as God;* but it is here declared that He *was God,* and that He was God in the beginning. This title, then, must be applied to Him in reference to His divine nature. Just say that Jesus Christ is God in nature, and all is plain. It does seem to me that much of the controversy concerning the Godhead of our blessed Redeemer might have been saved by this common-sense, and I will say Scriptural, view of the subject. Instead of contending that the Father and Son are one individual being, or personage, as some have been understood to do, let it be maintained that the unity is in nature; and I think but few who receive, as divinely inspired,

The Church the Body of Christ

the teachings of the apostles of Christ, will object. But let him object that will, such is the truth in the case. *Theos* may be regarded as the name of a nature—divine nature—and *anthropos* as the name of human nature. Now, these two natures were undoubtedly united in that wonderfully glorious being whose character we are now considering. Therefore, it was said of Him before He was born: "They shall call his name Emmanuel, which being interpreted is, God with us" (Matt. 1:23).

II. But I now pass to my second head of discourse, which is indeed the main subject on which I design speaking; namely, *"The body of Christ, the church."*

1. One object I have before me, in taking the very brief view of the exalted position and divine character of the Lord Jesus that I have done under the first head of this discourse, is to exalt the church in our esteem. As intimated in the foregoing discourse, I fear that we do not esteem the church as highly as we should; hence, the unceremoniousness with which persons frequently leave the church, and the little interest that many seem to take in the prosperity and welfare of the church.

Now, we generally estimate the worth and efficiency of a body by its head. A human body may be strong, well organized and healthy, but, if its head be idiotic, we attach but little importance to the body. So of organized societies; we look to the head for the honor and efficiency of the body. What estimate, then, should we place upon the church, when it is declared to be the *body of Christ?* If that glorious personage who is "the brightness of the Father's glory, and the express image of his person"—by whom all things were created, and who upholds all things by the word of His power—I say, if this transcendently glorious and divine being condescends to preside over the church, as its head—and permits Himself to be regarded, by all the shining hosts of heaven, as the head of the church, and the church to be considered His body—surely the church of God is no mean affair; and to be a constitutional member thereof is no small matter. Oh that I could make this thought sink deep into the heart of every one who may read this discourse! Are you, dear reader, a member of the church of Jesus Christ? How exalted, then, is your position! How highly should you prize your relationship in that body, of which Christ is the head; and how should you strive for the health and well-being of that body! But more of this in its proper place.

2. The second thought that I wish to suggest, in reference to the church, is, *that it is a unit—"the church is one."*

This word "church" is translated from the Greek word *ecclesia*, which literally means "assembly" or "congregation." *Ecclesia* is derived from

The Church the Body of Christ

ekkaleo—I call out, *the called out.* So the term "church" means a congregation called out from the world. This term, I admit, is applied, in the New Testament, to individual congregations, such as the church at Corinth, the church at Ephesus, the church at Philippi; and it is applied in the plural form to the churches in Galatia, Judea and Asia. (See Gal. 1:2, 22; 2 Cor. 8:1, 18, 23; 11:28; Rev. 1:11, 20.) In all these places these individual congregations are considered in their individual capacity, as embracing all these congregations in one general body.

When Peter made the good confession, Christ said to him: "Thou art Peter, and on this rock I will build my church," etc. He did not say *churches*, but *church*—in the singular. Now, no one will say that He meant the congregation at Jerusalem, to the exclusion of all other Christian congregations. Paul, reflecting on his former life, said: "I am not meet to be called an apostle, because I persecuted the church of God" (1 Cor. 15:9). He did not mean that he only persecuted one congregation, he persecuted the saints even unto strange cities; hence, he embraces the whole body of believers, wherever found, in the term "church." Again: "Husbands, love your wives, even as Christ also loved the *church,* and gave himself for it, that he might sanctify and cleanse it with the washing of water by the word [or, as Dr. McKnight renders it, with a bath of water, and with the Word], that he might present it to himself a *glorious church"* (Eph. 5:25, 26).

Now, in this whole connection, the apostle surely uses the term "church" in a general sense. And it is used in the same sense in our text: *"He is the head of the body, the church."* Thus are all the Christian congregations contemplated, in the light of apostolic teaching, as *one church—one body.*

I do not understand from this that the apostle intended to teach that all these congregations should be united by any general council, or by conventional rules; or that they should be united in one visible head, whether called bishop or pope; but that all who believed in Jesus Christ, and submitted to His authority, and stood upon the apostolic platform—namely, the one body, one Spirit, one hope, one Lord, one faith, one baptism, and one God and Father of all—were, by these holy principles, united in the unity of the Spirit and in the bond of peace, and were, therefore, to be regarded as *one body.*

3. My third remark, in reference to the mystical body of Christ, is that in the days of the apostles, when persons were prepared by faith and true repentance for a place in the church, they became members by baptism.

A reconciliation to God in all the feelings of the heart, and an entire reformation of life, are necessary to membership in that church. This change, or purification of heart, is effected by faith in the truth of God concerning the Christ, the Son of the living God; and this change of heart produces the change of life which is implied in evangelical repentance. Now, when a person is thus prepared for this society, he becomes a member by being baptized into the name of the Father, Son and Holy Spirit.

Paul said: "Know ye not, that so many of us as were baptized into Jesus Christ were baptized into his death?" (Rom. 6:3). Again: "As many of you as have been baptized into Christ have put on Christ" (Gal. 3:27). No one is, or can be, baptized into Christ literally, and yet, in the Scriptures just quoted, the apostle teaches most clearly that they were *baptized into Christ*. It follows, then, that they were baptized into the *body of Christ, the church*. Hence, all the members of this body were baptized, nor can it be shown that any person was ever regarded as a member of Christ's church without baptism.

4. The next item that I will notice, in relation to the church under the figure of a body, is the union that should exist among the members.

This subject is often spoken of in the Scriptures. The union of God's people was one of the great objects for which the Saviour taught and labored and died. It was the theme of His instruction, and the subject of His prayers. In one of His most solemn petitions to His heavenly Father, He said: "Neither pray I for these alone [the apostles], but for them also who shall believe on me through their word; that they all may be one; as thou, Father, art in me, and I in thee, that they also may be one in us: that the world may believe that thou hast sent me" (John 17:20, 21). How near and how dear must that union be, if it resembles the union between God, our heavenly Father, and Jesus Christ, the blessed Redeemer! We have seen in this discourse that they are one in nature; so should Christians be—all being partakers of the divine nature, through the exceeding great and precious promises of the gospel. And is not this as it should be? Should not all the members of a body have the same nature? and should not that be the nature of the head?

This union is often illustrated, in the apostolic teaching, by the union that exists between the members of a natural body. To the Ephesians, Paul wrote thus: "Wherefore, putting away all lying, speak every man the truth with his neighbor, for we are members one of another" (Eph. 4:25). To the church at Rome he said: "For as we have many members in one body, and all members have not the same office, so we, being many, are one body in Christ, and every one members one of another" (Rom. 12:4, 5). Now, who can conceive the nearness of the relation that exists between the members of my physical body? This, Christian reader, is but a figure of the holy union

The Church the Body of Christ

that should exist among all the members of Christ's mystical body, the church. The apostle teaches that it is the will of Christ that all the members, "speaking the truth in love, may grow up into him in all things, which is the head, even Christ: from whom the whole body fitly joined together and compacted by that which every joint supplieth, according to the effectual working in the measure of every part, maketh increase of the body unto the edifying of itself in love" (Eph. 4:15, 16).

What a beautiful description this is of the human body, and how forcibly does it illustrate the union that should obtain among the members of the church of Christ, which is His body. In the natural body, every joint supplies its place; the members are fitly (not unfitly) joined together, the parts composing the joint all adapted to each other; and then these parts are joined together by ligaments that hold the members in a very near relation to each other. Then they are compacted together by the outside membranes; and then, by the effectual working of every part, the body increases. So should the members of the body of Christ be united. Each should supply his place in the body, and all "be perfectly joined together in the same mind and in the same judgment" (1 Cor. 1:10), and then, by the effectual working of every part, of every member, whether preacher, pastor, elder, deacon, or private member, each working in his respective sphere for the general good, the body, or church, will grow, and increase in moral power as it grows.

The apostle Paul speaks at still greater length on the same subject in his first letter to the Corinthians. He says: "For as the body is one, and hath many members, and all the members of that one body, being many, are one body: so also is Christ. For by one Spirit are we all baptized into one body, whether we be Jews or Gentiles, whether we be bond or free; and have all been made to drink into one Spirit. For the body is not one member, but many. . . . If they were all one member, where were the body? But now are they many members, yet but one body. And the eye can not say unto the hand, I have no need of thee; nor again the head to the feet, I have no need of you" (1 Cor. 12:12-21). So should all the members of the church of Christ regard themselves—all united in the bond of peace, and all mutually dependent upon each other.

But the apostle labors this subject still further. He says: "There should be no schism in the body; but the members should have the same care one for another. And whether one member suffers, all the members suffer with it; or one member be honored, all the members rejoice with it." Thus are the members of my natural body united. If the lady's little finger is honored by wearing a gold ring, her head is honored; all the members partake of that honor. And if the most remote member of the natural body is pained, all the members sympathize with it. Thus it is that when one member of the body is diseased, the whole body becomes enfeebled. Why should a sound member be enervated by a disease in another member? It is because "all the members have the same care one for another." The forces and power of all the members are concentrated at the diseased part of the body, for the purpose of overcoming the disease and saving the member. So should it be with the members of Christ's mystical body. If one member is honored on account of devotion to, and usefulness in, the church, the whole body is honored by having such a worthy member in it; and hence, no one should be jealous of the influence of another, nor envious at his success in doing good.

And if one member suffer, all the members should sympathize with him; for, says the apostle, in making his application, "you are the body of Christ, and members in particular" (v. 27). If one member is morally diseased, all should feel for him. Suppose a member of the church has been overtaken in a fault, and has stepped out of the way: the members should not turn off from that member with cold indifference; they should not speak lightly of him, and express their fears of his stedfastness, and their want of confidence in the purity of his motives. This is not the way we treat the members of the natural body. The influence of the whole body is exercised in behalf of the diseased member, to save it, if possible. So, the care and influence and counsel and prayers of the whole church should be thrown around the erring member; yes, surround him with loving kindness, and make him feel that all are interested in his well-being. Amputation is never resorted to in the natural body until all hope is lost—until the very life of the body is jeopardized by its connection with a diseased, decaying member; and even then it is a painful operation. So should it be in the church of Christ. Exclusion should be the very last resort, and never should take place until all hope of saving the member is lost, and until the very life (spiritual life) of the body is endangered by the connection of the offending member with it.

Such is the union which should ever be maintained among the members of Christ's mystical body. Christian reader, what think you of it? Are you endeavoring to keep the union in the bond of peace? I fear that many who have talked and sung and preached and prayed much on this subject, the subject of *Bible union on Bible principles,* do not realize a moiety of the holy spiritual union that the gospel requires. We have said more on this subject than any other people during the last quarter of a century, and yet we do not exhibit to the world any more of that union than

The Church the Body of Christ

we ought. I speak to those who have taken the Bible as their only rule for religious faith and religious manners. Do we realize all that nearness of feeling, that identity of interest, that warmth of soul, that oneness of mind and purpose that we have professed? that the Saviour prayed for? that the foregoing Scripture quotations indicate? and that should always exist among the members of the same body? Ponder well these questions, Christian reader, and may the good Lord enable us to love one another, with pure hearts, fervently.

III. But let us now consider the relation and union that exist between the head and the body.

1. In all physical bodies which have animation, the head governs the body. This is emphatically true in reference to the human body, which seems to be the kind of body to which the apostle has more particular reference in this figure. The head is the seat of the judgment and will, by which all the members are controlled. One body, one head, one will, is Heaven's order. One body with two heads would be a monster, and such would be one head with many bodies.

No body could act efficiently if the members thereof were governed by different and conflicting wills. This is the secret cause of all the divisions among the professed followers of Christ. There are too many wills to be consulted, too many heads, too many lawmakers. Now, if we acknowledge Christ as the head of the body, the church, our wills should all be lost in His; self should be crucified with Him by the cross, and we should be buried with Him in baptism; then we should rise to walk in newness of life, and in all our future actions we should be governed by His righteous will. Paul says we have the mind, or will, of Christ. This we have in the Holy Scriptures. To this blessed Book, then, we should always come, in order to learn the will of Christ; and having learned His will, we should not stop to confer with flesh and blood; we should not consult our own views of propriety, or the views of our neighbor; but we should do the will of the great head of the church, and leave the results in His almighty hands.

2. I notice, in the second place, under this division of the subject, that the head is the seat of sensation—of sympathy. What is done to the members is felt in the head. The great sympathetic nerve, which connects with the head, divides itself into a thousand fibers, and runs through every ramification of the body, carrying the sensation of the smallest touch upon the most remote member, to the head, in the twinkling of an eye; and by this means all the members sympathize with each other, and all the members sympathize with the head, and the head sympathizes with all the members.

Now, let that nerve represent the love of God shed abroad in our hearts by the Holy Spirit given

The Church the Body of Christ

unto all the true members of the body of Christ, the church, and you have a very faint representation of the relation and sympathy that exist between Christ and His church.

I will only introduce two examples to show this relation—one of maltreatment, and one of benevolent treatment.

After Christ was crowned Lord of all, and His body, the church, was fully organized, there was a man of much influence and of great firmness and perseverance who set his face against this infant body, and determined on its destruction. In order to accomplish his designs, he persecuted the saints, even unto strange cities. On one occasion, he himself says: "I received letters unto the brethren, and went to Damascus to bring them that were there, bound unto Jerusalem to be punished. And it came to pass, as I made my journey, and was come nigh unto Damascus, about noon, suddenly there shone from heaven a great light round about me. And I fell to the ground, and heard a voice saying unto me, Saul, Saul, why persecutest thou me? And I answered, Who art thou, Lord? And he said unto me, I am Jesus of Nazareth, whom thou persecutest" (Acts 22:5-8).

Now, what was this man doing? He had no idea that he was persecuting Jesus. If he had ever heard His name, he believed that he had been justly crucified, and was then in the cold arms of mother earth. But he was persecuting

New Testament Christianity

those who believed in Jesus, and who had become the members of His body; and Jesus says, "You are persecuting me." As if He had said, "I am in heaven, seated on the throne of the universe, and the members of my mystical body are down here upon earth, yet I know them: I feel every pain that they endure for my sake; they are as dear to me as the apple of my eye; you can't touch them but I feel it; when you persecute them, you persecute me, and I hold you accountable for it, as if you had persecuted me face to face." How near, then, must be the union between Christ and His people! Oh, how careful we should be as to how we treat the members of the Lord's body!

The next case to which we refer is found in the twenty-fifth chapter of Matthew. In this chapter we have a very graphic description of the great and notable day of the Lord—that dreadful day when the destinies of men will be settled for eternity. In describing the scenes of that final day, Jesus says: "When the Son of man shall come in his glory, and all the holy angels with him, then shall he sit upon the throne of his glory; and before him shall be gathered all nations; and he shall separate them, one from another, as a shepherd divideth his sheep from the goats. And he shall set the sheep on his right hand, but the goats on the left. Then shall the King say unto them on his right hand, Come, ye blessed of my Father, inherit

The Church the Body of Christ

the kingdom prepared for you from the foundation of the world." Now, mark well what follows: "For I was hungry, and ye gave me meat; I was thirsty, and ye gave me drink; I was a stranger, and ye took me in; naked, and ye clothed me; I was sick, and ye visited me; I was in prison, and ye came unto me" (Matt. 25:31-36).

Oh, what a lesson this is for all who love the Lord; yes, and for those who love Him not, but treat His cause and His people with contempt.

It seems that these righteous persons do not fully understand the meaning of the Judge; and hence they shall say: "Lord, when did we see you hungry, and fed you? When did we see you thirsty, and gave you drink? When did we visit you in sickness, or in prison? We spent our days on earth, among the sons of men, while you were seated upon the throne, high up in heaven, surrounded by all the angelic hosts, who always delight to do thy will. How is it, then, we have performed these acts of kindness and mercy unto you?" Reader, hear the answer, and let it sink deep into your heart: *"Verily I say unto you, Inasmuch as ye have done it unto one of the least of these, my brethren, ye have done it unto me"* (v. 40). Lord, help us to feel the force of that declaration.

When the Philippians sent once and again unto the necessities of the apostle Paul, they may not have thought that they were administering to the wants of the blessed Lord. (See Phil. 1:7; 4:

14, 15.) Onesiphorus, also, may not have considered that he was bestowing favors on the Lord Jesus, when he so diligently sought Paul, the prisoner of the Lord, in the great city of Rome, and refreshed him with some of the good things of this life. (See 2 Tim. 1:16, 17.) But Jesus saw him, and regarded it as done to Himself, and will reward him accordingly. Reader, do you always reflect, when you speak of Christians, that Christ notes every word, as having reference to Himself? The Lord sees our hearts, He knows our motives, and He will remember how we treat the members of His body—the church.

You can not treat with contempt a member of a natural body without insulting the head. If you spit upon my little finger through contempt, my head is insulted; it would be regarded as offering an indignity to my head. So Jesus regards all the constitutional members of His church. Hence the apostle says: "We are members of his body, of his flesh, and of his bones" (Eph. 5:30). Such is the body of Christ. You can not offer an indignity to a member of the church without insulting Jesus, its head. Hence, He says that it were better that a millstone were hanged about a person's neck, and he be cast into the sea, than for him to offend one who believes in Christ.

IV. According to my fourth proposition, I am now to close this discourse with a few practical reflections:

The Church the Body of Christ

1. If we are members of the Lord's body, *we ought to love Him most devoutly*. We have seen the attachment that He has for the members of His mystical body; and should not this attachment be mutual? We should give Him the warmest seat in our hearts' affections, and we should always show our respect for Him and His holy cause, in all we do and in all we say.

2. *We should honor Him.* The members of any body, whether physical, political or ecclesiastical, should always honor their head, especially if the head be worthy. And I ask, What organism on earth has so worthy a head as the church? What head has ever shown such interest in the well-being of His body as the great head of the church has shown toward the body over which He presides? One witness hath testified that "he gave himself for the church, that he might sanctify and cleanse it with the washing of water by the word" (Eph. 5:25, 26). That is, He died for this body, that He might sanctify and save it; or, as Dr. McKnight renders it, "that he might sanctify her [the church], having cleansed her with a bath of water, and with the word." Now, if Christ has thus loved the church, should not the members honor Him? They should not speak a word, nor perform an act, that would be a reproach to the great head of the church; but all they do and say should reflect honor on the name and cause of Christ.

New Testament Christianity

3. *Christians should love one another.* If all true Christians are members of the same body, surely they should love each other sincerely, and always strive to promote the peace and happiness of one another. Read the following Scriptures on this subject: "Beloved, if God so loved us, we ought also to love one another" (1 John 4:11). "We know that we have passed from death unto life, because we love the brethren. He that loveth not his brother abideth in death. . . . Hereby perceive we the love of God, because he laid down his life for us; and we ought to lay down our lives for the brethren. But whoso hath this world's goods, and seeth his brother have need, and shutteth up his bowels of compassion from him, how dwelleth the love of God in him? My little children, let us not love in word, neither in tongue, but in deed and in truth" (1 John 3:14-18). "Seeing you have purified your souls in obeying the truth, through the Spirit, unto unfeigned love of the brethren, see that you love one another with a pure heart fervently" (1 Pet. 1:22). "Finally, be ye all of one mind, having compassion one of another; love as brethren, be pitiful, be courteous" (1 Pet. 3:8).

Surely, the love here recommended is more than mere natural affection, growing out of worldly considerations. This love is to proceed from pure hearts, and is to be fervent; which means "earnestly, eagerly, vehemently, with great warmth, with pious ardor, with earnest zeal, ardently."—*Webster*. This love to the brotherhood should be like the fire upon the golden altar in God's ancient temple. It should be holy, and be ever burning; it should never be permitted to go out. This will require much watching and prayer.

You remember, on one occasion the priests permitted the fire on the golden altar to go out. This happened on account of inattention on the part of these priests. So will it be without Christian love, which should ever be burning upon the altar of our hearts. If we neglect this altar, and give our attention too much to the cares of this world, the fire of sacred love will expire.

You also remember, reader, what those priests did. They put unsanctified fire upon that altar; that is, fire that had not been consecrated and set apart to a holy or religious use.

May we not virtually do the same thing? That is, may we not kindle the fire of Christian affection out of mere worldly considerations? How often do we see this thing, called Christian love, confined in its manifestations to certain grades and castes of society. Is it sometimes the case that our love to Christians is regulated by the fashions and etiquette of society? And how easily is such love cooled! A little inattention—even failing to return a fashionable call—cools all the affection that once existed between church-members. My brother, this is placing unholy fire upon God's altar.

New Testament Christianity

And do you not remember the fate of those ancient priests who thus defiled the temple of God? (Read in Lev. 10:1, 2.) God destroyed them for their neglect of duty and presumptuous wickedness. And should not all Christians examine themselves carefully, lest they be condemned at last? Remember that, if our Christian love is accepted of God, it must be kindled with a live coal from His altar; or, to speak without a figure, it must be inspired by the Spirit of the living God; but this they can only obtain and maintain by a union with Christ, the head of this body.

4. *We should co-operate in all the interests of the church.* That the body of Christ, the church, may be a healthy, growing body, it must be a working body. The strongest and most robust physical body would soon become feeble without exercise. And an individual member may be kept in a state of rest until its power to act is lost. Hence, you always see active, stirring persons most healthy, and the members that are most used become the strongest.

So is it spiritually speaking. The members of the church that never do much for the Lord's cause never feel like doing much, while those who work for Christ become stronger and stronger, and are thus able to do still more and more for the prosperity of the Lord's cause. If this should meet the eye of a moral dyspeptic, I exhort him to go to work in the cause of Christ, and it will do him good.

The Church the Body of Christ

But the thought that I wished to impress upon the reader's mind is the necessity of co-operation among the members of this body, for the welfare of the body. I speak now particularly to those who have taken their stand on the Bible alone; who have united on the foundation of apostles and prophets, Jesus Christ Himself being the chief corner-stone; who have become members of the body of Christ on Bible principles.

My brethren, should not the members of this body co-operate in all their general efforts for the enlargement of the borders of Zion—for the growth of the body—until it shall fill the whole earth? The brethren living in counties should form county co-operations for the purpose of sustaining the proclamation of the gospel in destitute portions of the counties. And districts and States should do the same. Why may they not? Are they not all members of the same body? And do not all of the members of my body co-operate for the general good of the body? So may the members of the body of Christ. Nay, they not only may, but they are in duty bound to do so.

5. *The members of this body should keep themselves pure.* Speaking of the Christian's hope, the apostle John says: "Every one that hath this hope in him purifieth himself even as he is pure" (1 John 3:3). If the head is pure, the members should be. Hear the great apostle of the Gentiles on this subject: "Know ye not that your bodies

are the members of Christ? shall I then take the members of Christ, and make them the members of an harlot? God forbid. What! know ye not that he which is joined to an harlot is one body? for two, saith he, shall be one flesh. But he that is joined unto the Lord is one spirit" (1 Cor. 6: 15-17). Thus reasons one who had the mind of Christ. Contemplating the purity of the great head of the church, he concludes that all the members should be pure; that it would be unjust, unnatural and unrighteous to form such an unholy alliance between the members of Christ's body and the base character just named.

But, if such an alliance with one species of crime is wrong, the same is true in reference to all sin. How appropriate Paul's command to Timothy: "Keep thyself pure." Shall I take the members of Christ's body, and introduce them into the ballroom? Shall I cause the Lord's feet to move in the giddy dance? If I do, do I not dishonor the head? Let every member of the mystical body of Christ endeavor, by divine grace, to "keep himself unspotted from the world," for this is one of the constituents of pure and undefiled religion.

6. *The head was raised from the dead and glorified in heaven; so shall the members be.* "Because I live, ye shall live also," said the blessed Lord. "If the Spirit of him that raised up Jesus from the dead dwell in you, he that raised up Christ from the dead shall also quicken your

The Church the Body of Christ

mortal bodies by his Spirit that dwelleth in you" (Rom. 8:11). "For if we believe that Jesus died and rose again, even so them also who sleep in Jesus will God bring with him" (1 Thess. 4:14). Then the desire of the Lord will be realized. "Father," said he, "I will that they also, whom thou hast given me, be with me where I am; that they may behold my glory, which thou hast given me" (John 17:24). "Then shall be brought to pass that saying that is written, Death is swallowed up in victory. O death, where is thy sting? O grave, where is thy victory?" (1 Cor. 15:54, 55).

Reader, are you a member of this body—the church of Christ? Then, be faithful unto death, and the Lord hath said you shall have a crown of life. But if you are not a member of this body, oh, be exhorted to come to the Saviour; believe on Him with all your heart, confess His worthy name, reform your life, and be baptized into the body of Christ.

THE KINGDOM OF GOD

BENJAMIN FRANKLIN

THE purpose of this article is to answer the following questions:

I. *What is the kingdom of God?*

II. *Was the kingdom of God fully established before the ascension of Christ to heaven?*

III. *Has the kingdom of God yet come, or been established?*

Without preliminary or ceremony, let attention be directed to these questions:

I. *What is the kingdom of God?*

That the same is meant by "kingdom of God," "kingdom of heaven," "his kingdom," and the "kingdom of his dear Son," as a general rule, there can be but little doubt, whether the same is meant in every instance or not. That which is called "his kingdom" (Matt. 16:28) is called "the kingdom of God" (Mark 9:1; Luke 9:27). The same kingdom mentioned in the phrase, "the Son of man coming in *his kingdom,*" is also mentioned in the phrase "the *kingdom* of God," for these are two reports of the same speech. The two expressions are simply two designations of the same kingdom.

The Kingdom of God

The same, precisely, that is called "the kingdom of heaven" (Matt. 19:23) is called "the kingdom of God" (Mark 10:25). In Matthew the record is: "That a rich man shall hardly enter into the kingdom of God." The "kingdom of heaven" at hand, as recorded (Matt. 3:2), is undoubtedly the same as the "kingdom of God" (Mark 1:14), for these are two records of the same thing. The same kingdom is meant (Matt. 13:11) in the words, "Because to you it is given to know the mysteries of the kingdom of *heaven,*" that is meant (Mark 4:11) in "To you it is given to know the mysteries of the kingdom of *God.*" "He that is least in the kingdom of *heaven* is greater than he" (Matt. 11:11), and "He that is least in the kingdom of *God* is greater than he" (Luke 7:28), are simply two records of the same thing, and the same kingdom is meant in both records.

In the following language the phrases "my church" and "the kingdom of heaven" are two designations for the same. That which is called "my church" is called "the kingdom of heaven." "I say also to you, that you are Peter, and on this rock I will build my church, and the gates of Hades shall not prevail against it; and I will give to you the keys of the kingdom of heaven; and whatever you shall bind on earth shall be bound in heaven; and whatever you shall loose on earth shall be loosed in heaven." (See Matt. 16:18, 19.) When we think and speak of what the

Lord calls "my church," we should keep in mind that He calls the same thing, in the same connection, "the kingdom of heaven," and that He calls the same "my kingdom" (John 18:36). Paul's "general assembly and church of the firstborn," to which he said "we are come" (Heb. 12:23), is the same as his "kingdom that cannot be moved" (verse 28 of the same chapter). It is the same as his "one body" (Eph. 4:4; 1 Cor. 12:13). All who enter the "one body" at all are immersed into it, or all who enter the kingdom at all, which is the same as entering the "one body," enter it by being born of water and of the Spirit. "Except a man be born again, he cannot see [or enjoy] the kingdom of God." (See John 3:3.) "Except a man be born of water and of the Spirit, he cannot enter into the kingdom of God." (See John 3:5.) The same community is styled "the house of God, which is the church of the living God, the pillar and support of the truth" (1 Tim. 3:13). "In Christ" is in the body, church or kingdom. To know what the church is, the body of Christ, the house of God, the temple of God, the building of God, is to know what the kingdom of God is. This view will assist much in ascertaining what the kingdom of God is, and several other things to be investigated in this article.

When we are thinking of the Lord's community as a *body*, we think of the head and the individual members, the life and support of the body. When we think of the same community as a *house,* or family, we immediately think of the head of the family, the members, the discipline and ruling of a family, the care and oversight of a family, the support and dependence of a family, the accession by birth or adoption, whichever figure may be used, and the losses by death, or those who have abandoned the family. When we think of the same community as a *temple,* or building, we think of the proprietor, foundation, the lively stones built together in it, and the builders. When we think of it as a kingdom, we think of a king, constitution, laws, territory, subjects. When we think of it literally, as the church, congregation or community founded by Christ, the only divinely founded religious community on earth, we think of God, who authorized it; of the prophets, who predicted its founding, with many of its stupendous and momentous surroundings—the Lord Messiah, who founded it; the great truth on which it is built; the authorized apostles and evangelists who first preached the gospel, called people together, under their new head, in the new community, or the church, making "one new man." It has Christ for its head; the gospel—the power of God—to turn the world to God; the teaching of Christ and His apostles for its edification and instruction. Christ is its supreme authority for everything. His authority is set forth in His own teaching and that of His divinely authorized and inspired apostles.

The church, or community of the living God, is composed of members, and has a head, gospel, teaching or territory. Bishops or overseers, and deacons, in their work, are limited to the congregation in their own vicinity, having no jurisdiction in other congregations. The church of the living God, the body of Christ, or kingdom of God, embraces all the local congregations, with the members, in all the world—all who are truly the people of God. As a whole, it is not an organized body, and has no method of acting in conventional form, in making decrees, laws or decisions. Its head has made, signed, sealed and delivered to it His laws and decrees, and demands of the church, or kingdom, implicit obedience. It is not the business of the church to *make* laws or decrees, but implicitly to *obey* and submit to the laws and decrees made by the head of the church.

This community, church or kingdom, of which Christ is the head or King, and all that pertains to it, was embraced in "the eternal purpose of God," but had no existence, in the form of a community, church or kingdom, only in the purpose of God, for ages. The same that was embodied in the eternal purpose—"a secret," "hid in God"—was subsequently embodied in the promise to Abraham. It was still a secret, a mystery, in a promise of a blessing for all the families of the earth, without any revelation explaining what that blessing was. That promise embraced the Messiah, the gospel, the church, and all the attendant blessings for the human race. Still, the church, or kingdom, did not exist in fact, and the blessings were spoken of as "good things *to come,*" and not good things *already come.* The same precisely, embodied first in the purpose, and then in the promise of God, subsequently filled a large space in prophecy, but still as "good things to come." Peter has the following comment touching the prophets: "Of which salvation the prophets have inquired and searched diligently, who prophesied of the grace that should come to you: searching what or what manner of time the Spirit of Christ which was in them did signify, when it testified beforehand the sufferings of Christ, and the glory that should follow. To whom it was revealed, that not to themselves, but to us, they did minister these things, which are now reported to you by them who have preached the gospel to you with the Holy Spirit sent down from heaven; into which things the angels desire to look." (See 1 Pet. 1: 10-12.) The kingdom of God is found, first, in the eternal purpose of God, then in the promise of God to Abraham, then in the prophecy, and then in the preaching of John the Immerser. In the preaching of John it is in different form, and a new item comes into the preaching. It is now "the kingdom of God *at* hand," "the kingdom of God *approaches*," etc. This opens the way for the inquiry:

II. *Was the kingdom of God fully established before the ascension of Christ to heaven?*

This question deserves a very full and satisfactory answer. That the kingdom, or church, was not fully established, in operation, and doing its work in the lifetime of the Saviour, is evident from the following Scriptures and considerations:

1. If the church, or kingdom, had been established fully, in operation, doing its work, and the apostles not only members of the church, or citizens of the kingdom, but active agents in it, the apostles and all His disciples, at that time, could not have been so greatly mistaken as they were, and as they remained till they had interviews with the Lord after His resurrection, in reference to the nature of His kingdom. In an interview with the Lord, after He rose from the dead, the disciples said: "Lord, wilt thou at this time restore again the kingdom to Israel?" (See Acts 1:6.) From this request, it is evident that they were not conscious. of His having established a kingdom; that they did not yet understand that His kingdom was to be one "not of this world," but expected a kingdom for Israel like the one in the time of David or Solomon, and that they were still looking for the kingdom to come. When He died they desponded, supposed His purpose was

defeated, and said: "We trusted that it was he who should have redeemed Israel." (See Luke 24:21.) But when He rose, their hope revived that He would redeem Israel from their oppression by the Romans, restore to them their national honors, and be their king; and, in view of this, made the request that He would restore the kingdom to Israel. This shows that they knew nothing about His having already established any kingdom. They certainly, as His ministers, would have known it had the kingdom been fully established. It was not then established.

2. After the Lord had entered His ministry fully, and was completely before the people, instead of His regarding His kingdom or church as established, He said, as quoted before on a different point: "On this rock I will build my church." Did He say, "I *will* build my church," when He *had* built His church? In the next verse (Matt. 16:19) he says: "I will give to you the keys of the kingdom of heaven: and whatsoever you shall bind on earth shall be bound in heaven; and whatsoever you shall loose on earth shall be loosed in heaven." At this advanced period in the Lord's ministry He was looking into the future for the building of His church, and the giving of the keys of the kingdom of heaven, or the power to open the church, to Peter. The church was not built, and the kingdom not opened, when the Lord uttered this language.

3. The first commission was limited to the "lost sheep of the house of Israel." Under this commission the preachers were expressly forbidden to go in the way of the Gentiles. John the Immerser came "preaching in the wilderness of Judæa, and saying, Repent ye; for the kingdom of heaven is at hand." (See Matt. 3:3.) "At hand" did not mean that it *had* come, or that it was *far off*. In the first commission, as recorded in Matt. 10:5-7, the Lord commanded the apostles to "go not in the way of the Gentiles, nor into any city of the Samaritans; but go rather to the lost sheep of the house of Israel. And as you go, preach, saying, The kingdom of heaven is at hand." This was the main theme under the first commission: to call the people to repentance, to immerse them, and prepare them for the near approaching kingdom, or reign of heaven.

4. In view of the approaching kingdom, or reign of heaven, the Lord taught His disciples to pray, "Thy kingdom come, thy will be done on earth as it is in heaven." (See Matt. 6:10.) This corresponds with the preaching. The disciples were commanded to preach that the kingdom was at hand, and to pray for it to come, and that "the will of God should be done *on earth* as it is in heaven." He certainly did not teach them to pray "Thy kingdom *come*," after the kingdom *had come*.

The Kingdom of God

5. The Lord said: "Verily I say to you, that there be some of them that stand here who shall not taste of death till they have seen the kingdom of God come with power." Did the Lord say this when He knew that they had seen the kingdom, and were ministers in it? Surely there can be no good reason for thinking so. They had been preaching that the kingdom was at hand, praying for it to come, and believed that it would come. They had forsaken their business and followed the Lord. They had preached and prayed, as He told them to do, but did not understand the nature of the main matter involved in their preaching and prayers. They were pressing the Lord for explanations in reference to things which it was not proper to open up yet. They expected pecuniary support, and probably office, or some kind of worldly honors and promotions in the Government, which they still kept in view, and frequently became restless and impatient. Such expressions as the one just quoted were intended and calculated to satisfy the disciples and pacify them, without a full explanation of what He did not intend to explain at that time, or that anybody should fully understand. It was true that the kingdom had not *then* come, but that some who stood there should not die till they *saw it come*.

6. The explanation that the Lord made before Pilate, "My kingdom is not of this world," as recorded in John 18:36, shows that the kingdom

was not yet fully established. Pilate inquired: "Are you the king of the Jews?" This question looked to the charge, "He is the king of the Jews," which was intended to fasten treasonable purposes on Him. Had He been then an established king of the Jews, or of His disciples, with a kingdom fully established and in operation as a distinct body, in any form, there would certainly have been no difficulty in identifying either the king or the kingdom. He, however, did not deny that He had a kingdom in view, but explained that it was not of this world—that He was no rival of Cæsar; that this kingdom was no rival of the Roman Government, or any other civil government, as it was not of this world, but a heavenly, a spiritual or a religious institution, entirely distinct from the governments of the world.

7. Beyond all doubt, the kingdom of God, or church, was not fully established while the apostles, who were the active and effective agents in preaching the gospel, making disciples, founding churches, setting them in order—advocating, maintaining and defending the faith—were erring, blundering and misunderstanding in reference to some of the clearest, most vital and fundamental matters of the kingdom, or church; while they did not believe the Lord's own clear statement touching His betrayal into the hands of enemies, His crucifixion, death and resurrection; while they were doubting and wavering; while they all had their hearts set

on an earthly king and kingdom, a mere worldly government; while one of His apostles was a traitor, engaged in a treasonable conspiracy which resulted in the betrayal of his Master, and another, fearing to be identified with his Lord, denied Him three times, and uttered bitter oaths; while the account of His resurrection, when reported to the apostles, "seemed to them as idle tales;" while they were all inquiring, "Wilt thou, at this time, restore the kingdom to Israel?" while the Lord, instead of acting in the capacity of the King, High Priest, filled the place of the suffering, bleeding and dying victim! Certainly the kingdom was not fully established before the Lord rose from the dead; before He gave the apostles the Great Commission, to "go into all the world"—to "preach the gospel to every creature"; before He ascended to heaven, "led captivity captive, and gave gifts to men"—"sent the Holy Spirit to guide the apostles into all truth;" before the great High Priest of the Christian profession had gone into the true Holy Place, of which the holy places on earth were only typical—into heaven itself, with His own blood, to appear in the presence of God for us—to make His one sin-offering in the end of the ages—the only sin-offering that can purge us forever from our sins. To say that the kingdom was fully established at any period while the matters here mentioned were transpiring, is certainly the culmination of all absurdity.

New Testament Christianity

It may be urged, in opposition to this, that the Lord said to some in His time: "The kingdom of God is in you." He certainly did not mean that the kingdom of God was *in the hearts* of those wicked and caviling Jews to whom He spoke. While it is true that the Greek preposition translated "in" literally means *in,* it is equally true that there are places where it should not be rendered *in.* This may be learned from the scope and connection generally. The case in hand is one of that kind. "The kingdom of God is *among* you," instead of *in you* or *in your midst,* is the true idea. In what sense was the kingdom of God among them? In its elements, its incipient or preliminary state; in John the Immerser, the people prepared for the Lord by him, by the apostles, and the seventy whom the Lord sent out under the first commission. It was in the Lord Himself, in those whom He sent, and the disciples they were making gradually coming forth, steadily developing itself, being more and more fully unfolded, till its full and complete establishment, in a visible form, on Pentecost.

Here we arrive at a grand culmination, a glorious period, and a full development of what has been preparing, unfolding and developing regularly, but gradually, for several years. Here we find the grand change in the apostles. Their erring, blundering, wavering and misunderstanding ceased. Their timidity, fear to be identified

The Kingdom of God

with Jesus, and want of independence ceased. Their ideas of a kingdom of this world at once vanished. Their unbelief terminated. Every man of them becomes bold, independent, and firm as the everlasting hills. No priests, no rabbis; no lawyers, doctors or philosophers; no jurists, statesmen or rulers of any sort—now intimidate them. They openly proclaim the gospel in the face of the world. What they say at the start they say all the time. Not a man of them ever relinquished his ground, departed from or repudiated a truth uttered by any one of them, from this time on. All that was done before this grand change in the apostles was preparatory and preliminary. What was done after this change was in carrying out their great commission in the new administration. After this period, they were acting under their new commission as the embassadors of the new King; making known the new law; using the keys in opening the new kingdom, or church; bringing light out of darkness, and order out of confusion. A more clearly marked line never was described between any old and new orders of things than the one between the state of things before the Holy Spirit came to guide the apostles into all truth, and the state of things after that event. Still, some are doubting whether the kingdom of God has yet come, or is yet established. Others are claiming that their doubts have all been removed—that they are convinced that the kingdom has not come—and are laboring with great zeal to prove this. This opens the way for the third question to be considered in this article:

III. *Has the kingdom of God yet come, or been established?*

To this question the following arguments shall be addressed. The question is not whether "the everlasting kingdom" has come, of which we read (2 Pet. 1:11); nor whether the kingdom, "delivered up to God, even the Father," as described by Paul (1 Cor. 15:24), or the kingdom in the glorified state, has come. The question to be considered relates not to the period when all the enemies of the Lord shall have been put under His feet—when the Lord "shall show who is the blessed and only potentate, the King of kings, and Lord of lords." That the kingdom in that state, and the time when the King will show this, has not come, all persons of good Bible intelligence will admit. But has the kingdom, in the sense in which John the Immerser speaks of it when he says, "The kingdom of heaven is at hand," or the kingdom of which John thus speaks; for the coming of which the Lord taught His disciples to pray, "Thy kingdom come;" the kingdom to which the Lord referred when he said to Peter, "I will give you the keys of the kingdom of heaven"—has this kingdom come? Is the kingdom in existence of which the Lord spoke when He said: "Except a man be born of water and of the Spirit, he cannot

The Kingdom of God

enter into the kingdom of God''? Is there any kingdom of heaven, or of Christ, in existence at this time? Is the Lord Jesus the Christ, King? Has Jesus any reign on earth? Has Messiah any kingdom on earth? It is affirmed in this article that the Messiah is King—that He has a kingdom. The following arguments are offered in proof of this:

1. The first argument offered in support of the position just taken is, that there is no way to account for the change from the first commission to the second, or for the difference between these commissions, except by admitting that the kingdom "at hand," as preached in the first commission, had come when the apostles commenced preaching under the second. John the Immerser, the Lord, the twelve apostles, and the seventy whom the Lord sent out under the first commission, all preached that the kingdom of heaven was at hand. Under the last commission they were not commanded to preach, saying, "The kingdom of heaven is at hand." The reason is that the "kingdom at hand," while they were under the first commission, had come when they commenced under the second. They were not simply not commanded to preach, under the second commission, saying, "The kingdom of heaven is at hand," but they never did thus preach. But if the kingdom of heaven has not come, was the preaching, saying, "The kingdom of heaven is at hand," true? It

was not true that it was *at hand then,* if it has not come yet.

2. The Lord, while the apostles were under the first commission, taught the disciples to pray, "Thy kingdom come." This was the grand theme during that period of preaching and prayer. The Lord did not teach them to pray for the kingdom to come after the kingdom had come. There is no account of any holy teacher ever teaching the disciples to pray for the kingdom to come after the Lord ascended to heaven; nor is there any intimation of any one ever praying for the kingdom to come after that event. The reason is, that the kingdom had come.

3. It is perfectly clear, from several Scriptures, that the apostles understood that all things proclaimed by John to be at hand were fulfilled when the church was established on Pentecost. Paul explains to the disciples of John, in Ephesus, that "John truly immersed with the immersion of repentance, saying to the people that they should believe on him that should come after him, that is, on Christ Jesus." (See Acts 19:4.) Here is clearly the general idea that what John preached as "at hand" had actually come; was fulfilled at the time when Paul made this comment. The same is clear from Paul's remarks as recorded in Acts 13:23, 24. He says, "Of this man's seed hath God, according to his promise, raised up to Israel a Saviour, Jesus," when John had first

The Kingdom of God

preached, before His coming, the immersion of repentance to all Israel. And as John fulfilled his course, he said: "Whom think ye that I am? I am not he. But, behold, there cometh one after me whose shoes of his feet I am not worthy to loose." These Scriptures, with other references to John and his immersion, show that the things by him proclaimed to be at hand, to come, and drawing nigh, were fulfilled, had actually come, when the apostles referred back to them. The central idea in the preaching of John was that the kingdom of God was *at hand*.

4. When the Lord was on trial in the Roman court, Pilate put the question to Him, "Are you a king?" Though He was then only prospectively a king, He did not deny being a king, nor of having a kingdom, though it was then in an incipient state, but explained: "My kingdom is not of this world." (See John 18:36.) Paul was accused of "saying that there was another king, one Jesus." (See Acts 17:7.) There is no intimation, in the whole record, of Paul's correcting this charge, or denying it. If he had not preached that Jesus was a king, he certainly would have denied the charge, or would have explained what he did preach, or Luke would have written out an explanation of their unfounded charge. But the truth is that He had a kingdom, when He was before Pilate, in its elements, like leaven at work in the meal; like the mustard-seed planted, but not

matured—not formed and perfected, but the kingdom *coming*. At the time Paul was charged with preaching that Jesus was a king, the kingdom had come, and the disciples were in the kingdom.

5. The Lord said to Nicodemus: "Except a man be born again, he cannot see the kingdom of God." Does not that imply that when a man is born again, he shall see or enjoy the kingdom of God? "Except a man be born of water and of the Spirit, he cannot enter into the kingdom of God." A man, then, enters the kingdom of God by a birth of water and of the Spirit. When does he enter the kingdom? At the time when he is born of water and of the Spirit, or at some subsequent period? Certainly at the time when he is born of water and of the Spirit. The time when he is born of water and of the Spirit is, literally, the time when he is converted. The time when a man is converted is the time, then, when he enters the kingdom. The kingdom had then come, in the time of the apostles, and the thousands turned to the Lord under their preaching entered the kingdom of God.

6. Before the kingdom was fully established, and before the door was opened, the Lord said to Peter: "I will give you the keys of the kingdom of heaven: and whatsoever you shall bind on earth shall be bound in heaven; and whatsoever you shall loose on earth shall be loosed in heaven." (See Matt. 16:19.) This work also related to the

The Kingdom of God

remission of sins, as may be seen by John 20:23: "Whosesoever sins you remit, they are remitted unto them: and whosesoever sins ye retain, they are retained." This using the keys was to be performed in their divine mission on earth, and in connection with the remission of sins. Certainly Peter did not use the keys of the kingdom of God in opening the kingdom, when there was no kingdom, or when the kingdom had not come. To use these keys of the kingdom, or to "remit sins," was to open the way to the remission of sins, or to open the kingdom and admit subjects into the new reign. Jesus, as the King, gave to Peter the keys of the kingdom, to use in his divine mission on earth. This he could not have done if there had been no kingdom on earth in his time. Peter did bind and loose *on earth,* and what he bound and loosed on earth was ratified in heaven. That binding and loosing on earth was in opening the kingdom of God—declaring the terms of remission of sins, *in the time of Peter, on earth.* There was, then, a kingdom on earth, in the time of Peter, to open, and it was a part of his work, in his mission, to open it.

7. Alluding to the same kingdom, in the same conversation, as recorded further on in the same chapter (Matt. 16:28), after saying to Peter, "I will give you the keys of the kingdom," the Lord said, "There be some standing here who shall not taste of death till they see the Son of man coming

New Testament Christianity

in his kingdom;" or, as reported in Mark 9:1: "Till they have seen the kingdom of God come with power." Some have supposed that this had its fulfillment in the mountain of transfiguration. But it can not, with any good reason, be said that the kingdom came there in any sense, or that it was even represented in vision. The King was there shown, and His divine majesty seen as it is now seen in heaven; and three witnesses—Peter, James and John—were enabled to say, as Peter did (2 Pet. 1:16-18): "For we have not followed cunningly devised fables, when we made known to you the power and coming of our Lord Jesus Christ, but were eye-witnesses of his majesty. For he received from God the Father honor and glory, when there came such a voice to him from the excellent glory, This is my beloved Son, in whom I am well pleased. And this voice which came from heaven we heard, when we were with him in the holy mount." The King was shown here, in divine majesty, as He would appear in the near approaching reign, to His eye-witnesses, that they might be able to testify, as Peter did. The promise, in the words, "There be some standing here who shall not taste of death till they see the Son of man coming in his kingdom," or "till they have seen the kingdom of God come with power," was not that they should see Jesus *in divine majesty*, or *the glorified Jesus*, but "see him coming in his kingdom," or "see the kingdom of God

The Kingdom of God

come with power." This they did not see in the mountain of transfiguration, but did see before they tasted death. The event described in the second chapter of Acts met and fulfilled not only what the Lord meant when He said, "See the kingdom of God come with power," but what was spoken of by Joel and other prophets. A complete change in the apostles followed the grand and sublime transaction on Pentecost—from wavering to stability, from unbelief to the full assurance of faith, from timidity to boldness, from doubts to certainty; from the first to the second commission; from errors, blunders and mistakes to infallible guidance of the Spirit of all truth and all revelation; from the long series of preparatory and preliminary work to the grand culmination in the kingdom, and the entrance of three thousand souls into the new kingdom.

8. "The seed of the kingdom is the word of God," and certainly "the seed of the kingdom," "the word of the kingdom," belongs to the period of the existence of the kingdom, and not some period when the kingdom has no existence. The sowing of the seed of the kingdom is preaching the gospel. The parables of the sower, the leaven in the meal, and several other parables, show that the fortunes of the kingdom are in this world; that the tares and the wheat were to grow together, if not in the kingdom, in the same territory, and at the *same time,* and that, at the end of the world,

New Testament Christianity

the Lord would send his angels and gather out all things offensive. (See Matt. 13:26-29.)

9. Paul, speaking of the kingdom of God, as existing in his times, tells what it *is not* and what *it is.* "The kingdom of God is not meat and drink; but righteousness, and peace, and joy in the Holy Spirit." (See Rom. 14:17.) The apostles proceeds in the next verse: "For he that in these things serves Christ is acceptable to God." The kingdom of God, of which Paul wrote, was in existence at the time of his writing, and men served Christ in it.

10. The Lord commissioned Paul to preach in the following words: "I have appeared to you for this purpose, to make you a minister and a witness, both of these things which you have seen, and of those things in the which I will appear to you; delivering you from the people and the Gentiles, to whom I now send you, to open their eyes, and turn them from darkness to light, and from the power of Satan to God, that they may receive forgiveness of sins and an inheritance among those who are sanctified through faith in me." (See Acts 26:16-18.) This work was to be done under Paul's mission, or during his natural life. Turning, then, from darkness to light was the same as delivering them from the power of darkness. This corresponds with the following language: "Giving thanks to the Father, who has made us fit to be partakers of the inheritance of the saints in light;

The Kingdom of God

who has delivered us from the power of darkness, and translated us into the kingdom of his dear Son." (See Col. 1:12, 13.) Those whom Paul here includes with himself were turned into the kingdom of God's dear Son. They were in a kingdom that had then come, that then existed, and not one that had no existence.

11. John the apostle, in addressing the seven churches in Asia, says: "I John, who also am your brother and companion in tribulation, and in the kingdom and patience of Jesus Christ, was in the island called Patmos, for the word of God, and for the testimony of Jesus Christ." While in this world, John the apostle, and those to whom he wrote, were *in the kingdom* and patience of Jesus Christ. The kingdom had come, and they were in the kingdom. In this kingdom the Lord Jesus shall reign till He has put all His enemies under His feet, and then He shall deliver up the kingdom to God, even the Father, that God may be all in all.

12. Paul says: "You are come to mount Zion, and to the city of the living God, the heavenly Jerusalem, and to an innumerable company of angels, to the general assembly and church of the firstborn, who are enrolled in heaven;" and speaking of the same body further on, he says, "Wherefore we receiving a kingdom which cannot be moved, let us have grace whereby we may serve God acceptably with reverence and godly fear." (See Heb. 12:21-28.) They had come to this

New Testament Christianity

"church of the firstborn," "general assembly," or "kingdom," and were exhorted to serve God acceptably with reverence and godly fear, when Paul wrote the letter to the church in Rome. It has already been shown that the "church" and "kingdom of God" are two designations for the same institution. To maintain, therefore, that there is no kingdom of God is the same as to maintain that there is no church of God, no temple of God, no building or house of God, or no body of Christ. It is the same as to deny that there is any "house of God, which is the church of the living God, the pillar and support of the truth," or that there was any, during the time the apostles were acting under the last commission, *actually existing*. Every reference, during the time the apostles were acting under the last commission, to the church, the body of Christ, the building of God, the house of God, as then in existence, is a standing refutation of the theory that there is no kingdom of God in existence at this time.

There was, then, a kingdom of God in the time of the apostles; Peter used the keys of the kingdom, opened it; persons "born of water and of the Spirit" entered it; that kingdom is now in existence, and men and women enter into it, and are, therefore, properly said to be *in the kingdom* and patience of Jesus Christ.

FAITH AND SIGHT

W. T. MOORE

"For we walk by faith, and not by sight."—2 Cor. 5: 7.

IN our present state, we are necessarily connected with two worlds—the natural and the supernatural—and from these we derive all the means of our temporal and spiritual life. The natural satisfies the senses, and is, indeed, the soil on which they grow; but only the supernatural can satisfy the conditions of the spirit, for its immortal longings reach far beyond the confines of sensuous and earthly things. These two worlds constitute man's entire area of thought and action, affording ample opportunities for the exercise alike of his physical and spiritual natures. In one, we walk by sight; in the other, by faith. Let it be distinctly stated, however, that there is no *necessary* conflict between the natural and the supernatural. These are complements of each other, and are both essential to meet the requirements of our organization, as well as to fulfill the purposes of God in us. It is time that the crude, irrational and unphilosophical conclusion that God, in His moral government, is forever contradicting the laws of the physical, had become obsolete—a fossil of a bygone, semichristian civilization. God does not contradict Himself, but is perfectly consistent in all His works. Hence, there is no necessary antagonism between spirit and sense; neither is there any between faith and sight. But, while this is true, it is equally true that Faith and Sight are exceedingly jealous of each other. No encroachments upon the boundaries of either must be made, for when it is otherwise, a conflict at once begins, which not unfrequently ends in the destruction of happiness and the ruin of the soul. Each has its distinctive province, and this is sacred against all interference. It becomes, therefore, a matter of grave importance to correctly define the boundaries of these, and whatever other relations they may sustain to each other. Hence, in order to treat the whole subject in a manner somewhat commensurate with its importance, I propose to observe the following plan:

I. SHOW THE DIFFERENCE BETWEEN FAITH AND SIGHT;

II. TRACE THE ANALOGY BETWEEN THEM;

III. ILLUSTRATE THE SUPERIORITY OF FAITH.

In presenting and developing these points, I shall avoid, as far as possible, everything like abstract or metaphysical reasoning, though, in the very nature of things, I shall be compelled to go somewhat out of the ordinary path of pulpit dis-

Faith and Sight

course. I will endeavor, however, to be as simple in my treatment as the character of the subject will permit; and trust that, by divine assistance, I may be able to present everything in such a way as that all may understand and be benefited by the investigation. Let us, then, consider:

I. THE DIFFERENCE BETWEEN FAITH AND SIGHT.

It will greatly facilitate our progress, in this inquiry, if we keep in memory what has already been stated in reference to the distinct province occupied respectively by Faith and Sight. It must never be forgotten that they do not belong to the same territory, and that it is only by keeping them *entirely separate* that harmony between them is preserved.

The term *sight,* in the text, may be defined as embracing everything *outside of faith.* Whatever belongs to the senses, or the reason, is clearly included in it. Hence, sense, reason and faith cover the whole ground of the natural and the supernatural, the visible and invisible, the temporal and eternal; and to understand the relation of these to each other, and to know how to appropriate the knowledge derived respectively from them, is the end of all study, the consummation of all effort.

I shall now attempt to illustrate these matters in such a way as that no one can fail to understand my meaning. If you look upon an object, the soul will be affected according to the qualities of that object. If the object is a beautiful landscape, the impression made will be *agreeable*—the soul will *enjoy* the view; but if the object is an ungainly thing—something possessing repulsive qualities—it will be *disagreeable,* and you will experience a· very unpleasant sensation. Hence, it may be affirmed that all sensuous knowledge— that is, knowledge derived directly through the senses—is either agreeable or disagreeable, pleasant or unpleasant; and that, therefore, it is the province of sense to determine the *qualities* of things.

If, however, you demonstrate that the "square described on the hypothenuse of a right-angled triangle is equal to the sum of the squares described on the other two sides," it can not be said that there is anything agreeable or disagreeable, pleasant or unpleasant in that. True, there is a sense of enjoyment when the conclusion is reached; but this is no part of the demonstration. The feeling experienced is *after the problem passes from the reason to the senses.* It is in the domain of the reason, and the knowledge which you derive from your effort may be denominated *rational,* because it comes from the *relation* of things, and not from their *qualities.* This is a new field upon which you have entered, and you no longer behold the enchanting sunsets, the meandering rivers and the beautiful landscapes which everywhere meet the

Faith and Sight

view in the world of qualities; nor do you any longer hear the ravishing music of singing birds, laughing rivulets and dashing waterfalls, as they mingle their strange and wonderful harmonies into a grand oratorio, the sound of which inspires all the region of the senseland. You have forgotten all these, and are now at work in the world of causes and wherefores, the possible and impossible, where sensation gives place to demonstration, and light comes only through the pure reason.

We have now briefly surveyed the dominion of Sight; but there are many things yet to be learned. We have done little more than cast a pebble into the great waters of the unknown. The past, with all its joys and sorrows, buried beneath the weight of six thousand years, and the future, with its hopes and fears, stretching out before us like a shoreless ocean, whose treasures can not be gathered, and whose mysteries can not be explained by either sense or reason, are yet unexplored. But, thanks to our heavenly Father, we are not left in darkness here. Over all this invisible land Faith holds undisputed sway. *Just at the point where Sight ends, Faith begins.* When Sense and Reason become helpless and blind, then Faith spreads her wings, and leads on through the regions beyond. Did such a man as the first Napoleon live and act the part ascribed to him in history? If so, how does it become a part of our stock of knowledge? Is it because it is agreeable or disagreeable? Or can it be demonstrated from the relation of things? Can either sense or reason reach back into the past, and bring this fact into the knowledge of the present? Who does not see that it is a subject entirely out of the range of either of these, and that, no matter how they may be affected by it, the *fact* is not changed in any way whatever? It is equally independent of the likes and dislikes of mankind, and the boasted power of human reason. All that you can say about it is, that it is either *true* or *false*. If false, nothing can make it true; if true, nothing can make it false. *Matters of faith, then, are matters of fact; and these can be determined only by the weight of testimony.*

If what has been already stated be true, it must be evident that there are but three ways in which knowledge can be derived; viz., through the senses, the pure reason, and by faith. And, for the sake of a convenient classification, we may call the first, sensuous knowledge; the second, rational knowledge; and the third, the knowledge of testimony. These comprehend all knowledge, and exhaust the area of the natural and the supernatural. In harmony with this classification, we have three systems of religion; viz., Paganism, rationalism and Christianity; and, upon investigation, it will be found that the characteristics of these correspond respectively to sense, reason and faith. Let us now examine these systems briefly, and see what their ruling principles are.

1. *Paganism is the religion of sense.*

It proposes nothing higher than the senses as an object of worship, and is constantly controlled by an unrelenting, sensuous philosophy. The appetites and passions become the gods of the godless religion. Under its teachings, men seek that which satisfies the lusts of the flesh while every grace of a higher civilization is either destroyed or driven into eternal banishment. Virtue is insulted in the arms of Bacchus; Righteousness is burned in the temple of Moloch; Truth is lost in the Pantheon; Innocence is chained to the car of Juggernaut; Love lies bleeding under the heel of Mars; and Peace hears nothing but eternal strife. And yet, all this exhibits but a faint picture of the blighting curse of paganism in its influence on the civilization of the world. But, if anything further is needed to illustrate the diabolical spirit of this sensuistic religion, it is only necessary to hear what the apostle says concerning its workings when the people were fully under its control: "Being filled with all unrighteousness, fornication, wickedness, covetousness, maliciousness; full of envy, murder, debate, deceit, malignity, whisperers, backbiters, haters of God, despiteful, proud, boasters, inventors of evil things, disobedient to parents, without understanding, covenant-breakers, without natural affection, implacable, unmerciful:

who, knowing the judgment of God, that they which commit such things are worthy of death, not only do the same, but have pleasure in them that do them'' (Rom. 1:29-32). These people were certainly the chief of sinners; and, after such an enumeration, can we wonder that the apostle gloried in the cross by which he was crucified to the world, and the world to him?

But what is modern ritualism but a refined paganism? Is not the principle of both precisely the same? What mean all the forms and ceremonies of ritualism, if they be not to charm the senses? From this standpoint it does not require much reflection to determine the secret of the success of Catholicism. Take away its liturgy, its ritual service—strip it of everything except what is legitimately Christian—and it will not be long before the pontifical throne is vacated, and the mistress of the world is humbled in the dust. Catholicism, as opposed to rationalism, is a religion of superstition; but, as opposed to Christianity, it is a religion of flesh.

2. *Rationalism is the religion of reason.*

As such, it is only a step higher than sensualism. It is simply more respectable. While one glories in the "lusts of the flesh," the other glories in the "pride of life." Rationalism may deplore the fearful consequences of sin as seen in the progress of sensualism; but it can neither account for that sin, nor offer an adequate remedy for it. It stands, in the presence of the world's greatest need, a condemned pretender, a vaunting hypocrite. It has yet to learn the palpable truism that *religion is philosophy, but philosophy is not religion.* What care I for the boasted powers of human reason, the wonderful revelations of science, and the splendid trophies of genius, *while all these perish with their using,* and offer nothing to the sad, sick and weary soul beyond the things of time and sense? What a cheat this rationalism is! And how impotent to meet our real wants! It has recently somewhat revived in Europe and this country, and, under the leadership of such men as Renan, Colenso, Leckey and Emerson, it promises great things. But it is the same old story of philosophy against religion, the natural against the supernatural, sight against faith, which has been the irrepressible conflict of ages. The apostle Paul found the same thing at Corinth; and the reason he gave for it then will account for it to-day: "The preaching of the cross is to them that perish foolishness, but unto us who are saved, it is the power of God" (1 Cor. 1:18).

3. *Christianity is the religion of faith.*

No higher encomium could be pronounced upon Christianity than is contained in this statement. Christ's kingdom is not of this world. Hence, the religion which He established is not carnal, but spiritual. Christianity, then, rises far above the sensuous and rational, and rests its claim on divine authority. "Which?" is the question paganism asks. It seeks after only the agreeable and pleasant—those things which satisfy the demands of the senses—while rationalism is equally persistent in pressing the everlasting "Why?" looking only for the cause or reason of things, and attempting to solve the mysteries of our present state by the revelations of science. But the question which Christianity asks is "What?" and has respect, not to pleasure or philosophy, but to *duty*. With all its qualifying words, it stands thus: *"Lord, what wilt thou have me to do?"*

It should ever be remembered that Christianity is not a religion of pleasure, but of self-abnegation, of self-crucifixion. We are constantly exhorted to "deny ourselves," to "keep the body under," to "crucify the lusts of the flesh," and to "suffer for righteousness' sake"; showing clearly that the enjoyment derived from the service of Christ is not sensuous, but spiritual. As followers of Jesus, we may expect to meet innumerable crosses; and if this were not so, we might question our final triumph, for it is only by the cross we reach the crown.

This peculiarity of the Christian religion seems to have been very generally overlooked by our modern system-makers, who would like to have the charities of the gospel include all the follies and pleasures of mankind; but, He who spake as never

Faith and Sight

man spake, said: "Wide is the gate, and broad is the way, that leadeth to destruction, and many there be that go in thereat: because strait is the gate, and narrow is the way, which leadeth to life, and few there be that find it" (Matt. 7:13, 14).

It becomes, therefore, a matter of great importance to determine by what principles we are guided in our religious acts. Is our service the "obedience of faith," or the obedience of sight? Are we seeking to gratify the senses, or to adorn and beautify the spirit? Is our service mere lip-service, or do we worship in spirit and in truth? A proper answer to these questions will do much toward determining our true relations to Christ.

If you wish to see how widespread and how desolating the religion of sight is, go to the people, and talk to them about obeying the gospel. You will constantly hear such expressions as these: "Everybody should belong to some church;" "I *prefer* the Presbyterian Church;" "The Episcopal service *suits me* best—it is so beautiful;" "I *like* Dr. A., and I will join *his* church," etc. All these clearly indicate that *self-satisfaction* is the principal thing aimed at. Esthetics, and not Christ, is the object of the worship of thousands. Poor sinners, this is not the kind of obedience Christ demands. What you like or dislike has nothing to do with your salvation, and is not the question for you to consider. You must walk by faith, and not by sight. The all-absorbing, all-important question is, *What does the Lord say?* When this is satisfactorily answered, you can go forward, with the blessed assurance that you can "do all things through Christ, who strengthens you."

But again: What business have you with the *reason* of the command? Can you expect to fathom the deep purposes of God? Why, you can not explain the most familiar thing. If, when surveying the legitimate realms of philosophy, you frequently stumble and fall, can you expect to walk by sight a single moment in religion? Should you entertain such an idea, let me assure you that faith alone can lead you through the darkness of the present to a bright and glorious future.

II. The Analogy between Faith and Sight.

The New Testament abounds in analogical teaching, but the great Teacher more especially excels in this method of presenting truth. Nothing could be more striking, and certainly nothing more instructive, than this method, when properly used. Besides the *particular* truth it unfolds, in any given case, it teaches us the *general* truth that material things are to be valued, not as an *end,* but as a *means;* and that, therefore, the senses and the reason are but instruments by which the soul travels toward the regions of faith, and are only useful while operating in their proper spheres. Hence they must not be allowed to tres-

Faith and Sight

pass upon the dominion of faith, for it can hold no partnerships, make no compromises; it must have undisputed and unlimited control over its own. Let us now examine the analogy between faith and sight. Sight clearly implies three things:

1. The organ of sight—the eye.
2. The medium of sight—light.
3. An object upon which to look.

Now, when these three things are perfect there will be perfect vision; but remove one—no matter which—and there can be no vision at all. Precisely so is it with faith. Three things are necessary to it also:

1. *There must be the organ of faith—the capacity to believe.*

Have we this capacity? Are we capable of believing truth when it is presented before us? Certainly no one ought to hesitate in answering these questions. But, strange to say, some men have doubted our capacity to believe—men, too, who are regarded as lights in the church, and whose opinions carry with them great weight. Surely, such men do not understand what they teach.

I do not propose to discuss this question. In fact, it is not a question within the range of legitimate discussion. It is a question of experience, and can be decided only by an appeal to every man's consciousness. Every man must decide for himself; no one can do it for him. True, the aggregate testimony of men can be taken, but the question then becomes a matter of faith, the ridiculousness of which will appear when an *individual* attempts to express himself in the language which this position forces him to use. "I believe that I can believe" is not very passable English, and certainly does not sound out with the same assurance as "I know that I can believe." The question, then, is not one of faith or philosophy, but of actual knowledge. In order to make my meaning more fully understood, I will illustrate: For several hours, upon a pair of scales, suspended by a rope, you have been weighing a thousand pounds at a time. A gentleman steps up, and, after examining the rope, and making a long and intricate calculation, he gravely informs you that he thoroughly understands the philosophy of ropes, and that this one is not now, and never was, capable of bearing up more than five hundred pounds. What would you think of this man's philosophy? And how long would you stop to reason with him about the matter? If you were to consume time with him at all, you would simply say to him that you did not care what his philosophy taught; that you had tried the rope sufficiently, and knew, from actual experience, that he was mistaken. So say to every man that doubts your ability to believe the gospel.

2. *There must be the medium of faith.*

The apostle says: "Faith comes by hearing, and hearing by the word of God" (Rom 10:17).

This, then, settles the question as to what is the medium of faith. Clearly, it is the word of God. And this at once elevates our view of the Word, and gives us better conceptions of the preciousness of faith. We bless the hand that bears us the gift. In what reverence, then, should we hold the word of God, which brings to us such a glorious gift as faith!

3. *Faith must have an object—something upon which to rest.*

What is this object? Let the Holy Scriptures answer: "God so loved the world, that he gave his only begotten Son, that whosoever *believeth in him* should not perish, but have everlasting life;" "This is the work of God, that ye *believe on him* whom he hath sent;" "He that *believeth on me* hath everlasting life;" "Ye believe in God, be*lieve also in me;*" *"Believe on the Lord Jesus Christ,* and thou shalt be saved." Many other passages could be quoted, but these are deemed sufficient to show that the object of our faith is the precious Saviour. And what a blessed fact this is! How consoling to the heart that is tired of the endless controversies about creeds and doctrines! And with what joyful trust does the poor, houseless wanderer come to this sure foundation-stone which God has laid in Zion! The Christian's faith is not *doctrinal,* but *personal;* not belief in a *theory,* but in a divine and glorious *character;* not the reception of a cold, lifeless *dogma,* but a hearty, earnest trust in One whose love is *stronger than a brother's;* who is "touched with a feeling of our infirmities"; who "knows our frame, and remembers that we are dust."

But let us notice in what particulars Christ addresses our confidence. *Is He worthy?* Certainly He who has been appointed "heir of all things"; "by whom the worlds were made;" who is the "brightness of the Father's glory, and the express image of his person"; who is "seated at the right hand of the Majesty on high"; whose "throne is for ever and ever"; who "loves righteousness and who hates iniquity," and whom all the angels worship," is worthy of our most unqualified trust and our highest adoration.

Has He done anything for us that entitles Him to our confidence? Read His history. Follow Him from His birth to the last scenes on Calvary. His life was one of toil, sorrow and self-denial, that He might teach us "how sublime a thing it is to suffer and be strong." But who can witness His last dying agony on the cross without exclaiming:

> "Were the whole realm of nature mine,
>   That were a present far too small;
> Love so amazing, so divine,
>   Demands my soul, my life, my all."

Will He certainly save us if we put our trust in Him? What penitent believer did He ever turn away? "He would not have any to perish, but all to come to the knowledge of the truth." Do we want a Saviour who is willing to save? *Jesus is ever willing.* Must He have the official character of a Saviour? *Christ is anointed to save.* But do you say He must have power to save? *The Lord is "able to save to the uttermost all that come to God by him."* Sinner, believe on the Lord Jesus Christ, and *thou shalt be saved.*

III. THE SUPERIORITY OF FAITH OVER SIGHT.

Numerous examples illustrating the truth of this proposition may be found in both the Old and New Testament Scriptures. In fact, from that memorable occasion in the Garden of Eden, when sight was first brought into antagonism with faith, till the present time, the history of the world is but a succession of events attesting the superior excellence of faith. Sight, when followed beyond its legitimate sphere, has ever led mankind astray. Its dazzling beauty, its splendid attire and its fascinating charms are well calculated to captivate those who trust in appearances. But it is only necessary to examine the records of the past, and our own experience, to understand how deceitful is all this display, and how unworthy it is of our confidence.

Not so of faith. It offers no enchanting prospects in this life. Its promises here are self-denial, toil, struggle, sorrow and disappointments; but its history is full of immortal heroes and glorious triumphs. After awhile its work will be accomplished, and then those who "have kept the faith" will, with the apostle Paul, receive a "crown of righteousness" which shall never fade away.

But let us now consider wherein consists faith's superiority.

1. *It has a more extended view than sight.*

Whoever attempts to walk by sight will not be long in finding out the shortness of his vision. He will find that life is full of labyrinths he can not thread, while everywhere he will meet untold mysteries he can not explain. Discouraged by his failures, and bewildered by the difficulties of his situation, he will very possibly despair of relief, and accept one of the inevitable alternatives of desperation; viz., dissipation, solitude or suicide, either of which will unfit him for the land of the great hereafter.

But the horizon of faith is not so limited. The apostle's description will help us to understand its extent: "Faith is the foundation of things hoped for, the conviction of things not seen" (Heb. 11:1). That is, it stands under all the future, and convinces of all the past. It is, therefore, master of the invisible world, and is to the spiritual world what sight is to the material. With this wonderful telescope we can survey every step of human progress, and understand every path of human duty.

Faith and Sight

2. *Faith is more truthful than sight.*

Things are not here what they seem to be. Deception lurks in the most inviting prospects. We see only the *outside*. We do not penetrate to the real *essence*. We are intoxicated with *qualities*, and show our aptness by compounding *relations*, but we only deceive ourselves, and demonstrate that

> "This world is all a fleeting show,
> For man's illusion given;
> The smiles of joy, the tears of woe,
> Deceitful shine, deceitful flow;
> There's nothing true but heaven."

Sight takes cognizance of things as they *appear;* faith sees them as they *are*. Sight sees that which is *visible;* faith sees only the *unseen*. One deceives, and often leads astray; the other deals honestly with us, and tells us the truth. When was any one ever disappointed who walked by faith? You will search the records of the past in vain for a single example. On the contrary, however, you will find that the "obedience of faith" has always been richly rewarded. I can refer to only a few instances.

As the children of Israel journeyed from Mount Hor, by the way of the Red Sea, to compass the land of Edom, they became much discouraged because of the way, and complained bitterly against God and Moses for having brought them out of the land of Egypt to die in the wilderness. And the Lord sent fiery serpents among them, to punish them for their unbelief and hardness of heart. From the bite of these serpents, many of the people died; after which, those remaining confessed their sins, and besought Moses that he would pray the Lord to have the curse removed. The Lord instructed Moses to make a brazen serpent, and set it upon a pole, and said it should come to pass that every one who was bitten, when he looked upon it should live.

Could anything have been more unphilosophical than this remedy? How unlike the *materia medica* of sight! Suppose some modern physician were to suggest such a remedy for the bite of serpents now, what, think you, would our learned doctors of medicine say of him? Would they be likely to regard him as sane? Not unless they should exercise more charity than they are in the habit of doing toward adventurers in their profession. But these Israelites were not to seek for the reason of the command; they were to walk by faith—simply to *look and live*. When they had obeyed, were they disappointed? No matter how unpromising the thing appeared, was not the faith of every poor, suffering Israelite, who looked to the remedy, instantly and amply rewarded?

The destruction of the walls of Jericho is another striking illustration of the fidelity of faith to her promises. What if some modern

Faith and Sight

Joshua should establish a school of military tactics in accordance with the programme of that siege? Does not the very thought excite a smile on the face of every war-worn veteran in all the land? Nevertheless, when the Israelites had compassed the city, as commanded, their faith met no disappointment—the walls of the city fell.

3. *Faith is more powerful than sight.*

There is nothing, perhaps, in which we are so constantly cheated as in our estimate of power. We are accustomed to look for it in noise and great display; but nothing could be more unwise, for *real* power moves in silent courses. It is not in the thunder's deep, portentous roar, but in the lightning which sleeps in the storm-cloud. Sight is forever thundering in our ears its arrogant boasts, while it is only able to make display; but *Faith goes on in silence, and overcomes the world.*

It would be both a pleasant and profitable exercise to notice the many conditions in life where faith manifests its superior power, but a few must suffice.

The most self-sacrificing service which God requires of us, faith can make easy. Abraham offering up his son Isaac is a fine illustration of this. What could have more severely taxed Abraham's fidelity to God than the act he was required to perform? It was paternal love and faith in conflict; a struggle between a father's affection for his son—his only son—and respect for the commandment of God. Faith gained the victory; and, on this account, Abraham is called the "father of the faithful."

Faith also enables us to endure the severest trials without murmuring. The Bible is full of splendid examples illustrating the truth of this statement, and the history of the church bears overwhelming testimony in its favor. With what eloquence does the long list of martyred saints speak on this subject? The names of such glorious heroes as John Huss, John Rogers and William Tyndale tell how true it is that faith in Christ is able to sustain us through the darkest hour of trial.

Again, it is a glorious fact that, when we are exposed to the greatest dangers, faith gives us courage and lights up our pathway. During a storm at sea, a ship, which had for a long time breasted the fury of the waves, was, at last, apparently about to go down. All on board were in the wildest state of excitement, except one man, who remained perfectly composed, and seemingly indifferent to the danger which threatened him. His wife, noticing his calm demeanor, and not understanding the meaning of it, asked him how he could appear so resigned in the presence of so great peril. He immediately drew a dagger, and presented it at her heart. Said he: "Are you not afraid of this dagger?" "No," she answered, as the tears streamed down her pale cheeks. "And why are

Faith and Sight

you not afraid of it?" he continued. "Because," said she, *"it is in the hands of my dear husband."* "Neither am I afraid of the storm," said he; *"because it is in the hands of my heavenly Father. I know that He loves me, and doeth all things well."* This man walked by faith, and faith gave him perfect resignation. "Though he slay me, yet will I trust him," is not the language of weak, hesitating, stammering sight.

Finally: Faith's conflicts, though they may seem doubtful for a time, never fail to end in victory. How many sad and weary hearts, worn down by the long, long night of toil, are inspired with a new hope and new life by the quickening rays of this blessed assurance! All along the lines of the struggling soldiers of the Cross, I see unmistakable evidences of a forward movement, as they unitedly pronounce the cheering words of the apostle: "Thanks be to God, who giveth us the victory, through our Lord Jesus Christ."

It is difficult to conceive how our heavenly Father could have given us more evidence than He has that faith is stronger than sight. We have seen that philosophy clearly suggests it; that history speaks but one voice on the subject, and that the heroes of the Bible, to whom we have referred, exemplify it in their lives. "And what shall I more say? For the time would fail me to tell of Gideon, and of Barak, and of Samson, and of Jephtha; of David also, and Samuel, and of the prophets: who, through faith, subdued kingdoms, wrought righteousness, obtained promises, stopped the mouths of lions, quenched the violence of fire, escaped the edge of the sword, out of weakness were made strong, waxed valiant in fight, turned to flight the armies of the aliens'' (Heb. 11: 32-35).

I feel that enough has been said to convince the most skeptical mind that only Faith is able to lead us to certain and glorious victory.

And now, in conclusion, let me urge upon you the importance of following the lead of Faith. The things of Sight can never bring happiness, though the world, with all its stores, were placed at your feet. The history of Solomon is re-enacted in the history of every man who seeks for happiness in the unsubstantial pleasures of this world: ''All is vanity and vexation of spirit, and there is no profit under the sun.''

But, even allowing that there is a degree of real pleasure in pursuing the things of Sight, they can not remain with you long, for decay is written upon them all—all is changing, passing, fleeting.

"The sweetest and dearest, alas! will not stay."

Where are the companions of your youth? ''The fathers, where are they? and the prophets, do they live forever?'' Look back upon the past. How many of life's fondest treasures lie buried there! How many cherished hopes and dazzling prospects sleep within that tomb of ages! When,

Faith and Sight

oh, when, will the world understand the folly of trusting the things of Sight!

Dear brethren, let us heed the voice of heavenly wisdom and "look not at the things which are seen, but at the things which are not seen: for the things which are seen are temporal; but the things which are not seen are eternal." "Let us not be weary in well-doing," but toil on and suffer, if needs be, *yet a little while;* "for in due season we shall reap if we faint not."

> "Soon shall close our earthly mission,
>   Soon shall pass our pilgrim days;
> Hope shall change to glad fruition,
>   Faith to sight, and prayer to praise."

THE MIDDLE WALL

ELIJAH GOODWIN

"He is our peace who hath made both one, and hath broken down the middle wall of partition between us."— Eph. 2: 14.

THIS text is only a part of a lengthy argument, employed by the apostle, for the purpose of settling a very *unpleasant controversy* which was agitating the public mind at that time. *This controversy had reference* to the rights and privileges which should be granted to persons who had embraced Christianity from among the Gentiles. *The Jewish believers opposed* their reception into the church, and even went so far as to forbid the apostles "to speak to the Gentiles that they might be saved." *Paul, being the apostle of the Gentiles*, defends their rights, devoting a great portion of this Epistle to that subject.

In the first chapter he shows that notwithstanding God had predestinated the seed of Abraham to the adoption of children by Jesus Christ, yet he had purposed "that in the dispensation of the fulness of times he would gather together in

The Middle Wall

one all things in Christ, both which are in heaven and which are on earth, even in him,'' thus showing that the original purpose of God was, finally, to unite all believers of all nations in one body.

In the second chapter he shows that the Jews have nothing to boast of above the Gentiles on account of good works. That, notwithstanding the Gentiles had "walked according to the course of this world, according to the prince of the power of the air, the spirit that now works in the children of disobedience," yet the Jews had had their behavior in the same way, "fulfilling the desires of the flesh and of the mind, and were by nature [practice, second nature] the children of wrath, even as others," as the Gentiles.

He then announces the great truth that the whole gospel plan of salvation was devised and put into operation *on the principle of grace,* so that all who are saved, whether Jew or Gentile, "are saved by grace, and not of works, lest any man should boast," thus showing that the Jews *had no constitutional rights in the gospel kingdom* which did not belong to the Gentiles on the same principles. Now, while prosecuting this argument, the apostle penned the text which I have selected as the theme of this discourse: *"He is our peace who hath made both one, and hath broken down the middle wall of partition between us."*

In the further investigation of the subject, we propose the following order:

New Testament Christianity

I. Show what is meant by this partition wall, and its designs.

II. Speak of the breaking down of this wall, and the purposes for which it was broken down.

III. Draw some practical conclusions.

I. According to this order, I inquire, *What is meant by this partition wall?* This the apostle explains in the following verse, thus: "Having abolished in his flesh the enmity, even the law of commandments contained in ordinances." *Then, the law of Moses,* with all its rites and ceremonies, is what is here called a *partition wall.* Of this law God was the author and finisher. He counseled with no intelligent being in the universe on the subject. He advised with no man or angel, as to what should be or should not be law. He gave it from the thick darkness that crowned the smoking summit of trembling Mount Sinai.

But for what purpose was this law given? What were its designs?

1. In order that man may be saved, he must have confidence in God. He must not only believe that *"God is,"* but he must believe that "he is a rewarder of all who seek him diligently" (Heb. 2:6). Now, in order that man may have this confidence in the Lord, it was necessary that He show himself *to be a covenant-keeping God;* that all that He promises He will perform. Now, God had made promises to Abraham, saying: "In thy seed shall all the families of the earth be blessed"

The Middle Wall

(Gen. 12:3; 22:18). *In order, then, to show* to heaven and earth that God had kept this promise, it was necessary to keep the seed of Abraham separate from all other nations until the Messiah should come; or, as Paul expresses it, "until the seed should come to whom the promise was made" (Gal. 3:19). *Had not this been done,* the seed of Abraham might have been lost in the ocean of human beings, and no man could ever have told whether the covenant was fulfilled or not. It might have been fulfilled to the letter, but, the lineage being lost, the skeptic would always have had the advantage. Hence, in order to keep the posterity of Abraham separate from all other people, and thus to show to heaven and earth that the Lord had kept His promise to the letter, He threw around the seed of Abraham, through Isaac and Jacob, the law of commandments concerning ordinances, and by it fenced them in from all the nations of the earth. This, then, was the first design of that institution.

2. But, in the second place, it was intended to hold that people in subjection; to govern them (Galatians 3).

The Jews are always spoken of as a stiff-necked and rebellious nation. They were constantly inclined to run away from God. Hence the Lord treated them as the husbandman treats his unruly stock; He *fenced them in.* Hence the law is called a governor, under which the Jews were placed during their minority, until the time appointed of the Father for them to be made free by the Son, that they might be free indeed, should come.

Peter, using another figure, calls this law a yoke, which, he says, "neither they nor their fathers were able to bear" (Acts 15:10). By a yoke he means law, government and thus shows that that partition wall was intended to hold the people in subjection to God. True, like unruly stock, they often broke over this wall, and ran away from God; but this does not disprove our last position in reference to the design of the law.

3. In the third place, the law was intended to teach that people, and thus prepare them for the reception of the Messiah when He should come.

The apostle says "the law was [not is] our schoolmaster to bring us to Christ" (Gal. 3:24). The Jewish nation was placed under the law as a tutor, to train, teach and prepare that people, in heart and character, for the coming dispensation. In reasoning on this subject, the apostle said: "Now I say, That the heir, as long as he is a child, differeth nothing from a servant, though he be lord of all; but is under tutors and governors until the time appointed of the father. Even so we, when we were children, were in bondage under the elements of the world" (Gal. 4:1-3). By "tutor" Paul means the law.

And I may be permitted to say that *there never was a more competent teacher than was this law.* No teacher was ever better qualified to accomplish the ends contemplated. That law, in all its rites and ceremonies, pointed to the gospel day; hence it is said, "The law had a shadow of good things to come." The loaves of the divine presence very fitly prefigured the Lord's Supper in the Christian church; the golden altar and burning incense were fit types of the spiritual devotion arising from hearts purified by grace under the reign of Christ; their bleeding, expiring victims, that bled for remission under that law, prefigured the great atoning sacrifice which was offered in the end of the Jewish age to put away sin. Indeed, their very temple itself was a type of the Christian church, and every rite performed within its consecrated walls was intended to develop the mind, enlarge the views, direct the affections, and prepare the nation for the coming Messiah.

It may be asked, If this teacher was so competent, why was the nation so poorly taught? Why were they so poorly prepared to receive the Saviour when He came?

I answer: It is not every student that is put under a good and efficient teacher that comes out an accomplished scholar. The student must be reconciled to the rules of the school; he must have some regard for his teacher; he must submit to the laws of the institution; and, above all, he must apply his mind to his studies. All these things the Jews failed to do. They fell out with their teacher; they refused to submit to his authority; they would not apply their hearts to his instructions; they added their own views of propriety to his commandments, insomuch that the Lord said, when He came, they had *"made void the law by their traditions."*

To this general charge there were *a few honorable exceptions;* and these were fully prepared to receive the Messiah. Good old Simeon was of this happy number. It is said of him that he "was just, and devout, waiting for the consolation of Israel." When Christ was circumcised, he "took him up in his arms, and said, Now, Lord, lettest thou thy servant depart in peace; for mine eyes have seen thy salvation, which thou hast prepared before the face of all people, a light to lighten the Gentiles and the glory of thy people Israel" (Luke 2:28, 29). Simeon saw salvation in this child for all nations; he saw, in the infant Saviour, light for the Gentiles, who had long been in darkness, and glory for the Israel of God.

Now, the only principle upon which we can account for the striking difference between this good man and the great mass of the Jewish nation is, that he studied his lessons, he obeyed his teacher, he satisfied himself with the requirements of the law, and was, therefore, prepared to enter the higher school, when the great Teacher, sent from God, appeared. And I fully believe that if the whole nation had thus submitted to that

The Middle Wall

schoolmaster and governor, they would all have been as well prepared for the reign of Christ as was this good man. The fault was not in the teacher, but in the students.

II. I now pass to my second head of discourse, which is to speak of the breaking down of this wall of partition, and the designs for which it was broken down.

This law stood in full force during the teaching of John the Baptist, and of Christ and His disciples, until the Lord's death. All the reformation and obedience that John required were to be performed according to that law. Christ Himself lived under that law, and hence, when He healed a man of the leprosy, He told him to "show himself to the priest, and offer for his cleansing those things that Moses commanded" (Mark 1:44).

But when the great antitype, the atoning sacrifice, expired, the law expired with Him; when He bowed His head and died, the partition wall fell. Then it was that He, who is our peace-offering, broke down the middle wall of partition, according to our text. Speaking in reference to this same matter, the apostle says He hath "blotted out the handwriting of ordinances that was against us, which was contrary to us, and took it out of the way, nailing it to his cross" (Col. 2:14).

That this partition wall had now fallen, God signified by rending the veil of the temple, at

New Testament Christianity

the death of Christ. That veil separated the Holy Place from the Most Holy Place; it concealed from public view the Most Holy Place of the temple, and might, therefore, be considered as an emblem of the partition wall between Jew and Gentile. But now the promised seed has come; the substance of all the shadows under the law is now manifested; the Lamb of God, which had been slain in type from the foundation of the world, was now slain in fact; upon the cross on Calvary He bows His head and dies, and the partition wall is leveled to the ground, and the veil of the temple is rent in two from top to bottom, as if God would say, We have no more need of thee: Christ has opened up a new and living way, through the veil of His flesh, into the Holy Place made without hands.

But, under this head, I am also to point out some of the designs of our blessed Lord, in breaking this partition wall down. Though these may be many, I will only mention two in this discourse.

1. The first design that I will notice is spoken of in the context thus: "To make in himself of twain one new man."

Now, by this "new man" the apostle means a new church, having reference to the Christian church under the gospel dispensation. This new church was to be composed of believers from every nation under heaven; but this could not be while the partition wall between Jew and Gentile stood. Therefore, before He organized the new church—

The Middle Wall

before He formed, of the two nations, one new man—He broke down the partition wall between them. Thus, we clearly perceive one of the main objects of the apostle in penning this text. The Jews, as stated in the introduction of this discourse, opposed the reception of the Gentiles into the church; they argued that the law forbade it; that that institution stood as a wall between them and all other nations; and, therefore, for them to unite with men of another nation in religious matters would be to overleap God's partition wall.

But, in answer to this, Paul speaks in the language of our text, saying: *"He is our peace who hath made both one, and hath broken down the middle wall of partition between us; having abolished in his flesh the enmity, even the law of commandments contained in ordinances, for to make in himself of two one new man."*

From this declaration, it is clear that Paul did not believe in the modern notion that the Jewish church and the Christian church were one; that they were identical. He does not say that He who is our peace has come to reform the old Jewish church, and "enlarge its privileges somewhat." But He declares that His object was to make a new man; a new ecclesiastical organization, the like of which never existed upon the earth before.

John the Baptist, the Lord Himself, and the disciples, all taught the same doctrine. John "preached in the wilderness of Judæa, saying, Repent, for the kingdom of heaven is at hand" (Matt. 3:2). Thus did He announce the near approach of a new kingdom, or church. "And when he saw many of the Pharisees and Sadducees come to his baptism, he said unto them, O generation of vipers, who hath warned you to flee from the wrath to come? Bring forth therefore fruits meet for repentance, and think not to say within yourselves, We have Abraham to our father; for I say unto you that God is able of these stones to raise up children unto Abraham. And now also the axe is laid unto the root of the tree; therefore every tree that bringeth not forth good fruit is hewn down and cast into the fire" (Matt. 3: 7-10).

John saw that these persons expected to obtain a place in the kingdom, or church of Christ, now approaching, by virtue of their relationship to Abraham. But he lets them know that, in that new organism, every man must stand upon his own faith and obedience; that every tree, whether of the seed of Abraham or not, that does not bring forth good fruit, shall be cast into the fire.

The disciples also were commanded to "preach, saying the kingdom of heaven is at hand" (Matt. 10:7). And Christ Himself "preached the gospel of the kingdom of God, saying the time is fulfilled, and the kingdom of God is at hand: repent ye, and believe the gospel" (Mark 1:14, 15); thus signifying the near approach of a new church, and

The Middle Wall

the necessity of a personal preparation for a place in it.

The Lord taught the same doctrine, both in parable and without a parable. On one occasion He said: "No man putteth a piece of new cloth on an old garment, for that which is put in to fill it up taketh from the garment, and the rent is made worse" (Matt. 9:16); thus intimating that He had not come to mend and patch up that old garment, or Jewish church; but that He intended to make a new garment, an entirely new church.

Again He said: "Neither do men put new wine into old bottles, else the bottles break and the wine runneth out, and the bottles perish; but they put new wine into new bottles, and both are preserved" (Matt. 9:17). By this parable the Lord teaches that He did not intend to pour the Holy Spirit, with all its quickening, sanctifying and miraculous power, into that old, moldy, leathern bottle, or national church; but that He was about to make a new vessel entirely—a new church—into which He would put the new wine of the kingdom, the Holy Spirit, with all its divine influences.

When Peter confessed the Lord, saying, *"Thou art the Christ, the Son of the living God,"* "Jesus answered and said unto him, Blessed art thou, Simon Bar-jona: for flesh and blood hath not revealed it unto thee, but my Father who is in heaven. And I say unto thee, That thou art Peter,

New Testament Christianity

and on this rock I will build my church; and the gates of hell shall not prevail against it" (Matt. 16:16, 17). The reader will please notice that the Lord speaks of His church as not yet built; He says, *"I will build my church."* Of course, when built, it would not be the old church improved, but a new church altogether, called, in the connection in which our text stands, *a new man.*

Jesus taught the same doctrine, virtually, to Nicodemus. This man was a ruler of the Jews, and, of course, occupied a high place in that old national kingdom, or church. He seems to have been well convinced that Jesus was the Messiah for whom his nation had long been looking. Hence he "came to Jesus by night, and said unto him, Rabbi, we know that thou art a teacher come from God, for no man can do the miracles that thou doest, except God be with him." Now, Jesus, no doubt perceiving the thoughts of his heart, said unto him: *"Except* a man be born again, he cannot see the kingdom of God."

This was a new doctrine to Nicodemus. It was not taught in the old covenant, on which the Jewish church stood, and therefore this officer in that church was filled with astonishment when, for the first time, he heard it announced. The Saviour explains by saying: "Except a man be born of water and the Spirit, he cannot enter into the kingdom of God" (John 3:3, 5). Thus the Lord teaches him, and us, and all the world,

The Middle Wall

that He was about to set up a new kingdom, or church, so different from the old institution that its members had to be born over again in order to obtain membership in the new church. Flesh and blood gave a title to membership in the old church; but faith, that works by love and purifies the heart, gives a title to membership in the new. Natural birth and fleshly relationship give no privileges in the church of Christ.

Though a person, applying for membership in this new church, might prove that his ancestry for ten generations back had all been members of the church, yet he can not be admitted unless he believe in Jesus, the Son of God. He can not come in on the faith of father or mother, or god-father or god-mother. And, on the other hand, if the person applying does believe in Christ with all his heart, and is willing to submit to His divine authority, he may become a member, though his ancestry for ten generations may all have been atheists.

I will only name one other point of difference between these two organisms, and then close my remarks on this item.

The prophet, speaking of those who should become members of this church according to the new covenant, says: "And they shall teach no more every man his neighbor, and every man his brother, saying, Know the Lord, for they shall all know me, from the least of them unto the greatest of them, saith the Lord" (Jer. 31:34). Now, this could never be said in the old Jewish church. Persons were born into this church of their earthly parents, and therefore had to be taught to know the Lord afterward. Not so in the new church of which we speak; in it all were to know the Lord; they were to be taught first, and then to come in, being found worthy. Hence the Lord said to His disciples: *"Go teach all nations,* baptizing them into the name of the Father, and of the Son, and of the Holy Spirit" (Matt. 28:19).

2. The second design that the Lord had in breaking down this partition wall, which I will notice, was to *make peace.* Paul says: "He abolished in his flesh the enmity, even the law of commandments contained in ordinances, for to make in himself of twain one new man, *so making peace."*

When the Lord appeared on earth, division and dissension prevailed everywhere. The Jews, within the bounds of the partition wall of which we have spoken, were much divided among themselves. There were the Pharisees and Sadducees, besides other minor sects, among them. True, they had not carried their sectarianism quite so far as some professed Christians have done. They all worshiped in the same temple; they offered their sacrifices at the same altar, and presented their gifts through the same priesthood; they did not lock the doors of their synagogues against a brother Jew because he belonged to a different sect. Still, they were much divided. Every man knew to which party he belonged, and thus the peace of Zion was much disturbed. And then, outside of the precincts of Judaism, all was division. The Gentile world had multiplied their deities to over forty thousand. Every god and demigod must have his altar and his priests, and these, by their teaching and mysteries, kept the people in everlasting contention. Such was the divided and distracted state of our world when the Star of Bethlehem appeared; when the great peacemaker from the skies appeared in human form. He came to hush, to silence warring elements—to say to the raging waves of the ocean of human passion, "Peace, be still;" and to unite in one holy brotherhood those who had been long divided. Well might the angelic hosts sing: *"Glory to God in the highest, on earth peace, and good will toward men."*

But it may be asked, If Christ came to make peace, why did He say that He came to send a sword? Why did He say, "I am come to set a man at variance against his father, and the daughter against her mother, and the daughter-in-law against her mother-in-law, and a man's foes shall be they of his own household"? (Matt. 10: 35, 36). Am I asked, How can this be reconciled with the idea that Christ came to make peace?

I admit that Christ did intend to draw one line of distinction—to mark out one division line, long and broad and deep—one that should be seen and known of all men. This separation line was to be "between them that serve the Lord and them that serve him not." (I fear that this line is not as distinctly seen in our day as the Lord intended it to be.)

When the gospel was first proclaimed, some embraced it, while others rejected it; the father would sometimes become a Christian, and the son would not; the mother would embrace the gospel, and the daughter would reject it—and thus the family would become divided, until a man's foes would indeed be those of his own household. And this division was more than nominal. The unbelieving party would even deliver up the believer, though it were a father or a son, unto death. To this state of things, doubtless, the Saviour referred when He said He had come to make division. Still, His great object was to make peace, and to make it on holy terms. These terms of union were to be so well adapted to the ends proposed—namely, the union of all believers—that the manifold wisdom of God should be visible in them; not only to men, but also to "principalities and powers in heavenly places" (Eph. 3:10).

The apostle refers to these principles in the twentieth verse of the chapter in which our text stands. Speaking to those who had become members of this sacred brotherhood, he says: "Now, therefore, you are no more strangers and foreigners,

The Middle Wall

but fellow-citizens with the saints, and of the household of God; and are built upon the foundation of the apostles and prophets, Jesus Christ himself being the chief corner-stone.''

Now, the constitution of any organized society is the foundation on which it stands. The Constitution of the United States is the foundation on which this great sisterhood of States is builded; the whole political building stands on this platform; destroy the foundation, and the whole building must fall into a thousand fragments—or, to speak without a figure, the Union would be dissolved. May so unhappy an event never obtain! Just so, the constitution of the church is the foundation on which it was organized, and on which it was to stand while sun and moon endure.

But what is meant by the foundation of the apostles and prophets? This must mean the teaching of these holy men of God, who spoke as they were moved by the Holy Spirit. Christ is called *the chief corner-stone* because these apostles and prophets taught as He directed. The chief corner-stone, in a literal building, is first squared and laid—and the whole foundation is squared by it. So, all the teaching of these divinely inspired teachers of Christ was fitted and squared and dictated by the mind of Christ, as revealed by the Holy Spirit.

Now, we have the teaching of these divinely authorized witnesses of Christ, in the Bible, which contains the Old and New Testaments. Thus we have found the constitution on which that new church was formed. The Holy Scriptures, given by inspiration of God, was their only book of faith and religious manners.

The apostle gives a compendium of this foundation of union and communion in the following words: "There is one body and one Spirit, even as you are called in one hope of your calling; one Lord, one faith, one baptism, one God and Father of all, who is above all, and through all, and in you all" (Eph. 4:4-6). These seven points embrace, in a compendious form, the great apostolic platform on which this new church is built and organized. All who acknowledged the one God and Father of all, and submitted to the one baptism, having the one faith, confessing the one Lord, came into the one body, and enjoyed the one Spirit, and rejoiced in the one hope.

What a beautiful arrangement was this. How well calculated to unite the good of all nations! All national peculiarities were to be forgotten here; the Jew was to be reconciled to his fellow-Jew, the Gentile to his fellow-Gentile—and the Jew and Gentile to be reconciled to each other; and on these divine principles to form the one body, and all in one body was to be reconciled to God by the cross of Christ, and thus peace was not only to be made on earth among men, but peace was to be established between heaven and

The Middle Wall

earth, between God and man. Hallelujah! praise ye the Lord!

But in every system there is one central idea— one fundamental truth—which may be regarded as the soul of the system, and which generally gives name to it. *The sun* is the central body in the system of worlds to which we belong, and from that body of light the system receives its name—the *solar system.*

The same is *true of all systems of human government. The central idea in the Constitution of the United States is expressed in these words:* "All men are born free and equal, and endowed by their Creator with certain inalienable rights." Now, the whole Constitution is framed in reference to this one great truth; and all the national and State laws of the Government must be in accordance therewith, and designed to maintain to every citizen that freedom which this simple declaration expresses.

So, in all ecclesiastical organisms, each has its own central idea. In one, that central idea is government by the congregation, so the body is called Congregationalist. In another, the central thought is government by the bishops, and the whole polity is organized accordingly, and the body is called Episcopalian—from *episcopos,* translated "bishop" in the King's Version of the Holy Scriptures. In a third, the central idea is government by the presbytery, or eldership, so this body is called Presbyterian—from *presbuteros,* translated "elder" in the Common Version.

Well, in the constitution of the new man, or church, which Christ built, there is also one central idea—one all-pervading truth—which may be regarded as the soul system. That central idea or truth is that *Jesus of Nazareth is the Christ, the Son of the living God.*

"When Jesus came into the coasts of Cæsarea Philippi, he asked his disciples, saying, Who do men say that I, the Son of man, am? And they said, Some say that thou art John the Baptist; some, Elias; and others, Jeremias, or one of the prophets. He saith unto them, But who say ye that I am? And Simon Peter answered and said, *Thou art the Christ, the Son of the living God.* And Jesus answered and said unto him, Blessed art thou, Simon Bar-jona: for flesh and blood hath not revealed it unto thee, but my Father who is in heaven. And I say unto thee, That thou art Peter, and *on this rock I will build my church;* and the gates of hell shall not prevail against it" (Matt. 16:13-18).

It is worthy of remark that, in this address to Peter, the Lord changes the gender. He says: "Thou art Peter [*petros,* which is masculine]; and on this rock [*petra,* which is feminine] I will build my church." Now, the Greek word *aleethia,* which means truth, is also feminine. This shows that Christ did not intend to build His church on

The Middle Wall

Peter, but on the great truth which he had just confessed. This truth, then, is the central idea in the kingdom of Jesus Christ. And hence, the *one Lord* is placed, by the apostle, in the center of the apostolic platform, upon which the unity of the Spirit is to be obtained and maintained. Read the seven items again, Eph. 4:5-7.

This truth is so interwoven with the whole revelation of God to man that, when it is believed, the whole system is believed with it. Hence the importance which is attached to this one article of faith, in the Holy Scriptures. When *the Ethiopian desired* to come into this sacred union, by baptism, "Philip said unto him, If thou believest with all thy heart, thou mayest. And he answered and said, *I believe that Jesus Christ is the Son of God*" (Acts 8:37). On this confession of faith, Philip baptized him, and he went on his way rejoicing. Why did not Philip ask him if he believed in the one God and Father of all? if he had the one faith? if he believed in the one body? or desired to enjoy the one Spirit and the one hope? Because no one could consistently acknowledge the one Lord, and reject these other items in the great platform on which Christ came to make peace.

Concerning those who had come into this bond of peace, Paul says: "There is neither Jew nor Greek, there is neither bond nor free, there is neither male nor female; for you are all one in Christ Jesus" (Gal. 3:28). Again: "There is neither Greek nor Jew, circumcision nor uncircumcision, Barbarian, Scythian, bond nor free; but Christ is all, and in all'' (Col. 3:11).

Thus we have ascertained the principles upon which the Christian church was formed. But when was it organized? When did it obtain a visible existence?

The materials for this new building were being prepared during the whole of Christ's ministry upon earth. Indeed, John the Baptist came to prepare the way for this new kingdom. All before the day of Pentecost was but the work of preparation; but on that memorable day the church received a visible form—or, to speak in modern style, it was organized.

This fact gives to this day an unusual importance. On this important occasion, the first additions to this church, the *new church,* that ever obtained, were made. This may be regarded as the birthday of the church of Jesus Christ. This is reason enough for any people, desiring to stand on apostolic ground, to be often found referring to that day. If all the mighty reformers that have arisen in the last three hundred years had taken their first lessons from Pentecost, and remained longer in the school of the holy Twelve, the multiplied divisions which have marred the work of God, and defaced the glory of the church, could never have obtained.

The Middle Wall

III. I now proceed to my third head of discourse, which is to draw some practical conclusions from the facts which have been developed.

1. My first conclusion, drawn from the premises now before me, is that God never had two churches, diverse one from the other, at the same time. That many individual congregations were organized at different points, for the sake of convenience, in the days of the apostles, is true; but these all belonged to the one body—they all had the same constitution and laws; namely, the teaching of the apostles and prophets of Christ, and that alone. This joined them all together, so that our one conclusion remains true. The Lord did not organize two different churches, on different constitutions, to be called by different names, and governed by different laws, and both to stand at the same time. He did not make the one new man while the old one lived. He did not organize the Christian church by the side of the Jewish, and tell the members to maintain their distinct and separate organizations, but still to love one another, and be as friendly as possible! No, verily! Before He organized the new church, He tore down the old one; He *took its constitution out of the way, nailing it to the cross,* that all legal barriers to an entire union of all believers might be removed, and that all necessity for two separate church organizations might be done away. Thus did God show

to heaven and earth that He intended to have but one church standing at the same time.

2. My second conclusion is that, if ever God determines to make a new church, He will give the constitution and enact all the laws for it, and appoint all its ordinances.

I come to this conclusion from the fact that He always has done so. When He was about to organize the Jewish nation into a church, or congregation, He did not tell Moses to assemble the elders of Israel together for the purpose of legislating for His people. He reserved all the legislative power to Himself. The only matter referred to them was, whether they would keep the law. "And they said, All that the Lord hath said will we do, and be obedient" (Ex. 24:7).

So, when He made the new man, or Christian congregation, He gave it all its laws. He assembled no general council, either of men or angels, to draft a constitution and enact laws for His church. He spoke, and it was done; He commanded, and it stood fast. He consulted His own will alone on the subject, and gave just such laws and ordinances as he saw would be best calculated to perfect the man of God, and thoroughly furnish him unto all good works. Now, judging the future from the past, is it not reasonable to conclude that if the good Lord should ever propose to organize another church, He will still hold all the legislative power in His own hands? That He will frame its constitution, enact its laws, and appoint all its ordinances? Most surely He will, as long as He reigns King of kings and Lord of lords.

3. My third conclusion is that, if God should even give organic laws for a new church, He will accompany the giving and promulgating of those laws with such miraculous gifts and divine manifestations as will leave no doubt as to their divine origin.

When He gave His law to His ancient people, He did not require them to receive it on the mere testimony of Moses. He did not leave the elders of Israel to guess or imagine, from secret impulses, what was the mind of God as to legal requirements. But the Lord communed with Moses from the thick darkness which overspread the mount of God; while the earth trembled, and the voice of words was heard, and the sound of a trumpet waxed louder and louder, until the affrighted hosts of Israel withdrew from the trembling, burning, smoking Mount Sinai, and entreated that the words should not be spoken to them any more. (See Heb. 12:18, 19.) These awfully grand and terrific scenes were intended to show that it was none other than God who gave that law; it was Jehovah's testimony to the divine authenticity of the law.

And when the constitution and laws of the new man, or Christian church, were given, they were attended by divine power. Even the Messiahship of the Lord Jesus was proved by His doing such works as no other man had ever done. And after He was crowned Lord of all, and the time came to organize the New Testament church, "suddenly there came a sound from heaven as of a rushing, mighty wind, and it filled all the house where they were sitting. And there appeared unto them cloven tongues, like as of fire; and it sat upon each of them, and they were all filled with the Holy Ghost, and began to speak with other tongues as the Spirit gave them utterance." Thus did the divine power testify as to the sacred origin of this new church. And then, during the entire ministry of these prime ministers of the kingdom of Christ, God "bore them witness, by signs and wonders, and divers miracles, and gifts of the Holy Spirit, according to his will" (Heb. 2:4), so that there was no room left to doubt the truth of what they preached. All who would reason honestly were bound to say:

> "The work, O Lord, is thine,
> And wondrous in our eyes."

Now, from all these facts, we conclude that if God should ever propose to build a new church, different from the one that was set up on the day of Pentecost, He will accompany the organization thereof, and the promulgation of its laws and ordinances, with such miraculous attestations as will prove its heavenly origin, and thus point it

The Middle Wall

out as *His church,* in contradistinction from every other ecclesiastical organization on the face of the broad earth.

4. My fourth conclusion is that *the church of Christ is no mean affair.*

If the whole Jewish economy was only a preparatory work for this church; if all the ancient prophets and seers of God spoke and taught in reference to it; if the whole ministry of John was only intended to prepare the way for it; if the partition wall, the law of commandments concerning ordinances, which had stood for fifteen hundred years, was broken down to make way for it; if Jesus died to blot out that old covenant which stood in the way of the Jews coming into the new church, and which was, therefore, contrary to their best interests; and if He sealed and ratified the constitution of this church with His own heart's blood—it must surely be an institution of no small importance.

I awfully fear that many who profess faith in Christ have not a proper regard for the church of God. I fear that many look upon the church about as they do on any human organizations, gotten up for mere worldly purposes. Hence, we hear men talk about *"the church of their choice,"* or of "selecting the church whose polity they prefer." Is not this treating the church of Christ as we do State governments and human organizations? Men choose to live in one State in preference to another, because of their difference in State polity. So, one man chooses to be a member of the Free Mason fraternity, but another prefers the Independent Order of Odd Fellows. And how many choose their church about in the same way. Now, my dear reader, all this is well enough in reference to mere human organizations, but when we speak of the church of God, the subject is too awfully great to admit of any such conferring with flesh and blood. In reference to His church, God has given no such volition; He organized it through the ministry of divinely inspired apostles and teachers, and the only choice left us is to adopt its constitution, submit to its laws, and become members according to gospel terms, and thus enjoy its blessings; or else to reject it altogether, and risk the consequences.

Reader, ponder these things well. Remember, we must all account to the great Judge of the living and the dead, for the manner in which we treat the "church of God, which he hath purchased with his own blood."

5. I conclude, in the fifth place, that it is the will of God that all partition walls, or human laws which tend to divide the people of God, shall be leveled to the ground. That the will of the Lord has not changed since the days of the apostles will not be denied; and that it will not change during the whole lifetime of the gospel dispensation must be admitted by all. Then it follows

The Middle Wall

that, if He broke down the old partition wall which He Himself built, even the law of commandments concerning ordinances, for the express purpose of making one new church, that He might thereby make peace, then is it contrary to His righteous purpose to have His people divided and subdivided into contending sects and parties, and kept apart by laws and usages which He has not ordained.

If these laws have not been attested by miraculous power, they are not of God, though they may have been enacted by the most august council ever convened since the days of the apostles; and if they are not of God, they should not be regarded as authoritative in His kingdom. And if they tend to divide and keep His people asunder, they should all be broken down, so that God's will may be done by His people on earth, as angels do it in heaven.

6. My sixth conclusion is that every disciple of Christ ought to be a *peacemaker*. Christ was a peacemaker, as we have seen; and He says: "If any man will serve me, let him follow me" (John 12:26). To follow Christ is to imitate Him. Then, as He made peace, so let His disciples endeavor to do.

When the Lord would make peace, He did not omit any duty for that purpose; He compromised no truth for the sake of peace; He made no league with sin; He broke down all legal barriers which stood in the way of the peace and union of believers of all nations, and then laid down a holy platform of union—a platform composed of a few plain, but mighty, truths—truths which permeate the whole volume of inspiration, giving life and power to the whole system of human redemption. Upon these sacred principles He formed a holy brotherhood, in which all was peace and love and joy, through the Holy Spirit.

Now, if we claim to be the disciples of Christ—to be learners of Him—then should we labor to make peace on the same principles. We should endeavor to impress these principles upon the minds of all over whom we have any influence, both by precept and example, so that all may see their beauty, feel their power, and be converted by the truth as it is in Jesus; that the peace of God may rule in the hearts and lives of all His people both now and for evermore.

GOD'S PURPOSE IN THE AGES

H. W. EVEREST

"Having made known unto us the mystery of his will, according to his good pleasure which he hath purposed in himself: that in the dispensation of the fulness of times he might gather together in one all things in Christ, both which are in heaven, and which are on earth; even him."—Eph. 1: 9, 10.

THIS paper will be concerned with three questions: What is God's purpose in the ages? Can we trace manifestations of this purpose? How is this purpose to be consummated?

I. At first sight, it seems absurd that one should think to know the purpose of God in the ongoing of the ages. Man is finite, God is infinite. Man lives but a moment, God inhabits eternity. Man opens his eyes on but a small part of God's creation, while God's knowledge and purpose comprehend all things and run on through all eternities. Can man measure the thought of God? On a closer view, the difficulties are vastly increased and the solution of this problem by man is seen to be absolutely impossible. The data on which a correct conclusion might be founded are not accessible. They are locked up in the infinite past and the infinite future. They include, not only what has been done, but what is yet to be done and what is as yet only in the thought of God. Moreover, the data from which the purpose of God might be inferred are not only inaccessible, but they are exceedingly complex. The scheme is a wheel within a wheel, and there is no end to the machinery, whether you go up to the revolving suns or down to the whirling atomic vortices. If man can not master the atom, how can he analyze and interpret the universe? Not only complex, but contradictory: progress and retrogression; solar systems evolved from cosmical matter and then slowly falling into the central vortex; systems of life rising into being and others passing away; desert wastes and fertile fields, pleasure and pain, righteousness and sin, life and death. Who can analyze the facts? Who can reconcile the contradictions? Who can discover the underlying laws? Who can arrange all the facts under these laws, and see the far-away end toward which all the stars and all the ages are moving? How can man, who fails in the simplest case, reach this highest generalization of all? How can he discover what was first and last in the mind of God and what has been His purpose concerning man during all the ages?

Riding along the street, you look up and see, through a dust-covered window in the tenth story, the glinting of a revolving wheel, and this only;

would you venture to infer the character of the building, the articulations of the machinery, the nature of the product, and the ultimate purpose of the builder? So, in the brief lightning-flash of life, you but dimly see earth and sky, faces aglow with life and faces pale in death; you experience the fleeting thrills of thought and feeling, of victory and defeat, and from these can you rise to the thought and purpose of God? Earth is a prison of Chillon. We pace its stony floor, listen to the dashing waves, see through the grated window the changeful sky, and clank the chain by which we are bound. The prison itself testifies to the power and wisdom of Him who reared its massive walls; daily food given by an unseen hand testifies that He has a purpose concerning us; but the chain that binds us and the graves opening at our feet leave us in terrible doubt. The storm rages without, but our prison stands; suns rise, but they are quenched in the coming night; stars shine, but they look coldly in upon our misery; thunders roll, but they are not the voice of God and make no disclosure of His purpose. We are but

> "Children crying in the night;
> Children crying for the light;
> And with no language but a cry;"

and infinitely pathetic is our condition, if there is no Father in heaven to hear our cry and bring in the light.

But what man can not discover, God may disclose to him. Indeed, it is the province of revelation to make known what man can not learn in any other way; to give man that truth which is the key to the mysteries of nature and of providence. Hence an apostle could write the words which I have read to you: "Having made known unto us the mystery of his will according to his good pleasure which he hath purposed in himself." We have Scriptures which were "given by inspiration of God." There were those who could truthfully say: "Eye hath not seen, nor ear heard, neither have entered into the heart of man the things which God hath prepared for them that love him; but God hath revealed them unto us by his Spirit; for the Spirit searcheth all things, yea, the deep things of God."

From these Living Oracles, then, we may learn what is God's purpose during all the ages. The analysis of this sublime oracle gives us the following facts: *First*, God has a high and holy purpose in man's creation and in all the centuries of human history. This world is not a result of fate nor a work of chance. It is not controlled by blind force nor ruled by malign spirits; but a God of infinite power, wisdom and love has a glorious purpose in it all. *Second*, this purpose is not an afterthought or an adjustment to unforeseen conditions; it was and is an eternal purpose. *Third*, this purpose originated in the mind and heart of

God's Purpose in the Ages

God. It is an expression of Himself, of the mystery of His will, of His good pleasure, of His divine nature. *Fourth,* this purpose has its manifestations, its limitations and its consummation in Christ. It was purposed in Christ Jesus before the world began. *Fifth,* this grand, divine purpose, running through all the ages, is the *unification of all things in Christ,* of God and man, of earth and heaven. *Sixth,* the period when this summing up of all things in Christ shall be accomplished is the dispensation of the fullness of the ages, is the gospel dispensation, is the reign of Christ.

God's eternal purpose culminates in man, in man's moral perfection. This purpose will be realized when man shall be brought into harmony with God, when love shall hold universal sway, when righteousness shall cover the earth as the waters cover the surface of the great deep, when Christ shall have put down all rule and all authority and power, and when all men shall be united in Him. It is the purpose of God that the kingdom of Christ shall triumph, that the hour must come when every knee shall bow to Him and every tongue confess to God. All else is but a means to this end. It is toward this glorious consummation that all the ages have been toiling; for it must be that the right shall be victorious, that righteousness and truth shall be enthroned in earth and heaven. Than this purpose none could be grander, none more consonant with reason, none more in harmony with our ideas of God, none more full of promise for the human race, and none more worthy of the struggling and rising ages.

II. Now, with the light of this revelation to guide our way, can we trace manifestations of this purpose? Can we see that nature and revelation are in perfect accord, and thus find a scientific basis and verification of our conclusion? In the great circle, the center of which is God's purpose, and the wide circumference of which is the consummation of this purpose, let us endeavor to trace out three radii of progress; viz., progress in nature, progress in human history, and progress in the evolution of Christianity. What God has done must be in harmony with His ultimate purpose. If we shall watch the divine Worker, we may see the material under His hand taking shape according to this purpose. If we shall see all lines of progress leading on to the accomplishment of one grand object, we must conclude that to accomplish this object has been the one all-comprehending purpose of God.

1. How is it with progress in nature? Has not the development and perfection of man been the goal toward which this progress has grandly moved during all the ages? From that first glimmer of light which shot through the primeval nebula, from the first appearance of life on through all material, biological and spiritual evolution, has

not man been the objective point and the crowning glory of the whole? Let us not be afraid of the word "evolution," as though it were the abode of an evil spirit. Let us cast out the demon; for there is a true evolution as well as a false one. Things do grow, there are gradations of organic forms, and nature has proceeded from the lower to the higher. But this evolution has not been without the wisdom and the power of God. Something was added to dead matter before it became a living plant; something more was added to the plant before it became a sensitive and moving animal; and infinitely more was added to the highest animal before it became a godlike man. There are chasms in this evolution so deep and wide that divine power alone can bridge them. Agassiz testifies that, from the appearance of the first paleozoic fishes, there was a constant approximation to man. The cephalic extremity was emphasized more and more. The vertebral axis continually approached the perpendicular, and some "cranks," political and religious, have gone so far as to lean the other way; there has been continual progress toward the higher intellectual and moral powers of man.

It is not a mere human conceit that man is the resultant of all lower forces and movements. It is not a mere conceit that without man nature would be meaningless and abortive; a foundation without a superstructure, a pedestal without a statue, a body without a soul, a vast complication of forms and forces, and of science and skill, and yet without a purpose. Without man, the mineral world would have less meaning than an Egyptian pyramid buried in the desert sands. Without man, the organic world during all the ages gone would have been climbing into the empty spaces only to fall back in cosmic dust. Without man, the embodiment of science and art in natural forms, the gleaming of divine thought from crystal and leaf, from flower and star, would have been useless, since it would have appealed to no corresponding intelligence, would have thrilled no immortal soul; all in vain the manifestations of beauty, the grandeur of the ocean, the sublimity of the mountains, and the glory of the sky. It was not till man appeared that the meaning of the whole could be seen, and not till then could all the sons of God have shouted for joy.

It is a sober and accepted demonstration of science that man is king over all terrestrial life, and that all things on the earth culminate and find their ultimate reason in him. The man of science finds many wonderful things: the microscopic world with its myriad forms; the telescopic universe with its innumerable suns and systems. He discovers mysterious and tremendous forces; he explains chemical and biological transformations; he describes many races of monsters that once tempested the oceans and roamed over the continents; but, after all, the man of science himself is the most wonderful being in all the world. All other things are but his toys, his material, his servants. He alone can understand their nature and the laws under which they exist. He alone can think about them and be thrilled with their perfections.

Those professions which are occupied with the development and training of human beings are of the highest rank. Parents, teachers and pastors stand near to God. It would be a great thing if one could be the engineer of a Brooklyn bridge, the builder of a modern battleship, the author and finisher of an interoceanic canal, or the founder of an empire; but it is a greater thing to develop the men who do these things and who are capable of doing unspeakably more; *men*, who are not means to an end, but the end itself; *men*, immortal and eternally progressive. Evidently nature during all ages has been working out God's eternal purpose.

2. God's purpose to perfect man intellectually and morally is clearly seen in the trend of human history. Man is a rising, and not a setting, sun. The movement may be slow, but it *is* a movement and it is upward. There are times and countries which seem to indicate the contrary. There are monsters of crime and times of popular madness; French revolutions and Armenian massacres. One shore is sinking while another is rising; but when

you have balanced elevations and depressions, you will find that every century the whole continent of humanity is higher and higher.

The facts of historic progress are undeniable. There are natural stages through which a nation passes—savage, barbarous, half-civilized, civilized and enlightened. What progress in government, from despotism to free republics and limited monarchies! What progress in science! Time would fail me to tell the triumphs of a single science—of chemistry, or astronomy, or psychology. What progress in art! Every article of food and clothing, every ornament, every tool, every instrument of observation and research; work, travel, music, literature and law—all illustrate the same facts of material and social advancement.

The panorama of human progress, passing before us with the passing centuries, exhibits great contrasts, especially between the first and last scenes on the canvas. Here at the beginning we see the earth but sparsely inhabited. Men are fishing and hunting, living on the spontaneous productions of the earth, naked, or clothed in the skins of animals, and contending with wild beasts for the possession of the dens and caves of the hills. But the last picture is the most wonderful, though so familiar to us. The whole earth occupied; farms, roads and cities everywhere; trains gliding over the continents and steamships crossing the oceans; commerce supplying every nation

God's Purpose in the Ages

with the good things of every land; and millions of people occupied in the promotion of science and the education of the young.

There are some, however, who question man's progress in morals, and the fact that any one is so pessimistic as to raise this question does seem to favor their contention. But ancient nations were sunk so deep in moral corruption that they did not know it. Our trouble about the wrong and outrage with which the world is filled is proof, not that we are growing blacker, but that we are rising into the light where the blackness of human nature can be seen. The daily press exaggerates the evil by giving a disproportionate report of the evil and the good. We do not know how wicked the world has been. Did you ever read the *Morning Chronicle* published in Sodom in the days of Noah? or a copy of the *Roman World* of the reign of Nero? or the London *Times* when, in England, two hundred crimes were punishable with death? Read these relics of the times when the earth was filled with violence, before you pass pessimistic judgment on the men of the present. Never before was woman so pure, man so righteous, nor the reign of just law so perfect. Never before was there such compassion for the suffering, such care for the helpless, and such self-sacrifice for the undeserving and the criminal.

This historical progress has been under the guidance of Divine Providence. Every nation has had its place in the procession of the ages, and its special work to perform. The ancient peoples—Hebrews, Chaldeans, Egyptians—laid the foundations of nationalities. The Greeks had a mission in behalf of art, oratory and literature. Rome gave the world lessons in law and lawlessness. The Germanic tribes stood for individual liberty and social equality, while it seems to be the work of the Anglo-Saxon race to bring the whole world under the sway of Christian civilization.

That this progress is working out the divine purpose, and is confirmatory of our conception of this purpose, is evident from the fact that this progress is the result of forces God implanted in the soul of man. God gave man's intellect, his wants, his desires, his conscience, his thirst for knowledge, his inventive genius and his power to lay all nature under contribution. Nor have these upward impulses spent their force. They have been gathering momentum during all the ages, and are energizing now as never before. The progress of the past and the velocity of our present advancement are prophetic of long and rapid marches toward the goal. All the centuries have been preparatory to the twentieth. We have the science, the instruments, the leisure, the wealth and the men; not a few men of genius only, as in former ages, but whole nations of educated people. We can avail ourselves of all the lasting results of human toil. We hold in our possession

God's Purpose in the Ages

principles and forces with which we can tunnel the everlasting hills and scale the vaulted skies. Man's progress is not an arithmetical, but a geometrical, series, and the ratio of this series is constantly increasing. All men who feel the throbbings of modern life are expecting great things in the near future. The future of human history, as well as the past, indicates God's purpose in the ages, and that we are sweeping on to its speedy and glorious accomplishment.

3. It is easy to trace manifestations of this purpose in the evolution of Christianity. He who does not see that Christianity is an evolution, and an evolution under the guiding hand of God; who does not see that it has a beginning, a progressive development and a consummation—can not understand the divine Book nor the religion taught therein. The Bible is not homogeneous from cover to cover, as some suppose. Like the crust of the earth, it is composed of many strata of truth—historic, moral and religious—deposited during many ages. The lowest stratum is the old Silurian of Genesis, holding the earliest appearance of life in the Edenic promise, and in the types of sacrifice and tabernacle. It has its Carboniferous, or Reptilian, age, with its rank growth of human institutions and its monsters of crime; with its many fossils of extinct species over which fossil theologians are wont to prophesy as did Ezekiel in the valley of dry bones. In the higher strata are still

clearer indications of coming eras in which the facts and principles of the true religion would be fully manifested. Then we have the eocene, the miocene and the pliocene of the New Testament; the epochs of John the Baptist, of Christ, and of the apostles. We have the gospel in promise, in type, in prophecy and in fact. We hear a voice crying in the wilderness, "Prepare ye the way of the Lord." We listen to Him who spake as never man spake. We shudder in the darkness which shrouds the crucifixion from the sight of the angels. We stand on Mount Olivet and hear the risen Christ giving the great commission to His apostles: "Go ye into all the world and preach the gospel to every creature." We see the ascending Saviour and we gaze up into heaven till a cloud receives Him out of our sight.

And yet this religion was not then fully developed. Jesus only began to do and to teach; His apostles were to complete the work. Jesus left His blood on Mount Calvary, and His apostles in Jerusalem. He commanded them to wait till they were endued with power from on high. On Pentecost this power came. The descent of the Holy Spirit, like a telegram from the throne of God, announced the coronation of Christ and filled the apostles with divine knowledge and power. They at once began to carry out their commission, nor was this commission fulfilled and Christianity fully revealed and confirmed till the last apostle had finished his course.

While Christianity is the product of a divine evolution, do not understand me as assuming that this evolution is still in progress. There are men who seem to think that Christianity is still in process of formation; who arrogate to themselves the authority of prophets and apostles, and who think to modernize it by adding somewhat and by subtracting a good deal. But Christiantiy is a completed system. Now for eighteen hundred years the heavens have kept silence, a silence not again to be broken till the trump of God shall sound and the dead shall rise. It is a revelation given once for all. It has in it nothing local or special; it is adapted to all ages and conditions; it needs no modification. Besides, there is no authority on earth to change it in the least respect; all who do it are usurpers and antichrists. Above the heads of those who dare to corrupt or attempt to improve what God has done may be heard the mutterings of the apostolic anathema: *"Though we, or an angel from heaven, preach any other gospel unto you than that which we have preached unto you, let him be accursed."* And the Bible, which gives this perfect system, is practically, to each one of us, *an infallible book*. If you *know* there are errors in it, however they have arisen, whether by translator, editor, copyist, amanuensis, or blundering apostle, such errors are no part of the divine Word; and if you do *not know* these errors, *you are not to assume that they exist*. To the Bible as the only source of Christianity we all must come. He who is wise or foolish above or below what is written in these Living Oracles is a fanatic, a fool or a knave. But while Christianity is perfect, we are exceedingly imperfect, and wherever any one of us stands there is large room for progress. As the scientist could not think to improve or abolish the laws of nature, but only to ascertain these laws and conform to them, so it would be absurd for the theologian to think to make progress except in his knowledge and practice of the divine law.

We conclude, therefore, that progress in nature, in history and in revelation is a sublime manifestation of God's purpose concerning man.

III. Our third and last question has to do with the consummation of God's purpose. "Watchman, what of the night?" Are there signs that the morning cometh?

Who is not troubled by the long delay? Who does not cry out in the anguish of his soul, "How long, O Lord, how long!"? As the tragedy of sin goes on with its myriad forms of crime; with its contending armies and murdered millions; with plague, famine and oppression; with blasphemy, debauchery and death—who does not pray that the curtain may fall, and soon rise again on the millennial age? And yet, in the arithmetic of Heaven, a thousand years are as one day and one day as a thousand years. Why was the Creator so long in evolving the world and the various ranks of organic life? Why was science so long in coming? Why does God employ human agencies? Why did He not make all things stand forth in perfection at once? Why did He not make heaven only, leaving out of His plan hell, the devil, and a wicked world? When you have answered these questions, you will know why God's purpose has been delayed so long.

It may be said that it is not mere delay of which we complain. The map is black with heathenism. Thrice fifteen hundred millions go down to the grave every century, and not one-third of them ever heard of Christ. The answer to this objection is not complete, but it may silence our murmurings. God is just, and no wrong will eternal justice ever do to a single immortal soul. Our Father in heaven pitieth His children. We can trust the God who "so loved the world." Ignorance and consequent folly stir not His wrath, but His compassion and mercy. Still further, numbers are not a standard of value. Noah and his family were worth more, in God's plan, than all the world besides. Even if few, comparatively, are saved, redemption will not be a failure. But nowhere do the Scriptures teach that only a few will be saved. The vision of the apostle John was that of "a great multitude which no man could number, out of every nation, and of all tribes and peoples and tongues." Besides, we are not to measure movements of the future by those of the past. There is a law of acceleration. A body falling to the sun from a great distance moves very slowly for ages, but very rapidly at the last. Whole nations may be converted in a day. The millennial age may be very long compared with the period of preparation; and so, at last, the lost may be to the saved as a drop to all the oceans, as a leaf to all the forests.

1. The present condition of the world is more favorable to this consummation than many suppose. Christendom comprises one third of the human race, and possesses more than three-fourths of the power, wealth and glory of the nations. The missionary army is very large: forty thousand in the foreign field; and at home many millions, for every Christian is a missionary of Jesus Christ. The controlling governments of the world are under the sway of Christian peoples.

But churches, colleges and Christian people are not all we have a right to claim. All science, all art, all invention, and the earth itself, improved in so many ways—cities, farms, roads, canals and mines—all these are ours, all are God's. The whole world of mankind is gradually approaching the kingdom of heaven, in morals, in social customs, in business honesty, in just laws, in hate of wrong, in benevolence, in Christian brotherhood.

God's Purpose in the Ages

When we feel these silent forces working in all departments of modern life, and when we see the whole world turning toward the Sun of righteousness, we may expect that it will soon be shining on all the nations in noontide splendor and power.

Indeed, it is a question whether the millennium has not already dawned upon us. This age is heaven compared with the hell of Nero's time, heaven compared with five hundred years ago. The world glided into the reign of Christ, but did not know it. And some men are so much inclined to look on the dark side that they will not know they are in heaven when they get there.

2. The providence of God may work mightily in bringing about the unification of all things in Christ. His purposes can not be thwarted, for to Him all things are possible.

> "God moves in a mysterious way
> His wonders to perform;
> He plants His footsteps in the sea,
> And rides upon the storm."

Queen Esther could not see how her people were to be saved from universal massacre, and yet it was done. We could not see how slavery was to be abolished, but God was marching on, and after the clouds of battle had rolled away, the sun of liberty and union shone out with unwonted splendor. So it may be in this case. Some remarkable advance of science, a more thorough exploration of ancient lands, the conversion of the Hebrew race, or a conflict of nations which shall desolate the lands and crimson the seas, may furnish the opportune hour when God will intervene.

3. The progress of man in science, invention and social order will tend powerfully to bring in this auspicious period. Knowledge, art and social institutions are God's means for the accomplishment of His purposes as well as the gospel of Christ. Already we are lifting the curse of labor and getting back to the Garden of Eden and the tree of life. Thistles are mowed down with a selfbinder, while briars and thorns are rooted out with steam-plows. Natural forces carry the heavy burdens and do the world's work. Science is constantly verifying Bible truth. Every precept of the Scriptures is found to be in harmony with mental and moral law. The gospel, as God's power to enlighten and save men, is exactly adapted to the intellect, the heart and the life of man, and the world is seeing this more and more. Commerce is bringing all nations into a brotherhood of industry and mutual dependence. Corporations and individuals dealing with one another from opposite sides of the ocean can not afford to be dishonest, and the time will come when all men will see that dishonesty and immorality do not pay. Christianity as it spreads throughout the earth will carry with it so many blessings of art

and social order, of health and life, that few will reject it. May we not hope that in the not distant future men will cease to slaughter one another in war; that arbitration will settle difficulties and not the carnage of battle? Have we not sense enough even now to see that this would be the better way? Will not the time soon come when all the treasures now expended on standing armies, navies and destructive wars will be spent in the arts of peace and in the work of saving men from barbarism and self-destruction? Then what rapid strides the nations will make toward that better era. Then men will see that Christianity is the only religion worthy of a civilized man, and the only hope of our race.

4. Even the enemies of Christianity are doing much to hasten its hour of triumph. Every attack brings out its defenders, and strengthens the weaker places in its walls. Every fifty years there comes a craze of infidelity, but the reaction is sure to follow. When the trainman puts his torch under the car and smites the wheels with his hammer, there is no danger that he will burn the train or demolish the wheels. It is well to find out whether any bolts are missing or any wheels broken. These so-called enemies are friends in disguise, pointing out the disarranged machinery and the unsafe men and the unsound articles of the creed, and still the train glides smoothly on nor falls behind its schedule time.

New Testament Christianity

So long as Christianity meets the great wants of the soul, so long it will not only endure, but go on from conquering unto conquest. Whatever may be said about the days of creation, about Jonah and the whale, about the interpretation of prophecy, the possibility of miracles, the doctrine of predestination, or about differences of ritual and government, still, so long as the Bible tells about our Father in heaven; so long as it gives peace to the troubled conscience and consolation to the breaking heart; so long as it gives a hope that is like an anchor to the soul sure and stedfast, and that reaches beyond the veil—it can never be in danger, it can never perish. The storm that sweeps over, convulsing the upper air, uprooting forests, and demolishing cities, does not disturb the humbler grasses nor diminish the supply of food for man and beast; so the storms of skepticism which now and then seem so black and dangerous, the "higher criticism" so destructive to some traditions and some men, do not affect the great masses of the people. Still the world loves Jesus and the church grows; still the children are taught to lisp His name; still the weary and heavy-laden hear Him saying, "Come unto me, and I will give you rest;" still men turn their death-dimmed eyes toward His cross; still the mourner reads, "Let not your heart be troubled; you believe in God, believe also in me;" and still those who have crossed the river send back the shout of triumph:

"Thanks be to God, who giveth us the victory through our Lord Jesus Christ."

6. The church of Christ is the chief instrumentality for the consummation of God's eternal purpose. It is the pillar which God has lifted up for the support of the truth; it is God's army under the leadership of Prince Immanuel, marching on to certain victory.

The church of to-day is living under a pressure of moral responsibility such as was never felt before. It is standing in the clear light of Christian civilization; it knows the condition of the heathen world; it is under the most solemn vows of allegiance to the Lord Jesus Christ; it has the wealth, the men and the opportunity. In the day of judgment we can not plead ignorance, nor poverty, nor inability. O my soul, what will be thy plea in that solemn day? Will it not be more tolerable for Sodom and Chorazin than for us? Will it not be more tolerable for the heathen than for those who refuse to send them the gospel? For what do we wait? That God may give another gospel and a higher manifestation of His love? That Christ may again come down from heaven and again arise from the dead? That the Holy Spirit may yield to our pleading and become more gracious? Nay, verily, the fault is with the church and not with the heavenly powers. But what does the church need? Does it not need this, the *Christianization of Christendom,* the conversion and consecration of those who are to be God's agents in the conversion of the world? This Christianization of Christendom implies and requires the following things:

First, the putting away of some great systems of evil. We must disband our standing armies and cease to learn the art of war. We must send to heathen lands more Bibles and less rum, more medicine and less opium, fewer drunken and lecherous sailors and more men of God. We must so reform that a Mohammedan could not point to the squalor and misery of our great cities, to the evils of intemperance, to brothels and gambling-hells, to oppressive commercial combines and to corrupt legislation, and thank God that he is not a Christian.

Second, it needs the evangelization of the unsaved millions of Christendom. How can we go to the heathen nations when two-thirds of our own people are against us? The home missionary work is an important part of the foreign work; it is the source of supplies and the best assurance of success. Blessed is the evangelist who every year converts hundreds and thousands! Blessed is the church that glories not so much in its great scholars as in its great preachers! Blessed is the church that crowds this evangelism in every suburb, in every school district and in every family. Do not say "we want quality, not quantity." We do want quantity; we want numbers, large numbers. We want all the people, all the world, for Christ. We do not pick for broadcloth and brain; every one rescued is a soul saved from death.

Third, the prayer of Christ must be answered, that His disciples may be one, that the world may believe that God has sent Him. There must be unity of testimony, unity of feeling, unity of prayer, and unity of effort. But we must be unified in God's own way, not hewing out for ourselves broken cisterns that will not hold water. "Other foundation can no man lay than that is laid, which is Jesus Christ." We must have union on the seven divine essentials: one Lord, one faith, one baptism, one body, one Spirit, one hope of our calling, and one God and Father of all. But Christian union implies difference and toleration in matters which do not affect the essential faith and practice. You can not so pack cannon-balls in a box that they will touch at all points; nor can you so pack men in a church that they will agree in everything. All have access to the same Bible, and each interprets this Bible according to his ability, or, rather, inability, and perfect agreement would be a miracle. The tacit agreement among Protestant denominations to let one another alone is a most *unrighteous* and *cowardly* state of things. As in science, so, at least, in religion, every man is under moral obligation to give and to receive; to *speak* the truth in love and to *hear* the truth in the same spirit. Storm is better than stagnation; discussion is better than dishonest acquiescence. It is only by letting our light shine that the darkness is dispelled and that we can come to a unity in our knowledge of the Son of God.

In the *fourth* place, we must cease wasting the revenues of the kingdom. We must not try to maintain a dozen churches in a village, where two are all that are needed. We must not segregate the church till no part has vitality enough to keep aboveground. Instead of competition, we must have a great religious trust, but not to raise prices. We must not waste our energies on unimportant issues. Hades and the Devil on the one hand, and a post-mortem gospel on the other, will take care of themselves. The higher criticism will get so high as to disappear with the German fog. Discord over church music is not promotive of harmony, and the decisions of the last day will not be determined by "tweedledum and tweedledee." We must not sit on the shore counting straws while thousands are going down in the deep sea.

It is a *fifth* requirement that the church shall preach the gospel as never before. We make progress in the industrial world by using the power of God in nature—wind, gravitation, heat and electricity. It is so in religion, and the gospel is the power of God unto salvation. The age of miracles is past. "Faith comes by hearing, and hearing by the word of God." The modern church folds its hands and prays that the Holy Spirit may come and convert the millions. The church is still in that upper room in Jerusalem praying for a promise which was fulfilled nearly two thousand years ago; but Christ says, "Go, preach the gospel to every creature."

Sixth, and finally, modern Christendom needs a reconsecration to the service of Christ. It needs to be able to say with Paul: "The love of Christ constrains me; for we thus judge that if one died for all, then were all dead, and that he died for all, that we who live should not live unto ourselves, but unto him who died for us and rose again." If all the church truly prayed "Thy kingdom come," millions of money would follow this prayer; thousands of missionaries would follow this money; and the speedy conversion of the world would follow this consecration of the wealth and power of the church.

By these means, and by others of which we can not conceive, God will bring about the consummation of His eternal purpose to unify, to sum up, all things in Christ, both which are in earth and which are in heaven, even in Him. But the time may be very long. Uncounted ages were occupied in the development of the material world, and it would not be strange if many ages more should precede this glorious consummation.

As the angel said to Daniel, so the Saviour would say to each one of us: "But go thou thy way till the end be; for thou shalt rest and stand in thy lot at the end of the days."

But what lies beyond this consummation? What lies beyond? Heaven beyond heaven, life beyond life, glory beyond glory, and progress beyond progress in the infinite universe of God, world without end.

SIN AND ITS CURE

AYLETTE RAINES

"For as by Adam all die, even so by Christ shall all be made alive; but every man in his own order."—1 Cor. 15: 22.

"Much more they who receive abundance of grace, and of the gift of righteousness, shall reign in life by Jesus Christ."—Rom. 5: 17.

THIS will exhibit itself from the nature of the topics which it is designed to embrace, under two general heads: 1 *Sin, or the disease.* 2. *The gospel, or the remedy, or cure.*

We shall not consider the evils of sin. That sin is in the world no Christian denies. How diversified soever may be our opinions with reference to other facts, there can be none with respect to the prevalence of sin. It is agreed, too, that its nature is malignant—its consequences most appalling. If sin were limited to the present world—if it could not, by any possibility, molest us beyond the grave—we see enough of it here, enough of its turpitude and of its tendency toward the production of misery, to demonstrate that it is an evil fraught with infernal venom, every way injurious and destructive, and above all things to be dreaded and abhorred.

In respect to the origin of sin, we have often been asked such questions as the following: "Why did God permit evil to be introduced into the world?" "Why did He not constitute or organize Adam upon principles such as would have rendered him incapable of sinning?" In answer to these questions, and all similar ones, we have but little to say. We have no disposition to perplex ourselves or our readers with bewildering speculations and disquisitions concerning things which have never profited those by whom they have been agitated. A few remarks, however, on these questions may not be without benefit to some plain, honest minds, which have been needlessly perplexed or confounded by unwarrantable speculations relative to the origin of sin.

We might ask, Why did God so constitute water that it will drown a man; and why did He permit fire to possess such properties that it burns the fingers of the cook, consumes the bodies of living men, and is in all respects, while a good servant, a furious and tyrannical master? A proper answer would be that were fire and water deprived of those essential principles by the misapplication or misuse of which physical evils are sometimes produced, they would cease to be fire and water, and would be, therefore, incapable of their beneficial results. The same is true in respect to man. To be a man, he must neither be a mole

Sin and Its Cure

nor an eagle, a mere animal nor the archangel. He must be that link in the long chain of created beings to which we apply the term "man." He must have all his native properties of soul and body—all his passions and appetites. And, to be an accountable being, he must be a moral agent. He must be placed under law. He must be capable of the feeling of approbation, on account of conformity to the law of God, and of disapprobation or guilt, on account of transgression. Any conceivable organization of human nature or constitution of the divine government, in which these principles should not have been recognized, would have placed man, with respect to morality and immorality, in a condition such as is that occupied by the brutal tribes—as incapable of virtue and vice, of rewards and punishment, of moral elevation and degradation, as is the mole, the oyster or the bat. He could have possessed no consciousness of merit nor of demerit, any more than a mere animal or a clock or a watch. The not conferring upon him those elements of nature, those faculties and powers, by the misdirection of which he might fall, would have deprived him of the ability to rise, and would, therefore, have cut him off forever from all those exquisite, those ennobling emotions consequent upon a sense of praiseworthiness, and of fitness for those rewards, rich with everlasting glory, which are treasured in the heavens for the obedient.

Evil, natural and moral, is incidental to the works of God, but forms no part of those works. "God cannot be tempted with evil," and therefore is not, can not be, the author of sin—"is the Father of lights"—"is the light, and in him is no darkness," and, therefore, the source of darkness He can not be! Teeth were contrived as instruments with which to eat—not in order that they might ache; just as sickles were contrived, not that they might wound the fingers of the reaper, but to cut the waving, golden grain. So God endowed man with faculties to glorify God, and to enjoy Him forever. If, therefore, moral evil has been produced, it is of human origin, and is incidental; the result of the perversion, misdirection or misapplication, on the part of man, of those elements of his moral nature which are as necessary to his moral weal as is the edge of the sickle to reaping, the heat of fire to render us comfortable, or certain properties of water to quench our thirst, to bathe our bodies, or to cleanse our clothing.

In strict accordance with these principles, Adam, being constituted a rational, a moral agent, was placed under law. The law under which he was placed seems to have been well adapted to the incipient state of his knowledge and experience. "Of every tree of the garden," said God, "thou mayest freely eat; but of the tree of knowledge of good and evil thou shalt not eat of it; for on the

Sin and Its Cure

day thou eatest thereof thou shalt surely die." Only one object, the fruit of one tree, in the midst of all the rich variety of trees and of fruits with which the garden abounded, was prohibited the first happy pair. On the circumstances of the first temptation and sin we need not expatiate. Suffice it to say that the serpent beguiled Eve; Eve gave to her husband and he did eat. Sin, the source of death, was born; and death came into the world. A stream of ills, comparatively small, commenced its onward flow, widening as it ran, until its black and filthy waters inundated the whole earth.

Indeed, no sooner was the first transgression committed than the malignant nature of sin began to be exhibited in its direful consequences. The eyes of our first parents were opened to contemplate the enormity of their crime, and they were overwhelmed with horror. Ashamed and affrighted, they sought concealment in the most retired recesses of Eden, foolishly imagining that they could hide themselves from the eye of God. But the Lord beheld them in their guilty retreat, penetrated their secret thoughts, and knew afar off the bitterness of their hearts. Adam attached the blame to his wife, and Eve to the serpent. But on their guilty heads the merited penalty must fall. God cursed the serpent, and He also cursed the ground for man's sake. And He declared to our first parents that this world should be to them a scene of sorrows and afflictions, of trials and woes, till they should return to the dust. He drove them from the garden, and placed cherubim and a flaming sword to keep the way of the tree of life, lest man, in his sins, should eat and live forever.

But sad, and even heartrending, as are these facts, when considered with reference to our first parents, the darkness of the picture is greatly increased when we contemplate the innumerable myriads of Adam's posterity, as all, to an alarming extent, involved in the same dreadful ruin. Our first father, not only for himself, but as the father and social head of the human family, had been cut off from the tree of life. He had by one act forfeited his title to that estate, one very important, nay, invaluable, item of which was this life-perpetuating tree. He had become a bankrupt. As, therefore, when a wealthy father turns spendthrift, and squanders his money or property, poverty, and sometimes shame, are entailed upon his children; or, as when, through luxury or other vices of parents, children are born the unhappy subjects of hereditary disease—so the posterity of Adam inherited a loathsome patrimony of evils on account of his defection from the divine law, as well as lost that which their father possessed in innocence; especially the tree of life, by a continued participation of which they might have inherited the fruition of perpetual health and life.

Sin and Its Cure

Could we bring into one group, and place under our close inspection, all the miserable beings who have suffered on account of the first transgression; could we with one glance behold all their writhings and contortions; could their sighs and groans and tears speak with emphasis into our ears the keenness of their pains, and the bitterness of their sorrows; could we behold them pale in sickness, cold in death, undergoing decomposition in the grave—then should we have in some good degree a view of the horrible nature of sin; for these are fruits or consequences of sin—the mementoes of God's righteous wrath against it—the indices which point to its malignity, its loathsomeness, its power to fit both soul and body for destruction in hell.

But, dark as is this picture, the half is not yet portrayed. Had Adam been the only sinner, good would it have been for the family of man. The dreadful truth, however, is that "all have sinned and come short of the glory of God." Thus, as by Adam's sin all mankind were made liable to death and all the miseries of the present life, so by their own sins have all mankind constituted themselves heirs of the second death and all the miseries of the world to come. But who shall describe the miseries of the future world? Neither the tongues of men nor of angels can give it an adequate expression. Only judgment and eternity can paint and exhibit this fiery picture. When the incorrigible shall stand in the presence of their Judge; when all their thoughts and words and actions shall be brought to light; when they shall be made to remember gospel privileges slighted, the great salvation despised, the authority of God contemned, the blood of the Lord Jesus trampled upon—ah! when sinking down into deep perdition, their souls, pierced with guilt, shrieking with terror, horrified with despair, will feel at their sensitive and convulsed center the inexpressible sinfulness of sin! "Cursed sin," they will say; "oh, fools that we were to serve sin in yonder world! Oh, wretched men that we are, who shall deliver us from this burning perdition? Oh, this blackness of darkness! Oh, this never-dying worm! Oh, this never-ceasing fire!"

Sin is a moral disease, destructive of both soul and body. Its advances may be imperceptible, but its effects are certain and its influence as deleterious as its guilt is deep and its nature damning. Not the less is it to be dreaded, nor the less feebly resisted, when its invasion of the soul is soft and noiseless; when it whispers peace and safety to its victims, lulling them into quietness and repose. Ah, how deceitful! Like the consumption, it is a flattering disease, but more to be dreaded; being in cases greatly more numerous, mortal, and bringing about, not the death of the body, but the death of the soul. Its delusive quietude is as the calm that precedes the tornado. The cloud that seems

Sin and Its Cure

to slumber above the horizon indicates "the wrath to come." The thunderbolt is in its bosom, but you hear no sound! The lightning is there, but you see no flash! Another moment, and the atmosphere is fraught with death, and destruction flies abroad on the wings of the winds. The sinner's disease has almost reached a mortal crisis, but he feels not his danger. The farther the hateful influence spreads, instead of becoming the more alarmed, and seeking with greater earnestness for deliverance, the more besotted and infatuated does he become—the more are his faculties and moral feelings steeped in insensibility. "A little more sleep," says he; "a little more folding of the hands, a little more indulgence in sinful pleasure." The cloud bursts, the disease reaches its crisis, and the sinner is whelmed in everlasting ruin! O sin, eldest born of hell! how hast thou deluged the world with pollution and misery! In every direction we contemplate thy direful ravages, we behold thy devastating footsteps. Insatiate murderer! thou art stained with the gore of thousands! thou art red with the blood of souls! God hates thee with a perfect hatred; and shall men love thee, and embrace thee, and be thy ignoble vassals?

Even the Christian, renewed as he has been in the spirit of his mind, and daily experiencing the efficacious remedies of the great Physician of sin-sick souls, feels that he has received a tremendous moral shock. He feels it in the shortness of his memory, in the defectiveness of his judgment, in the dimness of his reason, and in the sometimes capricious freaks of his imagination; he feels it in the coldness of his heart, in the lightness of his thoughts, in the barrenness of his mind, in the smallness of his joys, and in the poverty of his gratitude. He feels within him the law of sin and death—the flesh against the spirit, and the spirit against the flesh. He feels that when he would do good, evil is present with him. He feels that in his flesh dwells no good thing; and that before his body will be fitted to inhabit heaven, it must be changed from a natural to a spiritual body—from a vile body to the likeness of the glorified body of our Redeemer.

Upon this awful subject what shall we say more? The time would fail us were we to attempt to give the constituents of the whole black catalogue of sins now prevalent among men—the wraths, strifes, idolatries, heresies, envyings, immolations, murders, revelings, drunkenness, and such like! Sin is worse than Satan, for sin made him a Satan!—imparted to him all his diabolical principles, and clothed him with the horrid characteristics of the devil—all his subtilty, falsity, malignity, pride! And it is sin that makes, or will make, men devils! Compare the most depraved with the most excellent man. How great the difference! So is the difference between sin and righteousness! It is as the difference between

Sin and Its Cure

heaven and hell! Think of the most depraved human being with whom you have been acquainted, or of whom you have ever read or heard. How degraded! Sin has sunk him thus low, and may sink him lower, and would eventually, were there no remedy, plunge the whole family of man into the same yawning vortex of depravity. Thanks to God that a remedy for sin has been provided; that a Physician has been sent us from beyond the skies, endued with all divine skill; possessed of all the treasures of wisdom and knowledge; furnished with the whole *materia medica* of heaven; whose bosom overflows with perfect benevolence; whose heart bleeds at every prospect of human woe—melts at every symptom of human sorrow.

> "He comes the broken heart to bind,
> The bleeding soul to cure;
> And, from the treasures of His grace,
> To enrich the humble poor."

He has laid, in His own death, the foundation of human redemption. He has tasted death for every man. He ever lives, the Christian's intercessor and advocate—the sinner's friend, able to save to the uttermost all who will come to God by Him.

ii. Having now, as we know, very imperfectly sketched the consequences of sin, we proceed, as was proposed, to consider the *cure*.

This department of our subject is of vital importance. In order, therefore, to present appropriate truth, with all practicable intelligibility and force, we shall exhibit, as the first step of the discussion, an analysis both of the disease and of the remedy. In sin there are at least *five* prominent characteristics: 1. The love of sin. 2. The practice. 3. The state. 4. The guilt. 5. The punishment.

In the gospel there are not less than *five* points, or characteristics: 1. Faith. 2. Repentance. 3. Baptism. 4. Pardon. 5. The resurrection.

1. *Faith* destroys the *love* of sin. 2. *Repentance*, the *practice*. 3. *Baptism*, the *state*. 4. *Pardon*, the *guilt*. 5. *Resurrection*, the *punishment*.

To prevent mistakes, and to enable the reader to proceed with the greater satisfaction and intelligence, we would here offer a few explanatory remarks: 1. That when we affirm that the resurrection destroys the punishment of sin, we mean, not that it delivers us from the punishment of our own sins, but that it saves us from the consequences of the sin of our first father! This, in the proper place, we hope to make apparent. 2. When we say that faith destroys the *love* of *sin*, we do not mean that faith, considered in the abstract, accomplishes the work of destroying the love of sin, but that faith, connected with all the regenerating influences of the gospel, destroys the love of sin, in all hearts which fully and unfeignedly believe the gospel. Under this view of the subject, the reader may observe that we have not admitted into the pres-

Sin and Its Cure

ent arrangement one point which obtained in the first edition of this discourse—that the Spirit destroys the power of sin. The power of sin greatly consists, if not exclusively so, in its *love* and *guilt*. As, therefore, *pardon* removes the *guilt*, and faith the love, of sin, and as, also, the Spirit operates and produces all its purifying effects, and heavenly fruits, through faith, we deem our present arrangement much more neat and Scriptural than was the former arrangement. We proceed now, without further circumlocution or apology, to the capital points of this discussion.

Faith.—It makes no part of our present plan to write a dissertation on the subject of faith. That it comes by *hearing*, and this hearing by the word of God (Rom. 10:17); that without it we can not please God, or come to Him (Heb. 11:6); that all our works, which are to be esteemed good or righteous, are fruits of faith (Heb. 11:33); that without faith we can not obtain a victory over the world, but by its mighty workings may come off more than conquerors (1 John 5:4); that the Christian lives by faith (Gal. 2:20), walks by faith (2 Cor. 5:7), runs by faith (Heb. 12:1)—are truths, not only explicitly affirmed in the Scriptures, but admitted by all who deserve to be ranked among the friends of our Redeemer.

Faith is to the moral machinery of the soul what a mainspring is to a watch. When associated with all those principles and influences with which the gospel inspires the individual who believes with his heart unto righteousness, it puts all his moral faculties into motion. It propels the believer onward in the road of obedience. It enables him to obey from his heart the form of heavenly doctrine. It purifies his heart. It renews his mind. He is made a partaker of the divine nature. It is the medium through which he receives all things that pertain to life and godliness (2 Pet. 1: 2), escapes the pollutions that are in the world through lust, and will ultimately secure a permanent abode in the house not made with hands, eternal in the heavens.

There are various similes or illustrations by which the power of faith might be explained. *We sometimes assimilate it to a telescope.* We consider it as making visible the invisible, and as placing at a point apparently near to the observer objects that are afar off. Thus we are enabled to contemplate all the facts and things revealed in the Bible. The Father, the Son, the Spirit; creation, providence, redemption; heaven, earth, hell; time, eternity, judgment; eternal life and eternal death; motives which strike at the foundation of our moral nature; considerations the most weighty of which the human mind can possibly conceive—are not only rendered visible by faith, are not only brought near, but their relation to us is demonstrated. We are made to view them in the light of eternal truth. They are made to approach

Sin and Its Cure

us, to knock at the door of our hearts, and to pour into our souls a continual stream of spiritual influence, proportioned to the amount of our religious intelligence and faith. Thus, as, when we look through a literal telescope at the literal heavens, an indescribable influence comes streaming down from each planet and sun, overwhelming us with emotions indescribably sublime, so, through the telescope of faith, we contemplate the heavens of religion, more glorious than the literal heavens, and from God and Christ, and the saints' ultimate triumph—from the raptures of paradise, and the agonies of the damned—from every revealed object in time or in eternity—by the testimonies which originate and sustain our faith—by the promises which excite our hope, and by the threatenings which inspire us with godly fear, are our hearts filled with principles which stimulate, which purify, which elevate, which fill us with joy unspeakable and full of glory.

The word of God is said to be spirit and life (John 6:63); living and powerful (Heb. 4:12); to live, and abide forever (1 Pet. 1:23), and to be the power of God unto salvation (Rom. 1:16). This powerful Word being the basis of faith, and the atmosphere in which faith lives and moves and has its being, can not but impart to faith, or at least connect with it, its own potent principles. As when you receive a letter, in reference to the truth of which you have no doubt, which informs you of the death of a beloved relative, the words of the letter have power, from the very nature of the facts which it reveals, almost to break your heart, and to cause the streams of anguish to gush from both your eyes; so those facts and things which the gospel reveals render the Word "quick and powerful"—a hammer to break the heart, and a fire to melt it. Hence, it pleases God, by the foolishness of preaching, to save them that believe (1 Cor. 1: 21). Hence, too, the preaching of the cross is the power of God (v. 18), and the world is crucified to the Christian, and he to the world (Gal. 6:14). The spirit of truth becomes the spirit of faith, and the power of truth, which is the power and wisdom of God, the power of faith; as the life of truth is the life of faith. Truth, with all its wonder-working principles, is inseparably united, by the act of believing, with faith in the truth believed. So that the fruits of faith are the fruits of the truth, and *vice versa* (Col. 1:6), and the fruits of the Spirit (Gal. 5:22); the Spirit of God being the spirit both of faith and the gospel (John 15:26).

From the above it will be perceived that the faith of the gospel is not a mere inoperative or speculative principle. It works by love. It is intelligence in the head and love in the heart. It is light and heat. It brings head and heart together, in a state of happy harmony. It teaches that head religion, without the heart, is cold and dead; while heart religion, without the head, is ignorance of blind, and fanatical or enthusiastic. This faith, as it is a believing with the whole heart, takes the government of the whole man, leads the imagination and thoughts into the captivity to the obedience of Christ, and exhibits our religion, not upon the ends of our tongues only, but in a multitude of good works, like precious jewels, upon the ends of our fingers. The operative or fruit-bearing faith will destroy the love of sin—will break down the power of darkness within us—by purifying the heart; will renew us into the heavenly image; will save the soul. Call it historical, or what you may, still Heaven will approve; for if the tree brings forth good fruit it can not be an evil tree.

The operative faith, then, is adapted to the destroying of the love of sin, because, by the potent and efficacious principles with which it inspires the believer, it regenerates him, or changes his heart, and makes him a new creature. The remedy, therefore, in so far as faith is concerned, is precisely adapted to the disease.

Believing that our first point is now satisfactorily proved and illustrated, we proceed to the second consideration.

Repentance.—Repentance destroys the practice of sin. But that this proposition may be rendered indisputable, we ask, What is repentance? As one step toward the obtaining of an answer of truth, we shall refer to the ninth, tenth and eleventh verses of the seventh chapter of the second Epistle to the Corinthians. "For I rejoice not," says the apostle, "that ye were made sorry, but that ye sorrowed to repentance: for ye were made sorry after a godly manner, that ye might receive damage from us in nothing. *For godly sorrow worketh repentance* to salvation not to be repented of: but the sorrow of the world worketh death. For behold this selfsame thing, that ye sorrowed after a godly sort, what carefulness it wrought in you?" etc.

According to this text, repentance is preceded by "godly sorrow"; therefore, godly sorrow is not repentance. It is the cause, while repentance is the effect. The word here rendered "repentance" is different from that in the eighth verse, rendered "repent." This signifies mere regret; but that repentance which was the effect of godly sorrow evidently denoted a change of mind and of heart, which terminated in a thorough reformation of life. They put away the evil of their doings, as we learn from verse 11, in which Mr. Barnes very appropriately remarks as follows:

"We may learn what constitutes true repentance. There should and there will be deep *feeling*. There will be *carefulness*, deep anxiety to be freed from sin. There will be a desire to remove it, *indignation* against it, *fear* of offending God, *earnest desire* that all that has been wrong should be corrected, *zeal* that the reformation should be entire, and a wish that the appropriate *revenge* or expression of displeasure should be

Sin and Its Cure

excited against it. The true penitent hates nothing so cordially as he does his sins. He hates nothing but sin; and his warfare with that is decided, uncompromising, inexorable and eternal.''

As further proof that repentance is an *internal* change or amendment connected with an *external* reformation, let it be noted that when the men of Nineveh repented, "God saw their works, that they turned from the evil of their way" (Jonah 3: 10). They "believed God, and proclaimed a fast, and put on sackcloth" (v. 5), and the king commanded them "to turn every one from his evil way, and from the violence that was in his hands" (v. 8). To the same effect are those Scriptures in which men are commanded to "cease to do evil, and learn to do well"; to "break off their sins by righteousness, and their transgressions by turning to the Lord," and in which it is said, "Turn ye, turn ye, for why will ye die?" and "Let the wicked forsake his way, and the unrighteous man his thoughts, and let him return unto the Lord, and he will have mercy upon him, and to our God, for he will abundantly pardon." In all these cases, reformation is that which is most prominent as a fruit of repentance. And John the Baptist commanded the people to "repent and bring forth fruits meet for repentance." The case of the Pentecostians also is in point; for when Peter commanded them to repent, instead of being overwhelmed with sorrow, their hearts were filled with gladness. They were already sorry. They had been pierced in their hearts. This sorrow, therefore, wrought the repentance unto salvation which Peter commanded. It began in sorrow and sin, but terminated in gladness and reformation. Now, as repentance terminates in reformation, it follows that it destroys the practice of sin. This second position, therefore, being established, we proceed to the consideration of *baptism*.

In baptism the state is changed. As to what that action or ordinance is which is denominated baptism in the Scriptures, we shall leave the reader to determine; only remarking in passing that whatever may be said in favor of pouring and sprinkling, it is certain that immersion is valid baptism. It is also a very significant and solemn ordinance, being an emblem of the burial and resurrection of our Lord, things which can not, in truth, be said of sprinkling and pouring. They are not emblems of anything, and, therefore, in so far as emblematic significancy is concerned, are rites perfectly unmeaning. That either is an emblem of the outpouring of the Spirit is an assertion perfectly gratuitous. Why, then, should a dying man prefer ordinances which, possibly or probably, are not baptism, and which fall infinitely short of the solemnity and emblematic import of immersion, to that which, in any view of the subject, is a valid and most significant baptism? Let piety and honesty, not bigotry and prejudice, answer this question!

But to the point. When a foreigner takes the oath of allegiance, he passes from the state of an alien into that of a citizen; when persons are married, they pass out of the single into the married state; so when penitent believers put on the Lord Jesus Christ, they pass out of the unpardoned into the pardoned state. Observe, we do not affirm that the state of a sinner is never changed except in baptism. What *may* be done *out* of baptism is no part of the present question. We have, however, no great liking for the principles of those persons who are always inquiring how nearly they may approach the precipice of disobedience without falling over. Is baptism a divine command? or is it an unmeaning ceremony? Does it convey any blessings to the obedient? What are those blessings? What say the Scriptures? These are questions from which we can not turn away and be innocent.

"Baptism," say our Methodist brethren, "is not only a sign of profession and mark of difference, whereby Christians are distinguished from others that are not baptized, but it is also a sign of regeneration or the new birth" (Art. XVII.). And on page 107 of the "Discipline" they say: "We call upon thee for these persons, that they, coming to Thy holy baptism, *may receive remission of their sins* by spiritual regeneration." The Presbyterian "Confession of Faith," in answer to the ninety-second question, says: "A sacrament is a holy ordinance instituted by Christ, wherein, by sensible signs, Christ and the benefits of the new covenant are represented, *sealed and applied* to believers." If, then, the Methodists and the Presbyterians are right in the articles just quoted, we can not be wrong; or, in other words, if "baptism is a mark of difference whereby Christians are distinguished from others that are not baptized," and if in baptism, "by sensible signs, Christ and the benefits of the new covenant are *applied* to believers," certainly baptism must be an ordinance in which the state is changed; and, if possible, the more certainly so should the prayer of the Methodists be answered in granting the remission of sins by spiritual regeneration. This, however, only by the way, in proof of our orthodoxy! Our appeal is to the law and to the testimony.

It will, we presume, be granted by all that, if baptism is for the remission of sins, those who, in obedience to the gospel, are baptized, experience a change of state; that is, pass out of the unpardoned into the pardoned state. We affirm that baptism was, from the time of its first institution, for the remission of sins. "John did baptize in the wilderness, and preach the baptism of repentance for the remission of sins" (Mark 1:4). "And he came into all the country about Jordan, preaching the baptism of repentance for the remission of

Sin and Its Cure

sins" (Luke 3:3). "Repent, and be baptized every one of you in the name of Jesus Christ for the remission of sins" (Acts 2:38). "And now why tarriest thou? Arise, and be baptized, and wash away thy sins, calling upon the name of the Lord" (Acts 22:16). "He that believeth and is baptized shall be saved" (Mark 16:16). "Baptism doth also now save us" (1 Pet. 3:21). "Know ye not that so many of us as were baptized into Jesus Christ were baptized into his death?" (Rom. 6:3). "For ye are all the children of God by faith in Christ Jesus; for as many of you as have been baptized into Jesus Christ have put on Christ" (Gal. 3:26, 27).

We are utterly incapable of perceiving how any proposition could be more conclusively demonstrated than is that which affirms that baptism is for the remission of sins, by the Scriptures presented in the preceding paragraph. The testimony is positive, and most explicit. Not more fully can it be proved that Jesus is the Son of God; not more conclusively can any other proposition, within the whole range of human investigation and discussion, be sustained by evidence; for evidence more explicit and positive can not be adduced in proof of any proposition. May we not, then, say that if any person will not believe from the force of these positive declarations of Holy Writ, neither would he be persuaded though one should rise from the dead?

New Testament Christianity

Let it be deeply impressed upon the mind of the reader that although we teach that baptism effects a change of state, yet we do not believe that it effects this change in behalf of any who do not possess the faith and repentance of which we have spoken as prerequisites to its reception. A believing with the heart, and a repentance *in* and *from* the heart, we must possess before we can be recognized as qualified subjects of baptism. But, having these, "baptism," Peter affirms, "saves us." Not baptism alone! Eight souls were saved by water, not by water alone! Noah and his family believed and obeyed God; and in this faith and obedience were they saved from drowning. And we might add that not in faith and obedience only were they saved, but in and by the ark, into which they were introduced by faith and obedience. Thus it is under the gospel. We are not saved by faith alone, by repentance alone, by baptism alone, by grace alone, by hope alone, by blood alone, by the Word alone, by the Spirit alone, nor by any other one thing alone. As "man does not live by bread alone, but by every word that proceeds out of the mouth of God," so we purify ourselves," not by any one thing alone, but "in obeying the truth" (1 Pet. 1: 22), seeing that in obedience we become the subjects of the concentrated energy of all the gracious means appointed for our salvation. We are baptized *into Christ*, and have "put on

Christ''; we are, therefore, saved in our *ark*, Christ Jesus, by baptism, with which baptism are connected faith, repentance, the blood of Christ, the grace of God, all the saving energies and influences which God has been pleased to appoint in order to a perfect and most gracious salvation. Or, to change the illustration, as Mother Eve, by the internal act of believing a lie, and the external act of eating the forbidden fruit, passed out of a state of innocence into one of guilt, so we, by a cordial belief of the gospel in our heart, and an external submission to it from our heart, pass out of the unpardoned into the pardoned state. ''We obey from the heart the *form* of doctrine and are *then* made free from sin, and become the servants of righteousness'' (Rom. 6:17).

We have not space, in this discourse, for an extended discussion of this subject. One additional effort, however, we will make to convince the reader—if, indeed, he is not already convinced—that baptism is for the remission of sins. The reader will please to take his Book, and turn to the second chapter of Acts of the Apostles. In the thirty-eighth verse Peter commands the penitents to ''repent, and be baptized for the remission of sins.'' Now, the circumstances of the case prove incontrovertibly that, at the time at which this command was given, these penitents were in an unpardoned state. Their hearts were bleeding with convictions, and burning with remorse. In the bitterness of their pierced hearts, they were crying for mercy; were pleading to know whether or not pardon could be extended to blood-stained, heaven-daring, hell-deserving sinners, such as they felt themselves to be. That sudden springing up of joy which, by modern anxious-seat revivalists, is held as an evidence of pardon—but certainly without Scripture authority—they felt not, but, in its stead, dread alarm—inexpressible perturbations. We have a right, therefore, to consider them unpardoned at the point of time at which the apostle commands them to be baptized for remission of sins; and, if unpardoned, it follows that they could not otherwise have understood the apostle than as teaching that if they would repent and be baptized, their sins should be pardoned. This, together with the commission law—"He that believeth and is baptized shall be saved," or pardoned—makes assurance doubly sure; and we can not perceive how any person who venerates the Bible can withhold his assent from this doctrine, unless it may be accounted for by reference to the stubbornness of the human will; for, as the poet has said:

> "A man convinced against his will
> Is of the same opinion still."

Pardon.—This destroys the guilt of sin. "The blood of Jesus cleanses us from all sin." It "sprinkles us from an evil conscience." "We have redemption through his blood, the forgiveness of sins." We "are justified by his blood." The death and resurrection of Jesus are the great foundation facts of our holy religion. "He was delivered for our offenses, and rose for our justification." He entered the heavens by His own blood, and is there our High Priest, to intercede for us, and to make reconciliation for our sins. Upon the sacrifice of Jesus on Calvary, and the offering of Himself without spot to God, do we found our hope, in respect to the eternal inheritance. Without the shedding of His blood, there could be no remission. Glory and honor and power and praise and blessing and majesty be unto Him that sitteth upon the throne, and unto the Lamb for ever and ever!

From the whole premises, then, this is our conclusion. Pardon destroys the guilt of sin through the mercy of God and the blood of Jesus. The water of baptism can not cleanse from sin. But the blood of Jesus can cleanse us, when in the water, from all our past sins. The reader, perhaps, believes that the blood can cleanse from sin, at an anxious-seat, in the atmosphere, on dry land. And, pray, why may not the blood of Jesus as well cleanse the believing penitent in the water? Why not, we would say, better be cleansed by this blood, in baptism, as *"baptism doth even now save us"?* Does baptism save us without blood? Every place under heaven is suitable, with some people, for remission of sins but that place which God has explicitly appointed.

But not only does the blood of Jesus cleanse from the sins committed anterior to baptism; it also removes the guilt consequent upon sinning after we have become Christians. "If we [Christians] confess our sins, he is faithful and just to forgive us our sins, and to cleanse us from all unrighteousness" (1 John 1:9). Thus is the heart purged from an evil conscience, and the conscience from dead works through life. Thus is the ever-rankling thorn of guilt extracted from the human soul. And hence it will be that, upon the banks of deliverance, the Christian, whilst unearthly transport swells his bosom, and one thrilling ecstasy after another, inexpressible and full of glory, exhilarates his spirit, shall sing, "Thou hast loved us, and washed us from our sins in thine own blood, and hast made us kings and priests unto God, and we shall reign for ever."

Resurrection.—This destroys the punishment consequent upon the sin of our first father. The process exhibited under the four preceding heads presents a perfect remedy for all our personal sins. By faith, the love of sin is destroyed; by repentance, the practice of sin; by baptism, the state of sin; and by pardon, the guilt. But, renewed as the Christian is in the spirit of his mind, his regenerated soul remains incarcerated in a mortal, dying body—a body of sin and death. Oppressed

Sin and Its Cure

with labors and infirmities and afflictions, he sighs and groans, and prays for deliverance. He anticipates, through the hope of the gospel, the bright, salubrious morn when he shall be delivered from the bondage of corruption into the glorious liberty of the children of God; when his vile body shall be changed, and fashioned like unto the glorious body of our Lord Jesus Christ. Nor shall he groan and hope in vain. When Jesus shall make up His jewels, He shall sing the brilliant, ecstatic song of a resurrection triumph: "O death, where now thy sting? O grave, where now thy victory? Thanks be to God, who giveth us the victory through our Lord Jesus Christ." Then the cure of the soul and body shall be complete. "God will wipe away all tears from the eyes of the righteous; and there shall be no more death, neither sorrow, nor crying, nor pain." There, natural bodies shall have become spiritual bodies. We shall be like Jesus, and see Him as He is. But what will be the breadth and length and depth and height of our bliss and glory, neither human nor angelic eloquence can tell. It doth not yet appear what we shall be, but our inheritance shall be an infinite and an eternal weight of glory.

But we must hasten to the conclusion of this discourse. And, in order to reach this point in the most profitable manner of which we are capable, we must be permitted to remark briefly on three classes of our race: 1. Infants and idiots. 2.

Those who obtain pardon in this life, and die in a state of justification. 3. Those who live and die in their sins.

1. *Infants and idiots.* The Scriptures teach that God requires of every person according to his ability—according to what a man has, and not according to what he has not—according to his talents, whether one, two or five; and that to him that knoweth to do good, and doeth it not, to him it is sin. But infants and idiots know neither good nor evil, have no talents, possess no moral ability, and, therefore, can not be guilty of personal sin. Being, however, involved in the consequences of Adam's sin, without any act of their own, the second Adam will, without any act of theirs, redeem from all these consequences. As the offense came upon *all* to condemnation, so will the free gift come upon *all* to justification of life (Rom. 5:18). Thus, through the righteousness of Christ, and without faith, repentance, baptism, or the performance of any other conditions, will all infants and idiots be saved with an everlasting salvation.

2. *Those who obtain pardon, and die in a state of justification.* These, as well as infants and idiots, will need no other salvation, at the last day, than that which consists in a resurrection unto life, and glory which will follow.

3. *Those who live and die in their sins.* These, too, will be saved from all the consequences of

Sin and Its Cure

Adam's sin, but their own sins will be their ruin. They would not have Christ to reign over them. They would not come to Him that they might have life. They despised all His counsels, and would have none of His reproofs. A resurrection, therefore, shall be theirs, but it shall be a resurrection unto damnation. The fault will be theirs, not God's. They will be self-destroyed, having plucked down upon their own heads fiery, eternal destruction.

In addition, we shall present one argument against Calvinism, one against restorationism, and one against skepticism.

1. *Calvinism.* It is by virtue of certain relations which exist between all men and the first Adam that this sin affects them, and they are brought to the grave. Now, as the second Adam will raise all mankind from the grave, He must have sustained a relationship to all. But if there be a part of mankind for which Christ did not die, that part can not be raised from the dead; just as if, with reference to a part of mankind, Adam had not sinned, that part would not have died. Those systems of Calvinism, therefore, which deny that Christ died for all, are as certainly false as it is certainly true that all will be raised from the dead.

2. *Restorationism.* We have seen that, in order to our redemption from temporal death, Jesus must have died that death for us. We arrive at

this conclusion from the utter impossibility of imagining that the death of Christ would be a prerequisite to our redemption from one death, and not from another. But as Jesus has not died the *second death* for any man, therefore there is no redemption from the second death. It follows, consequently, that restorationism is false.

3. *Skepticism.* We have seen how admirably the *five points* of the gospel—each to each—are adapted to the removal of the *five points* of sin. Was there ever a more beautiful or wonderful adaptation? Surely the unbeliever will not say that this adaptation is a work of chance, or a production of clumsy priests. As well might he say that the adaptation of the glove to the fingers, of light to the eye, of sound to the ear, and of truth to the conscience, or that all the numerous adaptations, human and divine, in the whole universe, are works of chance. Men have never searched sufficiently deep into human nature, nor been so profoundly versed in moral pathology, as to invent a system such as is the gospel. No wisdom short of His who needed not that any should testify to Him of man, for He knew what was in man, was adequate to this adaptation. Hence, all systems of religion merely human, and perhaps all systems of education, are greatly defective; but the Christian religion reaches the whole man; it anticipates all his wants; it presents a remedy for all his moral maladies; it purifies, elevates,

glorifies him, and fits him for the most exalted heavenly society and enjoyments. This is the Lord's doing, and marvelous in our eyes. The grace of our Lord Jesus Christ be with all who love Him sincerely.

THE NEW BIRTH

A DISCOURSE BY ALFRED N. GILBERT

"'Jesus answered and said unto him, Verily, verily, I say unto thee, Except one be born anew, he cannot see the kingdom of God. Nicodemus saith unto him, How can a man be born when he is old? can he enter a second time into his mother's womb, and be born? Jesus answered, Verily, verily, I say unto thee, Except one be born of water and the Spirit, he cannot enter into the kingdom of God.''—John 3: 3-5.

I PRESUME there is no one of those here present to-day who does not believe in the sinfulness of man. We have too many evidences in the workings of our own hearts, in the developments of our own lives, in the fruits of our observation of those around us, in the universal necessity of means of enforcing the penalties of all systems of human law, to doubt for a moment that man is, by nature, sinful.

I assume, also, that there is no one of us, who believes in Christianity at all, who does not also believe in the necessity for some radical and vital change in man before he can be properly called a Christian. We realize that no man is a Christian by nature. We realize that his relationship to God, to Christ, to the Holy Spirit, must be essen-

The New Birth

tially changed before he can properly wear the honorable and sacred name "Christian." It will, I think, be also admitted that this change, whatever it may be, inducts into the kingdom of God; that, before it, man is outside of that kingdom; after it, inside the kingdom, so long as its effects shall continue. We shall agree that the man who has undergone the needed change is, by virtue thereof, a Christian, with all the rights, privileges and duties accruing to the rightful possessor of that name.

With these common premises before us, some questions will naturally arise, to the discussion of which I propose to address myself to-day, and to which I invite your thoughtful and prayerful attention with confidence, as every wise man and woman who accepts these premises must admit that no subject can be of more transcendent importance than this. I shall ask and try to answer:

First—What departments of man's nature does this change include and affect?

Second—By whom or what is it wrought?

Third—In what does it consist?

Fourth—How is it accomplished?

In the text which I have read to you, our Saviour speaks of this change under the vivid figure of a "new birth," and uses the most emphatic language with regard to it. He employs that peculiar form of speech with which He was wont to introduce solemn and profound truths,

"Verily, verily, I say unto you," than which nothing was better calculated to arrest and fix the attention of him to whom it was addressed, and then adds, "Except a man be born anew, he cannot see the kingdom of God."

Nicodemus had spoken with somewhat of a patronizing air to Jesus—"*We* know that thou art a teacher come from God"—but Jesus at once cut his pretension short with the assertion that until a man is born anew (or from above), he can not even see the kingdom of God—can not perceive the existence of such a kingdom, and therefore can know nothing about it. Jesus would accept no testimony of uninspired men. His testimony must come "from above," and therefore he who bore it must be informed and influenced "from above." Jesus would allow Nicodemus to occupy no other attitude to Himself but that of a humble learner from a superior. "Verily, verily, *I say unto thee,* Except a man be born anew, he cannot see the kingdom of God."

Nicodemus immediately vindicates Christ's estimate and declaration by asking, "How can a man be born when he is old?" evidently assuming that Christ referred to a second literal birth, and implying its impossibility. Whether this was sincere or ironical on his part, it equally involves his failure to catch the meaning of Jesus, and his ignorance of "the kingdom of God." We, of course, enlightened as we have been by the communica-

The New Birth

tions of the New Testament, will fall into no such blunder, but realize that Jesus is using figurative language to express a vital, radical change of relationship. And surely no language could more vividly express such a change than this. A "new birth" exhausts the idea of complete new departure.

But, having heard the question of Nicodemus, Jesus continues and amplifies His thought, again using His solemn form of affirmation: "Except a man be born of water and the Spirit, he cannot enter into the kingdom of God." The thought is now complete. Until the new birth is begun, the kingdom of God can not even be seen (or known) as such. I add "or known" because the original of "see" here is a word which, in a large number of instances of its New Testament use, means "know," and carries with it not merely the idea of impact upon the visual organ, but of recognition as a consequence of that impact. It therefore comes to be very frequently used where there is no physical seeing, but only mental recognition.

"The kingdom of God," in this passage, is evidently the church of Christ on earth, as our Saviour, in the twelfth verse, speaks of the communications He had made to Nicodemus up to that point as "earthly things," or things transpiring upon the earth, in distinction from "heavenly things," or things transpiring in heaven (the entrance upon eternal life), of which He subsequently speaks.

Until the new birth has begun, then, I repeat, we can not know the kingdom of God as such, and until it is complete we can not enter into it; or, in other words, no man can be a member of the church of Christ until he has passed through the "new birth." Passing through this, entrance is at once secured into the "kingdom of grace," the church of our Lord Jesus Christ.

But, entrance of *what* into the kingdom of God? Christ says, "Except a *man* be born anew." (Note.—The original is *tis*, but is here used as expressing a human being, as in so many places in the New Testament.) But what is a man? Is it the mind, or the heart, or the body? Is it the intellectual, or emotional, or volitional, or physical? We say "the mind of a man." The phrase involves the idea that the mind is a part of the man, but it also involves the idea that it is *only* a part. We say "the heart of a man," as expressing his emotional nature. This also involves the idea that "the heart" is only a part of the man. So with the expressions, "the will of a man" and "the body of a man." All these, then, enter into the composition of the man—thought, feeling, will and action; the mental, emotional, volitional and physical. With either wanting, the object is no longer a man, whatever else it may be. When, therefore, Jesus says, "Except a man be born anew, he cannot know the kingdom of God," the fair (may I not say the necessary?) implication is that the entire man participates in the new birth, and that it is not complete until the entire man has participated.

But when we go on to the completion of the Saviour's thought, this implied idea becomes explicit. "Except a man be born of water and the Spirit, he cannot enter into the kingdom of God." Here are two elements contributing to the new birth, one of which is visible, the other invisible; one is material, the other immaterial. The material element can have no direct impact upon the immaterial object; the immaterial element can have no direct impact upon the material object. At once there is forced upon us the conclusion that the internal and invisible, and also the external and visible, departments of man's nature alike participate in the new birth. In further elucidation of the thought, Jesus calls the attention of Nicodemus to the fact that two departments of man's nature come into existence in natural birth. "That which is born of the flesh is flesh," not "is fleshly," as so commonly interpreted; "and that which is born of the Spirit is spirit," not "is spiritual." John never uses the word here translated "flesh" in a figurative sense, as expressing moral condition. He always uses it literally of the physical man, and it is an entirely arbitrary exegesis, born of the necessities of theological teaching, which interprets it in any other way here.

New Testament Christianity

Nicodemus, by his question, conveys the idea that new birth applies only to the physical. Jesus reminds him that there are two natures which come into being in natural birth—"the spirit," or internal and invisible man, and "the flesh," or external and visible man. The mention of water, to one familiar with John's baptism, as Nicodemus doubtless was (and possibly with "proselyte baptism"), would at once suggest the Saviour's idea as far as the body is concerned. But the great difficulty of Nicodemus, as a Jewish rabbi, would be to grasp the idea of the new birth of the Spirit. At this point, therefore, Jesus amplifies: "Marvel not that I said unto thee, Ye must be born anew. The wind bloweth where it listeth, and thou hearest the voice thereof, but knowest not whence it cometh or whither it goeth; so is every one that is born of the Spirit."

In view of the words employed, it is astonishing how this verse has been misapplied and misunderstood as conveying the idea of the mystery and incomprehensibility of the new birth. Jesus expressly teaches Nicodemus that there is nothing to wonder at ("marvel not"), but calls his attention to the fact that, the spirit of man being invisible, the new birth of the Spirit is invisible. The word translated "knowest," in the eighth verse, is a form of the same word translated "see" in the third verse, and all that is necessary is to insert "see" to realize the meaning of Christ:

The New Birth

"The wind bloweth where it listeth, and thou hearest the sound thereof, but seest not whence it cometh or whither it goeth; so is every one that is born of the Spirit;" that is, the birth of the Spirit is an invisible thing, as are both the Divine Spirit and the human. The thought of the verse is invisibility, not mystery.

The teaching of the Saviour, that the new birth concerns both the external and internal man, has its analogies in both natural birth and the final change or transfer into the heavenly state. We live successively in three kingdoms—nature, grace and glory—and we enter each of these by a birth. In natural birth by which we enter the kingdom of nature, the intellectual, emotional and physical departments of our nature all come into existence. Each is only germinal, and is to be developed into powers marvelously transcending what it possesses at the moment of birth, but the germ of all those powers is present in birth. The mighty intellect of a Newton, the emotional nature of a Paul, the physical powers of a Samson, once existed germinally in the infant of a day old.

In like manner, when we pass over into the heavenly state, the mind is to participate in a radical change. "Now I know in part; but then shall I know fully, even as also I was fully known." But the *whole* nature is to participate. "We know that, if he shall be manifested, we shall be like him; for we shall see him even as he is. And every one that hath this hope set on him purifieth himself, even as he is pure." He endeavors to approximate to the perfect purity that is finally to be his. But one of the most glorious and inspiring thoughts in connection with this final birth is that the external nature, the body, is to participate. It was the favorite theme of the great apostle to the Gentiles—the resurrection and glorification of the body; the thought that, not as disembodied, but as embodied, spirits, we are to bask in the smiles of God in His own glorious dwelling-place.

What, then, would seem more natural than that all the parts of our being should be consecrated which are thus to be glorified? If, in the birth into the kingdom of nature, the intellectual, emotional and physical all participate, and in the final birth into the kingdom of glory they also have a share, what could be more naturally expected than that all should participate in that "new birth" which lies between the two, and inducts into the kingdom of grace, which is the connecting vestibule between the kingdom of nature and the kingdom of glory? The teaching of the Saviour, then, that the new birth is not complete until the entire man has participated therein, is just what we would have expected from the other teaching of the New Testament, and forbids alike the neglect and undervaluing of baptism on the one hand, and the undue exaltation of it upon

The New Birth

the other. The mind, the heart, the body, must all have a part in the "new birth," and thus we reach the answer to our first question, "What departments of man's nature does this change include and affect?"

Pass we now to our second question, *By whom or what is it wrought?*

John, in the first chapter of his testimony, says: "But as many as received him, to them gave he the right to become children of God, even to them that believe on his name: who were born, not of blood, nor of the will of the flesh, nor of the will of man, but of God." The author of the "new birth" is here definitely announced as being God, and to this purport are also the seven occurrences of the phrase "born of God" which are found in the letters of the same apostle. God, then, is the author of the "new birth," but so is He of all our blessings. "Every good and every perfect gift is from above, coming down from the Father of lights." God, however, employs various agents in the provision of the many blessings which He gives us. The question, then, naturally arises, Who is God's agent in the accomplishment of the new birth? This question is sufficiently answered by the Saviour when He says: "So is every one that is born of the Spirit." The words of the fifth verse also teach the same thought, "Except a man be born of water and the Spirit," for it is as illogical to conceive of the Spirit as an unconscious factor, as it would be to conceive of water as a conscious one. The agent of God in the accomplishment of the "new birth" is the Holy Spirit.

But we can conceive of the Holy Spirit as acting immediately, or through any one of various instrumentalities. The next question that arises, then, is, Does the Holy Spirit employ any instrumentality in the accomplishment of the "new birth," and, if so, what? Jas. 1:18 throws light upon this question: "Of his own will he brought us forth by the word of truth, that we should be a kind of firstfruits of his creatures." In this passage the instrumentality by which the "new birth" is wrought is undoubtedly declared to be the word of God. But Peter is equally explicit when he says: "Having been begotten again, not of corruptible seed, but of incorruptible, through the word of God, which liveth and abideth."

The "word of God," however, is a very comprehensive term, embracing the entire Bible, and, as the "new birth" is an exclusively New Testament revelation, and inquiry will naturally and legitimately arise whether there is not some more specific statement of the instrument of the "new birth," I would reply that such a statement does exist in the first chapter of Peter's first letter, in close connection with the last-quoted passage. After quoting,

The New Birth

"All flesh is as grass,
And all the glory thereof as the flower of grass.
The grass withereth, and the flower falleth:
But the word of the Lord abideth for ever,"
he then says, "And this is the word which by the gospel is preached unto you."

The circle of our inquiries is now greatly narrowed. We have ascertained that "the gospel" is the specific instrumentality of the Holy Spirit, who is God's agent in the accomplishment of the "new birth." The third verse of the first chapter of 1 Peter reciprocally illuminates and is illuminated by this thought: "Blessed be the God and Father of our Lord Jesus Christ, who according to his great mercy begat us again unto a living hope by the resurrection of Jesus Christ from the dead." We have only to turn to 1 Corinthians 15 and read Paul's definition of the gospel, in which he holds before us the death, burial and resurrection of Jesus Christ as its palpitating heart around which all else gathers, and we realize at once why Peter represents us as being begotten by the resurrection of Jesus Christ, in the same chapter in which he represents us as being born again by the Word which is preached in the gospel.

Let us now recapitulate the Scriptural answer to our second leading question, By whom or what is the "new birth" wrought? The answer is, God is its author, the Holy Spirit is God's agent, and the gospel of our Lord and Saviour Jesus

New Testament Christianity

Christ is the specific instrumentality employed, as the word of God. That "gospel" or "good tidings" of salvation through Jesus Christ is the direct offspring of 'the Holy Spirit. In its completeness, none but the Holy Spirit could have authoritatively spoken or dictated it. He it is who has taken the words of human language and combined them in intelligible sentences which must ever remain instinct with His own life so long as they continue in the combination which announces His divine truths. These words are spirit and they are life. Until they are placed in different combinations and embody other propositions, the Spirit of God can never be taken out of them, and the man who sneeringly uses the phrase "bare word," of the gospel, is guilty of blasphemy.

Our third leading question is, *In what does the new birth consist?* It is evident that in natural birth, as we commonly use the word, nothing comes into existence. An hour before birth the child is possessed of every member and faculty that it possesses an hour after birth. Nothing *comes into existence*, but the relationship and surroundings of every member and every faculty are changed. Birth is simply the entrance upon a new state which is marked by new relationships, and which involves a new destiny. We have no right to push the Saviour's figure out of or beyond the legitimate application of the literal fact from which it is derived. When the Saviour,

The New Birth

therefore, speaks of a new birth, it implies a change of state or relationship on the part of all which participates in it. As this new birth inducts us into the kingdom of our Lord and Saviour Jesus Christ, the prominent thought of this change of relationship must be in regard to Him. The essential idea of the new birth, therefore, must be a change of relationship, of all that is born again, to Jesus Christ. But we have already seen that the entire man, in all the departments of his being, is born again, consequently in the new birth there must be a definite change of relationship to Jesus Christ, of every department of our nature. If there be a plan of salvation laid down, equivalent in its details to the new birth as a whole, it will inevitably include details expressive of this change of relationship for each and every department of our nature as human beings. With this key in our hand, it will be easy to unlock all the (so-called) mysteries of the new birth.

Man may be divided into the intellectual, the emotional, the volitional and the physical. If there is more than this, I have not been able to find it. The normal relationship of each of these to Jesus Christ, and the claim which He makes upon humanity, is our first inquiry. That claim is belief of His divinity, love for Himself, subordination to His will and obedience to His commands.

The normal relationship of the *intellectual nature,* the thinking principle, is unbelief. We do not believe that Jesus of Nazareth is the Christ, the Son of the living God. It may not be disbelief. It may consist simply with want of knowledge. There may not be conscious rejection, for there may be no knowledge of such statement. But, stated in its simplest form, we do not believe this great truth. The most radical, vital change of relationship to Jesus Christ, for the intellectual nature, of which we can conceive, is to *implicit belief that Jesus is the Christ, the Son of the living God*. And in perfect accordance with this we find this laid down as one of the conditions of salvation through Christ, when it is developed didactically by the apostles.

The normal relationship to Christ of the *emotional nature* is indifference. It may develop, as in the case of Voltaire, into hatred, but this is exceptional. Indifference may be predicated of all. Stated in simplest form, we have no love for Jesus Christ. The most radical, vital change of relationship to Jesus Christ, for the emotional nature, of which we can conceive, is to warm love for Him as the Saviour. In perfect accordance we find *love to Jesus* laid down as one of the essential constituents of Christian life, Paul saying: "If any man loveth not the Lord, let him be anathema."

The normal relationship of the *volitional nature* or will to the will of Jesus Christ is insubordination. There is no purpose to obey His com-

The New Birth

mands. The purpose is to follow out our own desires. We care nothing for His will as revealed. We may *happen* to do some things that He has commanded. For instance, we may be upright in business dealings, we may be kind to the poor, we may abstain from immorality and obscenity, but it is not because we care for anything He has said, but from other motives. The most radical, vital change of relationship for the volitional nature of which we can conceive, is to the deliberate purpose to obey Jesus Christ, the acceptance of His will as ours. In perfect accordance with this we find *repentance*, which simply means such a change of purpose, laid down as one of the indispensable conditions of salvation.

The normal relationship of the *physical nature* to Jesus Christ is disobedience. It is not acting in accordance with the commands of Jesus. It is carrying out our independent personal will, or the will of some one whom we love or fear. Its motions have no reference to Jesus Christ or His commands. The most radical, vital change of relationship would be in the beginning of obedience to His commands, and the most striking exhibition of such obedience would be the performance of an act for which no known reason existed but the expressed will of Jesus Christ. If this act were of a character to *symbolize* the *complete* submission of the entire physical nature, it would possess a still greater fitness to express vital changes of relationship, a symbolic pledge of the physical to the future service of Jesus Christ.

In perfect accordance with this we find a physical act commanded in the plan of salvation, and so clearly and constantly associated with the remaining constituents of that plan that none can neglect it without putting asunder what God hath joined together. We find that act to be one of such a character that we could have no moral motive to its performance aside from the expressed will of Jesus Christ. We find that in its form it is more perfectly symbolic of complete submission of the whole physical nature to Jesus Christ than any other act could be. There is in its performance a complete suspension of every voluntary physical function, and even of that which is partly voluntary, the function of respiration. Of course, I allude to the ordinance of *baptism* or *immersion,* the prerequisite and accompaniment of which is the physical act of confession of the claims of Jesus Christ, which lifts it from a mere physical dipping to a religious act of consecration of the physical.

In these successive acts of the intellectual, emotional, volitional and physical departments of our nature, a change of relationship of the entire man has taken place. There remains no other department to be considered, and, therefore, at this point the new birth must be complete. Short of this point, and with any of these elements wanting,

The New Birth

it can not be complete. Consequently, just here, by divine authority, is located that "calling upon the name of the Lord" which brings salvation, that Lord unto whom the new-born has covenanted himself, and who is therefore bound to hear and answer his prayer for pardon. At this point also is located the beginning of that indwelling of the Holy Spirit which is "earnest" of the future glory, and of such as have thus been baptized. Paul says: "As many of you as were baptized into Christ did put on Christ."

Our fourth question is, *How is the new birth accomplished?*

Having found that the Holy Spirit, through the gospel, does this work, and having found in what the work must consist, this question becomes an interesting and important one. We have already found that the first work to be done is to convince the mind of the truth of the claims of Jesus Christ, so that belief may be produced. An intelligent conviction of the mind on any point can be produced only by suitable and adequate testimony. If faith is to be an intelligent one, the Holy Spirit must furnish testimony, and the conditions of the problem do not demand that He shall furnish or do anything more. Paul declares that "belief cometh by hearing, and hearing by the word of Christ." John says of his version of the gospel, "But these are written that ye may believe that Jesus is the Christ, the Son of God;"

and Jesus said: "If I go not away, the Comforter [Holy Spirit] will not come unto you; but if I go, I will send him unto you. And he, when he is come, will convict the world in respect of sin, and of righteousness, and of judgment; of sin, because they believe not on me; of righteousness, because I go to the Father, and ye behold me no more; of judgment, because the prince of this world hath been judged."

This prediction our Saviour made on the night of His betrayal. Its fulfillment began on the Pentecost day succeeding His resurrection. On that day the Holy Spirit convicted three thousand of the truth of the claims of Jesus Christ, and of His consequent righteousness. We are expressly told how He did this. He spoke through the lips of Peter in intelligible sentences which announced that the death and burial of Jesus had been followed by His resurrection, ascension and glorification. Thus God had vindicated Him and He was proved righteous. Being righteous, His declarations concerning Himself were true, and He had declared of Himself that He was "the Christ, the Son of the living God." It is the production of testimony to the truth of facts, which, if true, necessarily involve the reality of the great test truth of Christianity, "Jesus is the Christ, the Son of the living God." No man can believe the facts without believing the truth that arises from them. That testimony the Holy Spirit has fur-

The New Birth

nished through inspired men. They were the visible producers of the result, though he spoke through them, and it is for this reason Paul says of himself, to the Corinthians, "For though ye should have ten thousand tutors in Christ, yet have ye not many fathers: for in Christ Jesus I begot you through the gospel;" and again, to Philemon, "I beseech thee for my child, whom I have begotten in my bonds, Onesimus." Paul thus transfers to himself, by a figure, the work which the Holy Spirit did through him by the "word of faith" which he preached. This preaching of the apostles goes on, through the inspired record of the New Testament, as much now as in the first century. Whether read in the book or heard repeated from the lips of the preacher, the same process essentially takes place now as then. There is no intimation in God's word that there ever should be any change. And wherever this process takes place there the Holy Spirit is convicting the world, there the Holy Spirit is begetting men, there the Holy Spirit is present in the testimony He bears, and which only He can bear. No intimation is given of any other influence upon the unbeliever to produce belief beyond the authoritative presentation of this testimony by the Holy Spirit. They who assert any additional, extraneous influence present a mere speculation of their own brains for which they can produce no authority from God's word. We need be at no pains to deny it, and we certainly are under no obligation to accept it. It stands in the category of those "traditions" which the rabbis added to the law of Moses and the testimonies of the prophets. In the absence of any declaration in regard to it in the New Testament, there is but one other testimony which would be worth anything, and that is the production of a single man or woman who, without having ever heard in any way any testimony of the apostles to the divinity of Jesus Christ, has, by independent action of the Holy Spirit, believed and confessed that "Jesus is the Christ, the Son of the living God." No such instance has ever been produced, and in its absence it is an impertinent and gratuitous assumption and presumption which asserts on behalf of the Holy Spirit what He has never taught in regard to Himself. He declares that *the gospel* is "the power of God unto salvation to every one that believeth," and He represents the belief of divine truths as being produced by the same method by which the belief of all other truths is produced; namely, the presentation of suitable and adequate testimony. It is thus, then, that He approaches our *intellectual* nature. He testifies to the facts of the gospel. The man who believes these to have occurred necessarily believes the truth inseparably united with them, that Jesus is the Christ, the Son of the living God. But we have already found that this constitutes the *new birth* as it pertains to the intellectual.

The New Birth

It is necessary that the *emotional* shall have part therein. How, now, does the Holy Spirit reach the emotional, excite love for the Lord Jesus Christ? Through the gospel He presents to our hearts the most lovable Being, by universal consent, upon whom the world has ever gazed, and further presents this Being as manifesting toward the human race the most unselfish and self-sacrificing love. In this combination the motive powers that can appeal to the human heart for the excitation of a pure love are exhausted. It is impossible to add anything even in imagination. When this is brought to bear upon the emotional nature of man, the testimony of the gospel being believed, the love of the heart to Jesus must inevitably be excited if that heart be at all reachable. We love Him because He first loved us. The test of the new birth of the emotional is that it loves Jesus, and the Holy Spirit accomplishes this by presenting in the gospel the love and lovableness of Jesus.

It is necessary that the *volitional* shall have part in the new birth. How does the Holy Spirit reach the volitional through the gospel? The point to be reached is that the man shall be *willing* to take Jesus as Lord. There is a distinction important to be preserved at this point. It is not sufficient that a person shall perform certain actions, go through certain physical experiences, but that he shall do whatever Jesus has required, *willingly*. The action that results must result from his own deliberate purpose. If it is done unconsciously or under compulsion, it will have no value as far as the will is concerned. Consequently, it can be reached only by presenting truth to the mind and motive to the heart. Anything additional to this destroys the volition, and takes away the moral character of the resultant action. Whenever it can be shown that the Holy Spirit irresistibly, aside from the presentaion of truth and motive, saves a man, that moment it will be shown that the freedom of the will is destroyed, and that the time spent in appeals to men to accept Christ is time wasted.

But this has never been shown, nor do I believe that it ever will be shown. The Holy Spirit appeals to the will by presenting Jesus Christ as having all authority in heaven and on earth, as demanding the submission of our hearts and lives, as offering eternal felicity in heaven to those who accept and obey Him, and threatening eternal punishment to those who reject Him, as deserving our implicit obedience by the price He has paid for our redemption, as requiring of us nothing but what is in itself good and holy and noble. It thus brings to bear a wonderful combination of motives to induce us to repent, which means to change our purpose, to submit our will to the will of Jesus so that we take Him as our rightful ruler, our Lord. This is the new birth of the volitional

The New Birth

nature as wrought by the Holy Spirit through the Word of truth.

When the man has reached this point the only question he has to ask will be: "Lord, what wilt Thou have me to do? I believe in Thee, I love Thee, I am ready to obey and follow Thee. How shall I show my belief, my love, my repentance?" He does not ask in vain. His consecration is to be made complete by the consecration of the *physical*. The new birth so auspiciously begun is to be completed by the participation of the physical. To him, as to Saul of Tarsus, come the words of inspiration: "And now why tarriest thou? Arise, and be baptized, and wash away thy sins, calling on his name." The function of speech, which links itself with the intellectual, emotional, volitional and physical, which, indeed, may bring all together in its own exercise, is consecrated in the public confession of the Christhood and divinity of Jesus, and participates thus in the new birth.

All is now prepared for the carrying out of the great command which so enters into the apostolic commission to preach the gospel, that it can never be separated from it without such a wanton tearing to pieces of the Spirit's word as deprives it of its divine character and authority. Whatever it may be after this impious work of excision has been done, it is no longer the word of God as given to us by the Holy Spirit. That word is: "Go ye therefore, and make disciples of all the nations, baptizing them into the name of the Father and of the Son and of the Holy Spirit; teaching them to observe all things whatsoever I commanded you: and lo, I am with you always, even unto the end of the world."

Such was Jesus' own commission. When Peter stood, upon the following Pentecost, to fulfill that commission, the Holy Spirit spoke through his lips to the assembled multitude. "Repent ye, and be baptized every one of you in the name of Jesus Christ unto the remission of your sins; and ye shall receive the gift of the Holy Spirit." The baptism thus commanded was an act in water of such a character that the same Spirit could afterwards say of it, "Buried with him in baptism, wherein ye were also raised with him through faith in the working of God, who raised him from the dead," and was, therefore, immersion.

Thus the Holy Spirit completes the new birth in commanding the administration of the ordinance of baptism, a great symbolic picture of the complete surrender of our physical nature to the commands of Jesus Christ, as we confidently expect that nature to be raised from death and glorified by Him in the final birth into the kingdom of glory.

We have thus followed in detail the various steps of the new birth. We have found it to be wrought, from beginning to end, by the Holy Spirit through the Word of truth; we have found

The New Birth

it to comprehend the entire nature of man, intellectual, emotional, volitional and physical; we have found it to consist, for the intellectual, in the transition from unbelief to *belief;* for the emotional, in the transition from indifference to *love;* for the volitional, in *repentance,* or the transition from unwillingness to willingness to obey Christ; for the physical, in *confession* and *baptism,* or the transition to overt obedience of the body to the commands of Jesus. Thus the whole nature is brought into a new relationship to Jesus Christ, and of such a one it may be predicted that, being "born of water and the Spirit," he has entered into "the kingdom of God."

THE GREAT RENOVATION

JAMES M. MATHES

"Then answered Peter, and said unto him, Behold, we have forsaken all and followed thee: what shall we have therefore? And Jesus said unto them, Verily I say unto you, That ye which have followed me, in the regeneration when the Son of man shall sit in the throne of his glory, ye also shall sit upon twelve thrones, judging the twelve tribes of Israel."
—Matt. 19: 27, 28.

FOR a brief discussion of this subject we propose the following order:

I. *The Regeneration.*

II. *The Throne of Christ's Glory.*

III. *The Twelve Thrones Promised to the Twelve Apostles.*

IV. *The Judgments of the Twelve Tribes of Israel.*

As introductory to the subject, we shall briefly consider the case of the young man as recorded in the paragraphs immediately preceding our text. In the parallel passage, Mark tells us that when Jesus "was gone forth into the way, there came one running, and kneeled to him, and asked him, Good Master, what shall I do that I may inherit eternal life?" (Mark 10:17). Matthew informs us that

The Great Renovation

Jesus said unto this young man, "If thou wilt enter into life, keep the commandments;" and that he asked Him, "Which?" No doubt he, like many persons in the present day, was under the impression that the commandments are not all alike *essential,* and therefore he inquired *which* he must do. Jesus referred him to the commandments of the law. "And he answered and said unto him, Master, all these have I observed from my youth. Then Jesus beholding him loved him, and said unto him, One thing thou lackest; go thy way, sell whatsoever thou hast, and give to the poor, and thou shalt have treasure in heaven: and come, take up the cross, and follow me. And he was sad at that saying, and went away grieved; for he had great possessions" (Mark 10:20-22).

This otherwise good young man was covetous, and Jesus knew it, and therefore put him to the test. "Sell whatsoever thou hast, and give to the poor." This he was unwilling to do. If he could have obtained eternal life without making any sacrifices, he would have been glad to accept it; but, unwilling to make the necessary sacrifice, he walked sadly away. Jesus said unto His disciples: "How hardly shall they that have riches enter into the kingdom of God!" And then, to intensify the thought, He added: "It is easier for a camel to go through the eye of a needle than for a rich man to enter into the kingdom of God." That is, a rich man of that particular type—a covetous

New Testament Christianity

rich man, who loves his worldly possessions more than eternal life.

Now, after Peter and the other disciples had witnessed all this, and had heard the remarks of Jesus in regard to covetous rich men, they came to the conclusion that *they* had made great sacrifices and were poor enough. Peter, as spokesman for the twelve, said to Jesus: "Behold, we have forsaken all, and followed thee: what shall we have therefore?" The apostles were at that time expecting Jesus, as the son of David, to restore the fallen fortunes of the kingdom of David, and to sit upon the temporal throne of David. And in view of the speedy establishment of a great temporal kingdom, the question, "What shall we have therefore?" was equivalent to asking, "What offices of honor and profit shall we fill in your kingdom?" Jesus, without stopping to correct their mistaken views upon this subject, answered their question by saying: "Ye which have followed me"—that is, the chosen twelve, who had continued with Him in all His travels—"in the regeneration, when the Son of man shall sit on the throne of his glory, ye also shall sit upon twelve thrones, judging the twelve tribes of Israel."

I. *The Regeneration, or, More Literally, the Renovation.*—This means simply the gospel dispensation, embracing the whole period of time from the setting up of the kingdom of Christ on the day of Pentecost until the end shall come and

The Great Renovation

He shall deliver up the kingdom to His Father. This period is very properly called the Renovation, because the gospel of Christ, which is to be preached in all the world, is the power of God unto salvation to all, in every nation, who believe and obey it. It is the great renovating agent to purify and elevate human society. Jesus, the Son of God, and the Saviour of men, is the light of the world; and wherever the true gospel is preached, men are enlightened and drawn to Christ for salvation. The Renovation began on the day of Pentecost, when three thousand souls were "convinced of sin, of righteousness, and of judgment," and became obedient to the gospel. "Devout men, out of every nation under heaven," who were sojourners in Jerusalem at that time, were among the three thousand converts made on that day; and, returning to their homes, they carried with them the light and truth that were to renovate society everywhere; not only the twelve tribes, but the Gentiles as well, after their calling.

II. *The Throne of His Glory.*—During the period of the Renovation Jesus is to sit on the throne of His glory. He sat down upon the throne when He ascended up to heaven and was crowned King in Zion, forty days after His resurrection from the dead. David says: "Yet have I set my king upon my holy hill of Zion" (Ps. 2:6). Again: "The Lord said unto my Lord, Sit thou at my right hand until I make thine enemies thy footstool." These passages represent Christ as a King sitting upon His throne and reigning over the people. Once more: David describes the ascension of Christ to His glorious throne thus: "Lift up your heads, O ye gates; and be ye lifted up, ye everlasting doors; and the King of glory shall come in" (Ps. 24:7). Here He is called the "King of glory," when he ascends up to heaven, accompanied by thousands of angels and twenty thousand chariots of God. And on the day of Pentecost, when the multitude were together greatly wondering at the strange things that they saw and heard, and inquired of the apostles the meaning of it, Peter, standing up with the eleven, explained the whole matter to them by saying: "Therefore let all the house of Israel know assuredly, that God hath made that same Jesus, whom ye have crucified, both Lord and Christ."

III. *The Twelve Thrones of Judgment.*—The Saviour promised His twelve apostles that they should sit on twelve thrones in His kingdom, in the Renovation; and, according to this promise, they took their seats on their thrones on the day of Pentecost, and are to occupy these thrones during the whole period of the Renovation. Consequently they are on these thrones to-day as judges of the twelve tribes of Israel and of the Gentiles as well. And as they have no successors in office, they will continue to judge to the end of time. This fact is practically admitted by the whole

The Great Renovation

Protestant world. When differences arise among them, all agree to refer this matter to the apostles for decision. All parties go to the New Testament and find what the apostles have taught on the subject, and, their words being infallible, the question is forever settled. This is an admission that the apostles are yet on their thrones of judgment in the kingdom of Christ.

That we are correct in recognizing these twelve apostles as being on their thrones in the very commencement of the reign of Christ on earth, we further prove by the following parallel passage. Jesus says to the chosen twelve: "Ye are they which have continued with me in my temptations [trials]. And I appoint unto you a kingdom, as my Father hath appointed unto me; that you may eat and drink at my table in my kingdom, and sit on thrones, judging the twelve tribes of Israel" (Luke 22:28-30). That the thrones here referred to are the same twelve thrones promised in our text to the twelve apostles, no one can deny. And the apostles here are promised thrones, that they may eat and drink at His table in His kingdom while sitting on their thrones and judging the tribes of Israel. This settles the point.

But what are we to understand by *thrones*, in the text? Why, simply the apostolic office. The apostles were chosen by Christ to be His chief ministers, His ambassadors, to the world. Therefore, to sit on twelve thrones in His kingdom was

New Testament Christianity

simply to exercise the power and authority which they had received of Him as His apostles. And this authority was promised to them in the following Scriptures.

Jesus said to them: "As my Father hath sent me, even so send I you. And when he had said this, he breathed on them, and saith unto them, Receive ye the Holy Spirit: whosesoever sins ye remit, they are remitted unto them; and whosesoever sins ye retain, they are retained" (John 20: 21, 22).

Again: Jesus said to Peter and the other apostles with him: "And I will give unto thee the keys of the kingdom of heaven; and whatsoever thou shalt bind on earth shall be bound in heaven, and whatsoever thou shalt loose on earth shall be loosed in heaven" (Matt. 16:19). These Scriptures prove clearly that Jesus gave the apostles plenary authority, as His chief ministers, to judge the twelve tribes of Israel and to remit and to retain sins by teaching the people what they must do to be saved; to bind upon them "the law of the Spirit of life in Christ Jesus," and to loose the twelve tribes from the bondage of the law of Moses.

But it may be objected by some one that, as Judas had by transgression fallen, and lost his apostleship, and hung himself, before the kingdom of Christ was established on the day of Pentecost, there were only eleven apostles present on that

The Great Renovation

day, and that these could sit on eleven thrones only, which would leave one throne vacant. But such an objector seems to have forgotten that Matthias was chosen by divine direction to fill the place made vacant by the fall of Judas. (See Acts 1.) Luke says: "And he was numbered with the eleven apostles." This made the twelve, and of course there was no vacant throne on the beginning-day. And that the selection was sanctioned by the Holy Spirit is proven by the fact that the apostles are ever after referred to as "the twelve." Luke says: "But Peter, standing up with the eleven, lifted up his voice and said" (Acts 2:14). This proves that there were twelve apostles present on Pentecost, as eleven apostles stood up *with* Peter on that day. So, then, the twelve apostles were present on the morning of Pentecost, ready to take their seats on the twelve thrones as soon as they received the power from on high; which power came on them in the baptism of the Holy Spirit. This seated them on their thrones of judgment, in the kingdom of Christ, according to His promise. This brings us to our fourth division.

IV. *"This Judgment of the Twelve Tribes of Israel."*—In what did these judgments consist? It will be borne in mind that there were no others present on Pentecost but children of Israel, nor for some years after, when the Gentiles were called at the house of Cornelius the Gentile (Acts 10).

New Testament Christianity

The term "judgment" means *decision*. We use the term in this sense in common parlance. Some great question is brought before the court, and when the court decides it we call this decision the *"judgment* of the court." The twelve apostles upon their thrones of judgment were the high court of heaven, appointed by the King himself to decide all questions that might arise after the organization of the kingdom of Christ; and the decision of these matters authoritatively is what is meant by "judging the twelve tribes of the children of Israel."

Now let us see what great matters were submitted to them for their judgment or decision:

1. On the morning of Pentecost, when the multitude ran together, greatly wondering at what they saw and heard, "they were in doubt, saying one to another, What meaneth this? Others, mocking, said, These men are full of new wine." The multitude were in ignorance as to the meaning of the wonderful things which they saw and heard. And those who attempted to answer the question were entirely mistaken. These men were not full of wine. But Peter and the eleven other apostles now stood up to render their first judgment after being placed on their thrones. This decision of a very important question is recorded in Acts 2:14-36, and begins thus: "Ye men of Judæa, and all ye that dwell at Jerusalem." And at verse 22 he says: "Ye men of Israel, hear these

The Great Renovation

words." This shows that the apostles understood that their decision of this question was for the men of Israel—the twelve tribes. And the judgment closes, with verse 36, in these words: "Therefore let all the house of Israel know assuredly, that God hath made that same Jesus, whom ye have crucified, both Lord and Christ." This was the first judgment rendered after they received the power from on high and took their seats on their apostolic thrones; and it was an infallible judgment, and settled the question forever that Jesus Christ is the Son of God; and that, though the Jews with wicked hands had crucified Him, yet God had raised Him from the dead. "Therefore being by the right hand of God exalted, and having received of the Father the promise of the Holy Spirit, he hath shed forth this, which ye now see and hear" (v. 33).

2. This first judgment being satisfactory to a great number of the men of Israel present, Luke says: "Now when they heard this, they were pierced in their heart, and said unto Peter and to the rest of the apostles, Men and brethren, what shall we do?" (v. 37). They were now conscious that Jesus, whom they had denied and crucified, is indeed the Son of God and their long-promised Messiah. But they were in ignorance of the conditions of pardon; in fact, these conditions had not yet been made known by the apostles. Here, then, is one of the most important questions ever

asked by mortals, "What shall we do?" This called for a second judgment, or decision, from the men upon the twelve thrones. There they stand together, having the keys of the kingdom of heaven, gifted with plenary inspiration. They knew that their decision would be a finality on earth, and be ratified in heaven, as the conditions of pardon in all the coming ages. With a full knowledge of their responsibility, and of the vast interests involved in their decision, Peter, the chief speaker, announced the judgment of the twelve apostles as follows: "Then Peter said unto them, Repent, and be baptized every one of you in the name of Jesus Christ for the remission of sins: and ye shall receive the gift of the Holy Spirit" (v. 38).

This decision, coming from the inspired men sitting upon these twelve thrones where Jesus had seated them for the very purpose of deciding all these questions for the twelve tribes, forever settled the question of the conditions of pardon. And this decision, being ratified, or bound, in heaven, remains the law of pardon to-day, and will stand on the statute-book of heaven unrepealed until the closing up of Christ's mediatorial reign.

This second judgment rendered by the twelve was also satisfactory to many of the multitude. As Luke tells us: "Then they that gladly received his word were baptized: and the same day there were added unto them about three thousand souls"

The Great Renovation

(v. 41). Peter was the chief speaker on this occasion, as usual; but the decision he rendered was the unanimous judgment of the twelve inspired judges guided by the Holy Spirit. These great questions were therefore *authoritatively* decided for the twelve tribes, and for the whole world as well, and for all time. Other judgments were rendered by the apostles, but of these we can not speak now, further than to say that the apostles are our teachers, and that the words spoken by them are the words of Jesus, and must be believed and obeyed by us.

Reader, are you a Christian? Then we exhort you to stand fast in the liberty of the gospel; read and study the word of God; and never forget that the apostles are yet upon their thrones, and that their decisions, though rendered eighteen hundred years ago, have lost none of their authority. And to those who are not Christians we would say: The conditions of pardon as announced by the apostles at the beginning are the conditions yet. They are plain and simple. And we would exhort you to come to Christ. Delay no longer; now is the accepted time, and this is the day of salvation. Come!

THE WORSHIPING OF JESUS

M. P. HAYDEN

IT is the purpose of this article to present Jesus as an object of worship. Not Jesus risen, ascended, glorified, and crowned King of kings and Lord of lords; but Jesus the Nazarene, the Galilean prophet, who spake as never man spake, who went about doing good, who was a man of sorrows and acquainted with grief.

Before entering upon the investigation, however, it is proper to determine the *meaning* of the word "worship," for upon its meaning the argument very largely depends. The word "worship," in its various forms, is found in the Bible 191 times—113 times in the Old Testament, and seventy-eight times in the New. In the Old Testament it is *always* used to express the reverence and adoration which are due to the Supreme Ruler of the universe, whether the divine honors be paid to the great Jehovah, or wickedly given to the heathen substitute, the dumb idol. In the New Testament it is the translation of several Greek words, only three of which, however, occur more than once or twice. These three are *latruo, sebomai* and *proskuneo. Latruo* means *to work for a re-*

The Worshiping of Jesus

ward, to serve; hence, in respect to God, to serve or worship Him. This word is found twenty-one times, and seventeen times is rendered "serve," four times "worship." *Sebomai* means *to worship, implying* Deity as its object. This word occurs ten times, and six times is rendered "worship" and four times by an equivalent. *Proskuneo,* which is the *important* word in this discussion, occurs sixty times, and is *always* rendered "worship." Its general meaning is *to do reverence or homage* to a superior; with reference to the Deity, *to pay divine honors, to worship, to adore.* In the New Testament, however, it is always used *with the idea of bowing down, kneeling, prostration* (Robinson's "New Testament Greek Lexicon"), and it expresses that homage which our Saviour approves when He says: "The true worshipers shall worship the Father in spirit and in truth: for the Father seeketh such to worship him." It seems, then, from a full examination of the uses of the word "worship," that this word always signifies *the paying of divine honors.*

A single passage from the Old Testament, and one, also, from the New, will aid us in comprehending its meaning. After Solomon's prayer at the dedication of the temple was ended, after the glory of the Lord filled the temple, it is declared that "when all the children of Israel saw how the fire came down and the glory of the Lord upon the house,

New Testament Christianity

they bowed themselves with their faces to the ground upon the pavement, and worshipped and praised the Lord, saying, For he is good; for his mercy endureth for ever" (2 Chron. 7:3). Again, Paul says: "If all prophesy, and there come in one that believeth not, or one unlearned, he is convinced of all, he is judged of all; and thus are the secrets of his heart made manifest; and so, falling down on his face, he will worship God, and report that God is in you of a truth" (1 Cor. 14:24, 25).

One class of persons, while they utterly reject the claims of Jesus in divinity, extol Him as the grandest and loftiest of *human* characters. Another class, although they do not acknowledge Christ's divinity, yet, Nicodemus-like, recognize Him as a divinely inspired man, as a "teacher sent from God." In opposition to both these views, we propose to show that, while on earth, Jesus, "in whom," as Renan expresses it, "is condensed all that is good and lofty of our nature," received divine homage at the hands of His disciples, that He accepted worship *as God,* and, therefore, that He must be *divine.*

I. Before proceeding, however, to the proof of this proposition, it will be proper to premise some principles which will aid us in coming to correct conclusions.

1. It is a demonstrable truth that bad beings, whether human or superhuman, desire and freely accept worship. That wicked men desire and ac-

The Worshiping of Jesus

cept the worship of their fellow-men is evident to any one who understands the proclivities of human nature. Men, in their lust for fame, power and greatness, delight to have their fellows reverence and serve them, and in their *weakness* and *wickedness* approvingly behold their fellows bow down in humble adoration before them. If any instances are needed in proof of this, take the case of Alexander the Great, who drank the contents of Hercules' cup in order that his subjects might reverence and worship him as a god; take the case of Herod, who took the glory to himself when he made an oration to the people, and they declared it was the voice of a god, and not of a man (Acts 12: 20-23); take the cases of the Roman emperors, who, during their *lifetime*, caused their statues to be erected in the principal cities of the empire, and required their subjects to pay homage and sacrifice to them. And that evil spirits desire to be worshiped is well known to all who are familiar with the Holy Scriptures. (See Deut. 32: 15-17; Ps. 106: 35-38; 1 Cor. 10: 18-20.) This proposition will be clearly seen and readily accepted when we consider that Satan, the prince of the demons, especially desired to have Jesus fall down and worship him (Matt. 4: 9).

2. The Scriptures teach that good men and holy angels *refuse* to accept worship. That this is true of good men becomes evident when we consider an incident in the life of each of the apostles Peter

and Paul. When Peter came to the house of Cornelius to tell him words by which he and all his house might be saved, Cornelius fell down at Peter's feet and worshiped him (Acts 10:25). It is not sufficient for an objector to say that the word "him" is supplied from the context, and hence infer that it was not Peter who was worshiped; for the context plainly shows that it *was* Peter whom Cornelius worshiped. Nor does it avail anything for them to say that Cornelius was simply performing, according to the Oriental custom, an act of salutation; for, whatever might have been the purpose of Cornelius, Peter's answer, "Stand up; I myself also am a man," shows that *he* regarded it far otherwise; that *he* considered it to be such homage and adoration *as man has no right to receive*. If, then, it were merely an act of salutation, *much more* would it be wrong for man to accept worship.

An incident in the life of Paul and Barnabas, recorded in the fourteenth chapter of Acts, bears upon this point. When they fled from persecution at Iconium to Lystra, they preached the gospel there; and Paul healed a man who had been a cripple from birth, who never had walked. On account of this, the people of Lycaonia held them in so great veneration that they said, "The gods have come down to us in the likeness of men;" and they brought oxen and garlands, intending to offer sacrifice to the two apostles as to Jupiter and

The Worshiping of Jesus

Mercury. Did Paul and Barnabas quietly and approvingly hear of these proceedings? Far from it. "They rent their clothes, and ran in among the people, crying out, and saying, Sirs, why do ye these things? We also are men of like passions with you, and preach unto you that ye should turn from these vanities unto the living God. And with these words they scarcely restrained the people from sacrificing to them."

That holy angels do not suffer men to worship them is fully proved by an incident recorded in Revelation. (See 19:10, and 22:8, 9.) When John fell at the feet of the angel to worship him, the angel forbade him, telling him to worship God; and this incident is the more impressive from the fact that it occurred twice, with the same response from the angel.

3. The Holy Scriptures expressly and unequivocally teach that God only should be worshiped. They are very explicit upon this point. The passages to which reference has already been made imply this; but there are many others still more definite and unmistakable. A single passage from each of the Testaments must suffice for the present purpose. In the thirty-fourth chapter of Exodus, in the covenant which God, through Moses, made with the children of Israel at Mt. Sinai, He enjoins this command: "Behold, I drive out before thee the Amorite, and the Canaanite, and the Hittite, and the Perizzite, and the Hivite, and the

Jebusite. Take heed to thyself, lest thou make a covenant with the inhabitants of the land whither thou goest, lest it be for a snare in the midst of thee: but ye shall destroy their altars, break their images, and cut down their groves: *for thou shalt worship no other god:* for the Lord, whose name is Jealous, is a jealous God." Again, when Satan offered to Jesus all the kingdoms of this world and their glory if He would fall down and worship Him, the Saviour replied: "It is written, Thou shalt worship the Lord thy God, and him *only* shalt thou *worship* or *serve.*"

II. Since, then, wicked men and demons *covet* the worship of men, since good men and holy angels refuse to be worshiped, and since God, and God *only*, is a proper object of worship, let us examine a few passages in proof of the proposition that Jesus, while on earth, freely and repeatedly accepted worship from men.

1. Matt. 8:2: "And, behold, there came a leper and worshipped him, saying, Lord, if thou wilt, thou canst make me clean."

2. Matt. 9:18: "While he spake these things unto them, behold, there came a certain ruler and worshipped him, saying, My daughter is even now dead; but come and lay thy hand upon her, and she shall live."

3. Matt. 14:33: "Then they that were in the ship came and worshipped him, saying, Of a truth thou art the Son of God."

The Worshiping of Jesus

4. Matt. 15:25: "Then came she [the woman of Canaan] and worshipped him, saying, Lord, help me."

5. Matt. 20:20: "Then came to him the mother of Zebedee's children, with her sons, worshipping him, and desiring a certain thing of him."

6. Mark 5:6, 7: "But when he [the man with an unclean spirit] saw Jesus afar off, he ran and worshipped him, and cried with a loud voice, and said, What have I to do with thee, Jesus, Son of the most high God? I adjure thee by God that thou torment me not."

7. John 9:35-38: "Jesus heard that they had cast him out [*i. e.*, the blind man whose sight Jesus restored]; and when he found him, he said unto him, Dost thou believe on the Son of God? He answered and said, Who is he, Lord, that I might believe on him? And Jesus said unto him, Thou hast both seen him, and it is he that talketh with thee. And he said, Lord, I believe. And he worshipped him."

We have purposely omitted those passages which record the worshiping of Jesus while He was an infant or after he had risen from the dead, deeming it sufficient to consider the subject with reference to Jesus as a public teacher. Let it be observed, further, that if there were but *one instance* of Jesus' accepting worship, it might be argued that he was *led into it by mistake*, or "in time of temptation *fell away*," though this would be *admitting that Jesus had sinned;* but no such plea can be made, in view of the repeated instances that are found.

How striking the contrast between the conduct of Jesus, on the one hand, and that of Peter and Paul, on the other! When Cornelius offered to worship Peter, Peter forbade him, saying that he was but a man. When the people of Lycaonia were about to offer sacrifice to Paul and Barnabas, with what promptness and seeming frenzy did they attempt to check it! With what gestures and rending of clothes and vociferations did they strive to dissuade the people from accomplishing their purpose, and with what difficulty did they succeed! Thus these apostles, instructed in the Jewish law and in the teachings of their Master, *promptly checked* any attempt to worship them. How was it with the Master Himself? Worship is offered Him under circumstances which preclude the possibility of its being anything else than the paying of divine honors. How does the Master receive it? Does He forbid it, as did Peter and Paul and the angel spoken of in Revelation? Does He refuse to receive it, assigning the same reason that He did when He refused to render it to Satan? He does nothing of the kind. On the contrary, we find that Jesus repeatedly accepted worship, without any sign or word of disapprobation; and to our mind it is inconceivable that these writers, Jews as they were, should record these

The Worshiping of Jesus

acts of worship with no indications of disapproval, and not thereby express their sanction of them, and also the sanction of the Saviour Himself; for, if Jesus had disapproved this worship, He would have expressed such disapproval; if He had expressed such disapproval, the writers of the Gospels must have known it; if they knew it, they would have recorded it. The very fact, therefore, that such disapproval is wanting in the record, proves that the conduct was *approved* both by the writers and by Jesus Himself.

III. Since, then, Jesus did freely and repeatedly accept divine homage from men, the inquiry arises, How does this fact affect His character and claims? In the light of the principles which were laid down in the beginning, He can not be a *good being at all* unless He is more than a man. He must even be superior to the angels of God. We are driven to the conclusion that He is either a wicked person or a divine person. There is no middle ground —no place for compromise. Either He was a proper object of worship—that is, was the Son of God as well as the Son of man—or else He deserved to die the death of a malefactor for accepting worship. "He was worthy of worship or He was worthy of death!" He has done that which is sinful for men or angels to do. Hence, if it was lawful for Him to do it, He must have been superior to men and angels; that is, He must have been God Himself. If He was not superior to men and angels, then He was guilty of the *basest crime known to the Jewish law*, that of accepting worship due to God alone. Hence, if this last supposition be true, He was indeed a malefactor, an impious impostor and blasphemer, and the Jewish Sanhedrim was right in declaring Him worthy of death.

Was Jesus, then, a wicked, blasphemous person? Was He an impious impostor? It is not our purpose to argue this question at length, nor is it necessary; for there is no class of persons—indeed, scarcely a single person—in this age of the world, that affirms it. Infidels vie with Christians in extolling and honoring Jesus, in glorifying His humanity. Strauss says, "Jesus Christ is at the head of all men;" that is, in respect to morality, virtue and holiness. Also hear Renan: "Let us, then, place the person of Jesus on the summit of human grandeur." "In Him is condensed all that is good and lofty in our nature." "Whatever may be the surprises of the future, Jesus will never be surpassed. His worship will grow young without ceasing: His legend will call forth tears without end; His sufferings will melt the noblest hearts; all ages will proclaim that among the *sons* of men there is none born greater than Jesus." The author of *"Ecce Homo"* has a chapter on "The Enthusiasm of Humanity," which means, as explained by the chapter itself, a glowing love **for man** *as* **man.** In this chapter, speaking of the

The Worshiping of Jesus

human race, he says: "Of this race Christ Himself was a member; and to this day is it not the best answer to all blasphemers of the species, the best consolation when our sense of its degradation is keenest, that a human brain was behind His forehead and a human heart beating in His breast, and that within the whole creation of God nothing more elevated or more attractive has yet been found than He?" Also, in the concluding chapter is found this sentence: "The story of Christ's life will always remain the one record in which the moral perfection of man stands revealed in its root and its unity." Finally, I quote a sentence or two from Rousseau. Speaking of Jesus, he thus exclaims: "What sweetness, what purity in His manners! . . . what elevation in His maxims! . . . what empire over His passions! What prejudices, what blindness must they have who dare to draw a comparison between the son of Sophronicus and the son of Mary! What distance is there between the one and the other! Where could Jesus have found among His countrymen, that elevated and pure morality of which He alone furnished both the precept and the example?" We have made these quotations, not for the purpose of indorsing the statements of the writers, but for the purpose of showing that leading infidel or rationalistic writers bear the most decided testimony to the pure morality and elevated character of Jesus Christ as set forth in the Scriptures.

If, then, such be the testimony of infidels, if no class of persons can be found who affirm His wicked character, who justify the decision of the Sanhedrim, we may safely conclude that Jesus was *upright and holy*, and, therefore, *divine*.

We trust, then, in a *divine* Saviour, in Him who has life in Himself even as the Father hath life in Himself (John 5:26); we trust in Him whom angels worship (Heb. 1:6), and at whose "name every knee shall bow, of things in heaven, and of things on earth, and of things under the earth, and every tongue confess that Jesus Christ is Lord, to the glory of God the Father" (Phil. 2: 10, 11).

BAPTISM FOR REMISSION OF SINS IS JUSTIFICATION BY FAITH

J. S. SWEENEY

THE advocates of the doctrine of baptism for the remission of sins have no trouble in finding many passages of Scripture that not only seem to teach it in their most natural meaning, but also seem incapable of any other honest interpretation. Some passages teach so expressly, and others by fair and seemingly unavoidable inference. And it is clear, also, that those who deny this doctrine labor under a felt difficulty in their efforts to dis pose of these passages.

It comes within the purpose of this article merely to recite the most of the passages that are nearly always brought into the discussions of the doctrine in hand.

Mark 1: 6: "John did baptize in the wilderness, and preach the baptism of repentance for the remission of sins."

Luke 7: 29: "All the people that heard him, and the publicans, justified God, being baptized with the baptism of John. But the Pharisees and lawyers rejected the counsel of God against themselves, not being baptized of him."

New Testament Christianity

John 3:5: "Except a man be born of water and the Spirit, he cannot enter the kingdom of God."

Mark 16:16: "He that believeth and is baptized shall be saved."

Acts 2:38: "Repent, and be baptized every one of you in the name of Jesus Christ for the remission of sins."

Acts 22:16: "And now why tarriest thou? Arise, and be baptized, and wash away thy sins, calling on the name of the Lord."

Rom. 6:3, 4: "Know ye not that so many of us as were baptized into Jesus Christ, were baptized into his death? Therefore we are buried with him by baptism into death: that like as Christ was raised up from the dead by the glory of the Father, even so we also should walk in newness of life."

Eph. 5:25, 26: "Christ also loved the church, and gave himself for it, that he might sanctify and cleanse it with the washing of water by the word."

Tit. 3:5: "He saved us by the washing of regeneration and the renewing of the Holy Ghost."

1 Pet. 3:21: "The like figure whereunto even baptism doth also now save us."

These passages, just as they read in the Common Version of the Scriptures, seem to teach baptism for the remission of sins about as clearly as anything else is taught in the New Testament; and, indeed, as clearly as anything could be taught

Justification by Faith

in language. So that if they do not put the matter beyond question, it is simply because it is impossible for language to do so. Moreover, the result of translation and criticism of these passages, which the controversy has given rise to, has not in the least weakened the cause of the advocates of the doctrine, while it is more than sustained by the history of the church in all ages.

What, then, the question naturally arises, is the reason this doctrine is so earnestly opposed by so many Protestants, and its advocates counted as unevangelical for holding it? It is not unreasonable that a new doctrine, sustained only by questionable inferences from Scripture and analogical reasoning, should be opposed; but why should one, taught in every century of the church's history, taught expressly in the Scriptures, and sustained by the fairest inferences from Scriptures and the strongest analogies, be so generally counted unevangelical by so large a portion of Protestant Christians? It will be attempted in this brief paper to show what the difficulty is.

The doctrine of "justification by faith" has been so conspicuously and so generally taught by Protestants since the Lutheran Reformation that it has come to be styled "the great doctrine of the Reformation," and is made a sort of test of Protestant orthodoxy; so that whatever teaching or practice seems to conflict with justification by faith is, for that reason, condemned. Nor is this doctrine to be questioned in this article. It is certainly Protestant, and as certainly a New Testament doctrine. This being herein assumed and so generally received and insisted on, it becomes needless to recite any of the many passages that so teach. And here it is that the trouble with which the Disciples of the nineteenth century, who have conspicuously taught baptism for remission, have had to contend, has arisen. In the estimation of many, "baptism for remission of sins" seems to conflict with "justification by faith." Hence the former is condemned as untrue. The argument against it that is really most potent is substantially about this: Whatever teaching conflicts with justification by faith is unscriptural; but the doctrine of baptism for the remission of sins does so conflict, therefore the doctrine of baptism for the remission of sins is unscriptural. It may be justly said that no one has ever discussed the doctrine of baptism for remission, negatively, without experiencing much difficulty in disposing of the Scriptures adduced in its support, even to his own satisfaction. This is not meant to apply, of course, to the ignorant and bigoted partisan, but to the scholarly and fair-minded Protestant. But may not both doctrines be Scriptural? Is there any such conflict, when both are fully understood, as is generally assumed? Men are apt to see conflict too soon. Many truths have been condemned, on this ground, that were really

Justification by Faith

in harmony with all other truths, the only difficulty being that the harmony was not seen. This weakness of men has been developed in all departments of investigation. And this fact should cause men to think.

Now, there are two conceivable methods of justifying a sinner. Justification by law is entirely out of the question. No sinner can ever be justified by mere law. It is the nature of law to approve the obedient and condemn the sinner. It will be admitted that, should any one render perfect obedience to law, he would be just. He would be just before the law, but not a *justified sinner*. He would be approved before the law, because he had not violated it. Should any one render perfect obedience to moral law, he would be just before God. But this is not the kind of justification the New Testament treats of. The justification of a sinner, or one condemned by law, is the problem it grapples with. So that justification of a sinner by law is not conceivable. Justification by *works* is one method. The Jews supposed that in the ceremonial works of their law there was something really meritorious or compensative in its nature, affording the worker somewhat of merit or compensation to set over against his sins, to go to his credit against past delinquencies. Such works were called "works of righteousness." Romanists had at the time of the Reformation, and some have yet possibly, some such notion of works of penance.

This, as was said, is a conceivable method of justifying a sinner. It assumes for the works done a meritorious and compensative character. The works of the Jewish law had a value as types and shadows of good things to come, which they mistook for a real intrinsic value. This mistake led them to lay hold of the shadow and reject the substance; to hold on to the type and reject the antitype. This was the difficulty with which the apostles, and Paul most conspicuously, had to contend. Justification by this method was justification without Christ. It rejected Christ, who, in fact, gave all the value to them that there was in all the gifts and sacrifices of the law of Moses. This was what was in the mind of Paul when he excluded "deeds of the law," or "works of righteousness," from justification; holding that whoever would be justified by the deeds of the law merely, would be profited nothing by Christ.

The other, which is the New Testament method, is one of grace, mercy, pardon. It justifies one who is condemned by law, and has nothing he can do or offer as a compensation. It is, therefore, opposed to the method of work. The condemned sinner, whether Jew or Gentile, is justified freely by the grace that is in Christ Jesus, and all ground of boasting save in the cross of Christ is excluded. By His death Jesus procured justification, bearing therein Himself the sins of the world. But the question meets us here, Why is justification on this

Justification by Faith

method of grace, or mercy, said to be by faith? This is so because faith is the means by which we appropriate and enjoy that which was procured by the sacrifice of Christ. Faith is not a work of merit, or of righteousness, in the sense before indicated. Faith takes hold of Jesus and His sacrifice, and rests in Him. Faith lays hold of and claims the grace of God in Christ Jesus. "Therefore," says the apostle, "it is of faith that it might be by grace." Faith lays hold of and appropriates what only the death of Jesus could procure. Faith is itself, in one sense, a work. It is a work of the mind. But it is not a work of the kind that the apostle excludes from justification. It has in it no idea of merit or compensation, but exactly the opposite—that of trust in and reliance upon another. For the same reason, also, *deeds* of faith are not excluded from justification. Not only so, but they, like faith, are necessary to justification. Deeds of faith partake of this character. Indeed, they are but faith expressed, or actualized. Baptism is simply an act of faith. It is that act under the gospel in which faith first actualizes or expresses itself. It is, therefore, of faith, and in all proper classifications belongs on that side. So the apostle Paul classifies it in the following passage: "Not by works of righteousness which we have done, but according to his mercy he saved us, by the washing of regeneration and the renewing of the Holy Ghost" (Tit. 3:5). Here, "works of righteousness'' are set on the one side, and baptism on the other; these excluded from our salvation, and the other connected with it. Baptism is an act of faith, and not only does not belong with works of righteousness, but is exactly opposed to them. Now, that baptism is, under the gospel, that act in which faith becomes an actuality and is expressed, is quite clear to the unbiased mind from the commission of our Lord to the apostles, and from their practice under it; but for the benefit of another class of readers, it may not be amiss to cite here a few extracts from an eminent and a standard theologian, with those who advocate justification by faith as opposed to baptism for remission of sins—Richard Watson:

"The design of this institution . . . was to *express faith* in Christ, on the part of those who were to be baptized" (*Watson's Dictionary*, p. 130).

"To the covenant in this new form he also requires a visible and formal act of acceptance, which act, when *expressive of the required faith*, makes us parties to the covenant, and entitles us, through the faithfulness of God, to its benefits: 'He that *believeth* and is baptized shall be saved'" (*Institutes*, p. 622).

Again, commenting on 1 Pet. 3:21, he says:

"It is thus that we see how St. Peter preserves the correspondence between the act of Noah in preparing the ark as an act of faith by which he

Justification by Faith

was justified, and the act of submitting to Christian baptism, which is also obviously an *act of faith* in order to the remission of sins" (*Institutes*, p. 624).

Moral law is addressed to the moral sense in man, and obedience thereto is morality; while positive law is addressed to faith in man, and obedience is piety. Adam was put under positive law in the garden, when the fruit of the tree of knowledge of good and evil was forbidden. There was no apparent reason why that fruit should not be eaten, only that God had forbidden it. This was, therefore, a trial of Adam's faith, a test of his piety. And so it was in the case of Abraham, when he was commanded to offer up his son Isaac. When he obeyed God in the thing that doubtless, to him, seemed not good, that seemed even to conflict with moral law, with the law of nature; when he obeyed God in the thing commanded, his faith triumphed gloriously; "and the scripture was fulfilled which saith, Abraham believed God, and it was imputed to him for righteousness" (Jas. 2:23). And Abraham was made the example and father of the faithful. We are justified now on the same principle that Abraham was. His faith was made actual, "made perfect," by doing the thing God commanded: our faith is made perfect by doing what Jesus has commanded us. Faith may express itself differently; that is, in different acts, that being varied by what is commanded. But the principle is the same. We are justified on precisely the same principle that Abraham was. He believed God, perfected or actualized his faith in doing what God commanded him, and was justified. We believe, now, our faith is expressed or perfected in doing the things God has commanded us, and we are justified.

Our faith in the Lord is brought out in doing just what He had commanded. The sinner now who seeks to be justified has not to offer Isaac, or to bring his gift to the altar, but to be baptized. Baptism without faith is nothing. It has in it no merit or compensation for justification. It is what it is because it is expressive of faith in the Lord. He who believes and will not be baptized has not actual, living faith. His faith is as a thing unborn, as an idea unexpressed; it is dead, being alone.

But one is ready to say, What of the person who believes, but, being honestly in error as to baptism, fails to do what the Lord has commanded—fails really to be baptized? Perhaps no one is authorized to say what of such a one. He certainly fails to express his faith in the Lord's appointed way. That, indeed, is assumed in the case; it would not be safe to say that he does not express faith at all, if he does what he honestly thinks the Lord has commanded. The case is a supposable one, it is true, but not one upon which

Justification by Faith

any man is authorized to speak, only to deliver his opinion. It is generally held that one is not guilty of crime unless he has *intentionally* done what is criminal. One obeys the law when he intentionally does what it requires, and disobeys it when he intentionally refuses to comply with its requirements. The case supposed falls under the head of neither obedience nor disobedience of the Lord. It is a case wherein there was a good intention resulting in a wrong action. It is a case, therefore, not justly to be tried in the court of law, but falls more properly into the divine equity, and that is a court mortals are not licensed to practice in.

But extraordinary cases do not set aside a general rule, and we should not lose time on them. The fact is, however Abel, or Abraham, or anybody else before Christ, or during His personal ministry, might have expressed his faith, the commissions make it the duty of the believer to *be baptized*. Baptism, therefore, is simply actualized faith. Baptism for remission of sins is justification by faith. Baptism is faith acting and appropriating justification to the believer. And hence the seeming conflict between baptism for the remission of sins and justification by faith is only a seeming one; and the two classes of passages in Scripture, which have to some seemed somewhat in conflict, are in fact in perfect harmony.

THE ROYAL PRIESTHOOD

JOHN A. BROOKS

THE priestly function is not peculiar to any nation or age. Through the mediation of the priest, the human heart has ever intuitively sought to bridge the chasm between the holy One and fallen man. No effort of genius has ever taken, or can ever take, from the conscience of humanity the necessity of this mediation. It will not avail the skeptic to say it is a relic of the barbarous ages; for, alike with the roving tribes of Asia, and the ignorant hordes of Africa, the most enlightened minds of Europe and America have felt this truth and acknowledged its necessity. The false philosophies, sciences and civilizations of those ages have long since been discarded; but the combined efforts of infidelity, adorned by the greatest genius, and wielding the logic and rhetoric of every age, have only served to deepen this universal conviction.

Whence, then, the priestly office? Human wisdom could not have originated it; but, when once revealed, the necessities of man's fallen nature impelled him, intuitively and forever, to appropriate it. How one sinful creature can become the

The Royal Priesthood

sanctified and accepted mediator between his fellows and the just and holy One is far beyond the ken of human vision. But when that holy One, by His own will and ceremonial law, sanctifies to Himself a holy priesthood, the heart intuitively accepts it as the divine basis of human redemption, and hence the only hope of a lost and fallen world.

The first intimation of a priesthood that we have in the word of God is in connection with him whose order was destined to become illustrious throughout the cycles of time. Melchisedec is called "king of Salem, and priest of the most high God"—a royal priest to whom even Abraham paid tithes. Again, in the days of Joseph, we read of Potipherah, priest of On, or Heliopolis, in Egypt; and of the priests generally, as a distinct and greatly honored class in that country. Afterward, we read of "Jethro, priest of Midian," who so kindly received and entertained the future lawgiver of Israel. During all this period, we find no divine statute consecrating any family or class to the priestly order. Nor was the sacerdotal office reckoned among the rights of primogeniture, as some suppose. These the Scripture itself limits to pre-eminence among the brethren, and a double portion of the inheritance (1 Chron. 5: 1-4). In the patriarchal age, while no one was forbidden the altar, yet the father, by common consent, and of right, as the head of the family, stood before God and interceded in behalf of his children. As families grew into nations, kings, as national heads, and for the same reasons, sometimes, and especially upon great festive occasions, performed priestly duties. But we are not to conclude, from all this, that God did not signify His choice and divine acceptance of His faithful priests, else whence the glory and renown of Melchisedec, not only among his own people, but among all the nations of Asia? By His providences, God had marked him as the "blessed of the Lord," "the priest of the most high God." During this dispensation every man could build his own altar, and offer thereon his sacrifices. There was no tabernacle, with its consecrated altar, upon which all sacrifices must be offered. The humble worshiper of God might build his altar upon Ararat, in the grove of Mamre, or in the vale of Shechem, and offer there his sacrifices.

But, in the lapse of time, the tabernacle is spread, and the brazen altar erected. God has chosen a people from among the nations of the earth, and a new order of priesthood must be consecrated, in harmony with the divine economy now established. Jehovah proposed now to dwell in person among His people, to manifest His presence in the house to be built for Him. It was proper that the house in which God should dwell should be built in accordance with His own designs; hence Moses built it exactly after the pattern shown him in the mount. But now that the tabernacle

The Royal Priesthood

is set up, the glory of God is descended upon it, and His Shekinah is within, whose feet shall now tread those sacred precincts, consecrated by the glory of His presence? Evidently only His chosen and consecrated priesthood. Of the twelve tribes, He chose that of Levi to minister to Him, and for the people, in sacred things; and, from this tribe, the family of Aaron to officiate in the tabernacle.

It is foreign to our present purpose to institute any inquiry as to the reason of Jehovah's choice. Suffice it to say that the same God who called Israel from the nations, also called out of Israel this tribe and family, and consecrated them to the priestly office.

To this priestly order, then, as the type of another and more enduring one, we invite attention for a time.

First: *Their qualifications.* The purity, perfection and holiness of their calling were indicated by all the outward and bodily ceremonies of the law concerning the priesthood. Everything tended to impress the fact that they were separated from the world—set apart to God. 1. They were to have no bodily defilements whatever. Only a perfect and unblemished body could stand before the Lord. 2. They were to serve in the tabernacle only during the strength and vigor of manhood. Neither the feebleness of childhood, nor old age, was tolerated within its holy precincts. 3. They were to avoid every occasion of bodily defilement, such as contact with the dead, except in cases of near relationship; cutting and disfiguring the beard, as in times of mourning; marrying a woman of bad fame, or one that had been divorced; and the high priest, as being in his own person the most sacred, was still further restricted, in that he was not to defile himself even for his father and mother, and should marry only a virgin. 4. Their garments of white linen, promoting cleanliness, as the use of them always does, indicated purity of life; hence, the white garments of the heavenly inhabitants are, in the language of revelation, expressly declared to mean "the righteousness of saints." For this reason, also, the pure white robes worn by the high priest on the day of atonement are called the "garments of holiness," and upon his mitre was written, "Holiness to the Lord."

Second: *Their consecration.* They were taken to the door of the tabernacle, and their bodies washed in the waters of the laver, the priestly garments put upon them, and their heads anointed with oil—the washing in the cleansing element of water again indicating purity of soul and life, and the anointing with oil declaring them to be chosen of God and consecrated to His service. But all these external purifications only served to reveal to them the immeasurable distance between themselves and the holy One, in whose presence they were about to stand. They were now, in some degree at least, prepared to comprehend the

The Royal Priesthood

necessity for the blood of atonement. This again was provided in such a manner as not only to impress them with its necessity, but also with a vivid consciousness of the absolute purity of those who would serve at the altar of Jehovah. "For first of all there was presented, for the expiation of sin, the bullock of sin-offering, of which nothing save a little fat was offered (on the altar), because the offerers were not yet worthy to have any gift or offering accepted by God. But after they had been so far purged, they slew the burnt-offering to God, which was wholly laid upon the altar. And after this came a sacrifice, like a peace-offering (which was wont to be divided between God, the priest, and the offerers), showing that they were now so far received into favor with God that they might eat at His table." The blood of the victim was then sprinkled upon the altar and the priest, indicating that God accepted the life (in the blood) of the animal slain, instead of his own; the blood also was sprinkled upon his right ear, hand and foot, consecrating the ear to hear the commands of God, the hand to extend offerings unto Him, the foot to tread the holy precincts of His court, and hasten in the ways of His righteousness. Now, to complete the consecration, the oil and blood, commingled, were sprinkled upon him, signifying that their consecrating and cleansing influence would ever be present with him, so long as he obeyed the commandments of God. Thus, every ceremonial act of consecration displays the holiness of the infinite One, and, at the same time, discovers the woeful depths of human degradation. Here, too, the boundless grace and mercy of God are ever present in the blood of atonement, but only attained through a priesthood consecrated in every respect as the infinite Father has directed.

Third: *The duties of the priesthood.* The tribe of Levi received no lot with the other tribes, but was wholly consecrated to the work of the Lord. To this tribe, while sojourning in the wilderness, was given in charge the tabernacle. Around it they encamped at night, and bore its various parts when traveling in the day. When, at last, they became located in Judea, it was their duty to prepare all things necessary for the temple worship, and to teach the law to the people, among whom they were located, and by whom they were supported. But to the priests were confined the duties of the sanctuary. They were the mediators between God and the people. Theirs was the duty to offer the various offerings of the ceremonial law, to officiate at the morning and evening sacrifices, and, upon the occasion of all national festivals, to keep in order all things about the temple, and unfold the law to the people. (Lev. 10:11; 33:10; Mal. 2:7.) The high priest alone entered the Most Holy Place once a year, to make atonement for the sins of the people.

The Royal Priesthood

To the most casual observer there are, in the Jewish priesthood, evident imperfections. The high priest himself needed a mediator. With his people he had sinned, and, like them, he needed a sin-offering. Separated from the people, a priest unto God, and yet himself in need of a priest. Propitiating the divine favor in behalf of Israel, and yet himself standing in the presence of God, only through the boundless grace of His infinite love. The offerings, too, were equally imperfect. No philosophy, human or divine, can demonstrate how it is possible for the blood of bulls and of goats to take away sins, or how the blood of an innocent victim can propitiate Deity. But these are imperfections that must ever attach to all merely human priesthoods. The divine wisdom alone can supply the deficiency. The consciousness of this fact laid hold upon the sweet Psalmist of Israel when he said: "The Lord said unto my Lord, Sit thou on my right hand, until I make thine enemies thy footstool. The Lord shall send the rod of thy strength out of Zion: rule thou in the midst of thine enemies. Thy people shall be willing in the day of thy power, in the beauties of holiness from the womb of the morning: thou hast the dew of thy youth. The Lord hath sworn, and will not repent. Thou art a priest for ever after the order of Melchisedec." In this, and other Jewish Scriptures, a new order of priesthood is plainly indicated. Still, strange to say, this pretension to the priestly function is the very rock over which the Jews stumbled when they crucified the Lord of glory, and which ever after proved a stumbling-block to many Hebrew Christians.

Against these claims of the Christ, two grave objections presented themselves to the Jewish mind: 1. Coming of Judah's tribe, how can he be a priest of Aaron's order? 2. If not of that order, then His is a new one, and without authority. Paul, in his Epistle to the Hebrews, meets these difficulties. He frankly admits that Christ could not belong to the Levitical priesthood; for "he sprang from Juda, of which tribe Moses spoke nothing concerning the priesthood" (Heb. 7:14). Besides, if, on earth, He could not minister at that altar, seeing there is a distinct order appointed by the law, and this order is taken from another tribe (Hebrews 8), by what right, then, does He claim to be a priest? By divine right—the call of God Himself, the apostle replies. "No one takes this honor to himself, but he that is called by God, as Aaron also was called. So also the Christ did not take upon himself the honor of becoming a high priest; but he gave him this honor who said to him, Thou art my Son, this day have I begotten thee. As he says also in another place, Thou art a priest for ever after the order of Melchisedec" (Heb. 5:4-6). Again: "He is made a priest, not according to the law of fleshly commandment, but according to the power of an endless life. For

The Royal Priesthood

he testifies, Thou art a priest for ever after the order of Melchisedec'' (Heb. 7:16, 17). Again: ''He is made such by the oath of the living God, which cannot be said of Aaron's order.'' Thus, from their own Scriptures, he demonstrates the necessity for another order of priesthood. These Scriptures find their fulfillment in Christ, and the order in which He is high priest.

This new order, while in many particulars it resembles the former, yet in its essential characteristics is altogether superior to it. It is a royal priesthood. This high priest is possessed of power and authority. We no longer listen for the sound of the bells upon His robes to assure us that He lives while standing in the midst of the *Shekinah* of God. His is an unchangeable priesthood, and He lives and abides forever to make intercession for the saints.

Made a priest by the "oath of God," and "the power of an endless life," He entered upon His official duties, not because of lineal descent, but because of the eternal fitness of things. In His person the necessary defects of the former priesthood are done away. He alone of all born of women is spotlessly pure. He alone can stand with unveiled face in the *sanctum sanctorum* of the universe. Sinless, He needs no sin-offering for Himself, no priest to stand between Him and His Father in heaven. What a glorious high priest is this—our Brother. tempted as we are tempted, and yet without sin; and, also, our Redeemer and King, who lives and abides forever! Nor does He enter the Most Holy Place without the blood of atonement; yet, not the blood of bulls and goats, which can not cleanse from sin, but by His own precious blood, shed for the remission of the sins of many. Thus the divine wisdom has presented a perfect mediation through the son of Mary—the Son of God—as human as His mother, as divine as His Father—a priest forever after the order of Melchisedec.

Now, since in Him we "live, and move, and have our being," and our "life is hid with Christ in God," we, too, are royal priests with Him; having been consecrated and brought near to God, "an holy priesthood, to offer up spiritual sacrifices, acceptable to God by Jesus Christ," we are constituted in Him "a chosen race, a royal priesthood." O Christ, Thou art He who "hast redeemed us to God by thy blood, out of every tribe, and tongue, and people, and nation; and hast made us to our God kings and priests, and we shall reign on the earth."

To conclude the argument, the apostle declares that to have been simply the type of this, the services of the Jewish tabernacle only "copies" of the things in the heavens. To this typical relation we invite attention for a time:

1. As the people of Israel could approach their God only through the mediation of Aaron and his

The Royal Priesthood

sons, so now we can only come to God through Jesus the Christ. Thus has God ordained; and the result of Korah's rebellion should teach the Roman priest the infamy of his pretension, and the inevitable doom that awaits him. Christ is the one Mediator, and no man can come to God but through Him.

2. The sacrifices, consecrations, garments, purifications by water and blood were all typical of the personal holiness of Christ, only His was not acquired, but original, inherent holiness. He was the "lamb without spot or blemish," covered from His youth with a spotless garment of righteousness.

3. The high priest, entering the Most Holy Place with the names of the twelve tribes upon his breast, typified Christ entering heaven, bearing His people upon His heart before the throne of God.

4. The clear and perfect revelation of the Father's will was prefigured by the *Urim* and *Thummim* of the Jewish high priest, "through which the priesthood gave auricular decisions in regard to the things of God." In short, the covenant of Sinai was typical of a better covenant, and all the ceremonies of the tabernacle service "copies of the things in the heavens" (Hebrews 9 and 10).

We conclude, then, with great confidence, that the consecration and anointing of the Aaronic priesthood was typical of the consecration and anointing of the Christian priesthood. It would be strange, indeed, if it were not so. That which preceded and which came after the anointing was typical; then, why not the anointing itself? Indeed, the "various immersions" spoken of by the apostle in this chapter constitute a part of the consecrating ceremony.

We have already invited attention to the order of consecration peculiar to the Jewish priesthood. They were washed in the laver, their garments put upon them, their heads anointed with oil, the sacrifices offered, and the consecration completed by the blood of sprinkling.

For the fulfillment of all righteousness, whether exhibited in positive commands, or in the shadows of the law, the body of Christ was washed in the laver of baptism, and, the heavens opening, He was anointed Prophet, Priest and King by the descending Spirit of God. Unlike Aaron, He needed no sprinkling of blood upon Himself. One with the Father, He had no divine favor to propitiate. Sinless, He had no guilt to cleanse, but with His own blood He entered the Most Holy Place once for all, to make atonement for the human family. Christ was anointed Priest at His baptism.

Against these conclusions the following objections will be urged:

1. An objection based upon Heb. 7:11-14: "If, then, there had been a perfect expiation by means

of the Levitical priesthood (for with reference to it the people received the law), what further need was there that another priest should be raised up after the order of Melchisedec, and not be called after the order of Aaron? It is evident that, when the priesthood is changed, there is of necessity also a change of the law. For he of whom these things are said belongs to another tribe, from which no one attended upon the altar. For it is very clear that our Lord sprang from Juda, of which tribe Moses spoke nothing concerning the priesthood.'' There can be no valid objection based upon this passage. Some of the Jewish Christians taught that the law of Moses had not been abrogated, and was therefore binding still upon all the followers of Christ. Paul meets this declaration by pointing to their own Scriptures, which declared that God would raise up a "new order" of priesthood. That Christ was a priest, they themselves acknowledged; but that He could not belong to the Levitical priesthood was evident, for He came from the wrong tribe, but is, rather, a royal priest after the order of Melchisedec. Hence, the priesthood being changed, there is of necessity a change of the law. This is the logical conclusion of the apostle. That He was a priest *then* is conclusively demonstrated. This, and no more, upon that question.

2. Heb. 8:1-7: "Now, concerning the things that have been spoken, the principal point is this:

New Testament Christianity

We have such a high priest, who has taken his seat at the right hand of the throne of the Majesty in the heavens; a minister of the holy places, and of the true tabernacle, which the Lord pitched, and not man. For every high priest is appointed to offer gifts and sacrifices: wherefore, it is necessary that this one also have something which he may offer. For if he were on earth, he could not be a priest; because there are priests who offer gifts according to the law: and these serve the copy and shadow of heavenly things, as Moses was admonished of God when he was about to make the tabernacle. See now, says he, that you make all things according to the pattern shown you in the mount. But now he has obtained a more excellent ministry, inasmuch as he is the Mediator of a better covenant, which is established with reference to better promises.''

The apostles, in this context, declared the tabernacle erected by Moses to be ''the copy and shadow of heavenly things''; that Christ serves ''a minister of the holy places, and of the true tabernacle which the Lord pitched, and not man.'' He does not serve in the former, and if He were on earth He could not be a priest in that line and serve in that tabernacle. But why not? Because there are already priests that offer gifts according to the law. This Christ could not do if on earth, for, as we have already seen, He does not come from the right tribe. Hence the conclusion: He has obtained

The Royal Priesthood

a more excellent ministry, inasmuch as He is the Mediator of a better covenant, which is established with reference to better promises. This is clearly the logical import of the apostle's argument, and beyond this we can not legitimately press the interpretation.

3. Heb. 1:9: "Thou hast loved righteousness, and hated iniquity; therefore God, thy God, hath anointed thee with the oil of gladness above thy fellows." This prophecy the apostle applies directly to the Saviour; and, indeed, it is applicable to none other. If it be said that the anointing was completed even when the prophecy was first uttered, the conclusion is fatal to the objector. If, as it most certainly was, the anointing was yet a future event, then this passage does not throw any light upon the time and place of the anointing, and hence the objection based upon it is invalid.

4. Acts 2:36: "Therefore, let all the house of Israel know assuredly that God hath made this same Jesus, whom you crucified, both Lord and Christ."

This passage simply forms the conclusion of a grand argument in demonstration of the Messiahship, which the apostle has just completed, but the time and place of the anointing the context does not determine.

5. Finally, it is urged that He did not begin at once to officiate as priest, and could not until

the Jewish sacrifices had ceased. This we readily grant, but the conclusion does not affect the fact that He was anointed priest at His baptism. Time, indeed, elapsed between the anointing and the beginning of the official work, but the Old Testament Scriptures abound in illustrations entirely similar. The Lord sent Elijah from Horeb, on the way to the wilderness of Damascus, to anoint Hazael to be king over Syria; Jehu, the son of Nimshi, to be king over Israel; and Elisha to be prophet in his stead. Elijah faithfully fulfilled the commands of the Lord, but long years supervened before either of these anointed ones began his official work. It was at least seven years after this before Elijah was taken up to heaven, and left his mantle with Elisha; and it was, probably, twice that time before the death of the kings of Syria and Israel gave room for Hazael and Jehu to assume the scepters of their respective kingdoms. Long years of trials, likewise, intervened after the son of Jesse was anointed king, before the shepherd of Bethlehem assumed the royal purple. So with his illustrious antitype, "the Prince of the house of David." He was anointed at His baptism, but three years of bitter trial had passed away when He began His work as priest; and the rending of the veil indicated the abolishment of the Levitical priesthood.

In confirmation of this proposition, we submit the following proofs:

The Royal Priesthood

1. Luke 4:17-21: "And the volume of Isaiah the prophet was given to him: and when he had unrolled the volume, he found the place where it was written: The Spirit of the Lord is upon me; because he hath anointed me to preach the gospel to the poor, he hath sent me to heal the brokenhearted; to proclaim liberty to the captives, and recovery of sight to the blind; to set free the oppressed; to proclaim the acceptable year of the Lord. . . . And he began to say to them, This scripture which you have heard is this day fulfilled."

Here the Master declares Himself to be already anointed to do a work which necessarily involved the priestly function. That is, "to heal the brokenhearted; to proclaim liberty to the captives, and recovery of sight to the blind; to set free the oppressed;" but without the shedding of blood there is no remission of sins, no such thing as setting free the oppressed or giving liberty to the captives. Hence, we conclude, with positive certainty, that He had, in this early period of His ministry, been anointed to offer the sacrifice of atonement, to shed His blood for the remission of the sins of many; but only a priest can accomplish this work.

2. Acts 10:36-38: "The word which he sent to the sons of Israel, preaching peace by Jesus Christ [He is the Lord of all]: that word, you know, which was published through the whole of Judæa,

beginning from Galilee, after the immersion that John preached; how God anointed Jesus of Nazareth with the Holy Spirit and with power." The "word" sent to the sons of Israel, and which was published through the whole of Judea, was that God had anointed Jesus. But where was this "word" published? It began in Galilee, after John's immersion. Why had it not been proclaimed before? Because God had not before anointed Him. Why proclaimed just after John's immersion? Because at His immersion He was anointed with the Holy Spirit and with power. This is absolutely certain, and since there is not a single intimation, in all the Book, of any other anointing, we conclude that He was here anointed Prophet, Priest and King.

3. In his confession Peter said: "Thou art *the* Anointed, the Son of the living God"—the Prophet, Priest and King. Thou *art* the Anointed; not will be, but art now. This is simply exhaustive. There can be no other anointed one, no other anointing. "Upon this truth I will build my church." But if the priestly function constitutes no part of that truth, then his priestly relation constitutes no part of the foundation. Hence we conclude again that He was the anointed priest.

4. "I adjure you by the living God, that you tell us whether you are the Christ, the Son of the living God." "Jesus said to him, You have said." Under oath He affirmed Himself *the*

The Royal Priesthood

Anointed of God, the Prophet, Priest and King. This ought to be conclusive.

5. Into the first tabernacle the high priest went *not* until he was anointed, and then not without blood (Hebrews 9). Even so *the Anointed* entered the Most Holy Place, not without the blood of atonement, which He sprinkled upon the mercy-seat. But only the consecrated and anointed priest of God could have offered that spotless lamb, or stood with the "blood of sprinkling" in the presence of the eternal One. We conclude, then, that Christ was anointed priest at His baptism, and began His work as such when He offered Himself upon the cross, and with His own blood entered the heavens to make atonement for the sins of the world.

We have already seen that all the service of the first tabernacle was typical of the service in the true. In the former service the high priest was washed in the brazen laver, his priestly garments put upon him, his head anointed with oil, and then declared symbolically sanctified by the sprinkling of the blood of atonement. In the true tabernacle services, our great High Priest was washed in the laver of baptism, and anointed by the Spirit of God descending upon Him. He needed no robes of righteousness, for these had ever been around Him, nor did He need any sprinkling of the blood of atonement, for sinless He stood in the presence of the universe.

New Testament Christianity

That the washing of the laver was typical of baptism is, we think, demonstrable, if the whole service of the tabernacle was a type of the Christian economy. Altars in that dispensation were typical of altars in this; sacrifices of sacrifices; blood of blood; sprinklings of sprinklings; pourings of pourings; and washings of washings. In that dispensation, blood, or its substitute (ashes mingled with water), was sprinkled upon the parties to be cleansed. Water alone was never sprinkled upon any one by divine authority. So now, in the New Testament, we read of the sprinkling of blood (Heb. 10:22; 12:24), but never of water. There also the blood was poured out upon Calvary for the sins of the world. In that economy their bodies were washed wholly in water; so now in this also. In that the oil of anointing was poured on Aaron's head, and ran down upon his beard, even upon his garment; so in this the Holy Spirit was poured out upon Christ without measure, "anointing him with the oil of gladness above his fellows."

Again: That the washing of the laver was typical of baptism is positively affirmed by Dr. Fairbairn, of Glasgow, the greatest of all expounders of Scriptural types. In proof of the proposition he quotes the following (Heb. 10:22): "Having their bodies washed in pure water," "where [he says] the symbolic language is entirely retained." Again (Tit. 3:5), "The wash-

The Royal Priesthood

ing of regeneration," and (Eph. 5:26), "Sanctified and cleansed by the washing of water, by the word."

As Aaron was inducted into the priestly office, so were all the Levitical priests. We also are a "royal priesthood," "kings and priests" with Christ. As He was consecrated and anointed, even so we also should be consecrated.

He was washed—went down into the Jordan, and came up out of it again. We also must be washed. But we, being sinners, must have put on the priestly robes of righteousness, without which we could not officiate at the altar; but "he is our righteousness," hence "as many as have been baptized into Christ have put on Christ." In both dispensations the candidate attained to his priestly robes through the washings of the laver, and by baptism, respectively.

Again: As in the former service all things were cleansed by blood, so, in this, "we come to the blood of sprinkling, that speaks better things than the blood of Abel;" but when do we come to this "sprinkling of blood"? Certainly not until we come into the death of Christ. "Know you not that as many of you as were baptized into Christ Jesus were baptized into his death? Therefore we are buried with him, by baptism into death." The Jewish priest passed through the washing of the laver to the sprinkling, we through the waters of baptism; hence, "draw near with a true heart, in full assurance of faith, having our hearts sprinkled from an evil conscience, and our bodies washed with pure water.''

Finally, as Christ was anointed with the Holy Spirit after baptism, so we receive the gift of the Holy Spirit after baptism. Christ went down into Jordan, and came up out of it. The force of His example is deeply felt by the religious world, hence the constant effort made to break it. Christ's baptism, we are told, is no example to us, for, unlike us, He had no sins to be forgiven. True, but He was to become our great High Priest, and this, in harmony with the fulfillment of all righteousness, could not be, unless His body was first washed in the laver of baptism.

Are we, then, consecrated priests? If not, how dare we officiate at the altar? Have our bodies been washed in the laver of baptism? Have we gone down into the tide and come up out of it as did the Saviour? If not, let the fate of Korah and his companions be a warning to us. If, in the type, men perished because they approached the altar without consecration, how much greater their punishment in the antitype!

Christ's immersion is then, indeed, an example to us. Then, let me stand, like the blessed Saviour, on ''Jordan's strand''; yea, let me put my feet in the tracks He left in its yielding sands; like Him, lie beneath its liquid wave, and rise with Him, a royal ''priest for ever.''

THE FELLOWSHIP

ISAAC ERRETT

IT does not need to be argued here that the second chapter of Acts contains a record of the first sermon that announced a complete redemption; the first accomplishment of the promised mission of the Holy Spirit to convict sinners and comfort saints (John 16:7-14); the first authoritative announcement of Jesus as Lord and Christ; the first publication of the law of pardon under the reign of the new Lawgiver, and the planting of the first church of Christ. Its importance, therefore, as a starting-point in our labors to restore New Testament Christianity, can hardly be exaggerated. That we have succeeded in developing, from this chapter, the beginning of the reign of the Christ, the mode of the Spirit's operation in the conversion of sinners, the unchanging law of pardon and of initiation into the church of Christ, the infallible authority of the apostles to administer the affairs of the absent Lord, and the simple, spiritual worship of the primitive church, is also, we think, beyond question.

On one subject, however, there has been dimness—that of the fellowship. That the first church adhered as stedfastly to the fellowship as to the teaching of the apostles, is positively affirmed; but precisely what is meant by fellowship, and how they continued in it, has been matter of so much doubt as to leave our churches largely destitute of the blessings of fellowship, and render them failures, so far as this feature of primitive Christianity is concerned.

We propose, therefore, an examination of this word, and of its application in Scripture, that we may ascertain if any definite conclusion can be reached as to its Scriptural import.

If it can be said to have any definite meaning among us, it is understood to signify the weekly contribution of money for benevolent purposes. Taking this as its strict import, there has been among us no other such instance of trifling with a divine ordinance; for the paltry contribution, week by week, of dimes and half-dimes by one-fourth or one-fifth of the members present at a church meeting, is a shameful slurring over of any just idea of *fellowship* in a solemn duty enjoined on all the saints. It is a custom, we take it, "more honored in the breach than in the observance;" for there is just enough done to lull the conscience of the selfish into quietness, and to belittle one's ideas of Christian benevolence, while, for all the great purposes of the true church life, it is so insignificant as to merit only contempt. It is offering the bran to God and keeping the flour

The Fellowship

to ourselves. Is this what is meant by fellowship? Let us see.

Koinonia, here rendered *fellowship*, is not a term of doubtful import. In classic use *koinos* signifies *common, shared in common;* in social and political relations, *common to all the people, public, the common weal;* of disposition, *lending a ready ear to all, impartial; connected by common origin, kindred,* especially of brothers and sisters. These are its principal classic uses, as given by Liddell and Scott. The same authority defines it *communion, community, intercourse.* Its sacred use is given in New Testament lexicons as *fellowship, partnership, participation, communion, aid, relief, contribution in aid.*

It will be seen, at a glance, that unless the Scriptures make a rigorous application of this term to some one specific act or ordinance, the word itself would suggest nothing of the kind, but would rather lead us to think of community of interest or of obligation—of the spiritual kinship established in Christ, the *partnership* of duties, of interest, and of destiny which is peculiar to the great brotherhood called the church of God.

We ask, then, Do the Scriptures limit this term to a specific act or ordinance? The best answer to this is found in the texts in which the word occurs:

Acts 2:42: "They continued stedfastly in the apostles' doctrine and *fellowship.*"

Rom. 15:26: "To make a certain *contribution.*"

1 Cor. 1:9: "Called unto the *fellowship* of his Son."

1 Cor. 10:16: "Is it not the *communion* of the blood? is it not the *communion* of the body of Christ?"

2 Cor. 6:14: "What *communion* hath light with darkness?"

2 Cor. 8:4: "And take upon us the *fellowship.*"

2 Cor. 9:13: "For your liberal *distribution.*"

2 Cor. 13:14: "The *communion* of the Holy Ghost."

Gal. 2:9: "The right hands of *fellowship.*"

Eph. 3:9: "What is the *fellowship* of the mystery?"

Phil. 1:5: "For your *fellowship* in the gospel."

Phil. 2:1: "If any *fellowship* of the Spirit."

Phil. 3:10: "And the *fellowship* of his sufferings."

Philemon 6: "That the *communication* of thy faith."

Heb. 13:16: "And to *communicate* forget not."

1 John 1:3: "May have *fellowship* with us; and truly our *fellowship* is with the Father."

1 John 1:6: "If we say that we have *fellowship.*"

1 John 1:7: "We have *fellowship* one with another."

We add to these the occurrences of

The Fellowship

Matt. 23:30: "We would not have been *partakers.*"

Luke 5:10: "Which were *partners* with Simon."

1 Cor. 10:18: *"Partakers* of the altar."

1 Cor. 10:20: "Ye should have *fellowship* with."

2 Cor. 1:7: "As ye are *partakers* of the sufferings."

2 Cor. 8:23: "He is my *partner* and fellow-helper."

Philemon 17: "If thou count me, therefore, a *partner.*"

Heb. 10:33: "Ye became *companions* of them."

1 Pet. 5:1: "And also a *partaker* of the glory."

2 Pet. 1:4: "Be *partakers* of the divine nature."

It will be readily seen that the term is not restricted to a special use—is limited to no specific application as indicating a particular act or observance of a particular ordinance; but is freely used to express almost every phase of that precious spiritual fellowship which links Father, Son and Holy Spirit with those who are baptized into these sacred names, and all the baptized in one great copartnery. The joint privileges, responsibilities and duties of all the members of this spiritual family, as well as their common relationship to God as their Father, to the Son as their Redeemer, and to the Holy Spirit as their Comforter, all find expression in this word.

It is readily granted that this word is sometimes used in reference to money—joint contributions for benevolent purposes. It is not only readily granted, but we are anxious to have it known, that it may be fully understood that in regard to outlays of money for all good purposes there is a *joint responsibility*—a partnership, from the duties of which no member of the firm is to be allowed to escape. But what we now are desirous to impress upon our readers is, that this does not exhaust the applications of the word; that it has a much wider range, and conveys a much larger idea of our relationships and duties, than can be found in it when this specific application is urged. It expresses partnership in the blessings of the death of Christ (1 Cor. 10:16); in the strength and comfort of the Holy Spirit (2 Cor. 13:14); in the sufferings of Christ (Phil. 3:10); in all the blessings of the gospel (Phil. 1:5); in the favor and protection of God (1 John 1:3).

Nor is it necessary to deny that there is a somewhat special use of the term in the immediate application of it in Acts 2:42. Verses 44 and 45 favor the idea that in its first use it was meant to describe that generous outflow of regenerated hearts in which all participated; but as none of those for whom we are now writing insist on this as any part of the permanent order of the church,

The Fellowship

we have a general agreement that this does not exhaust the import of *the fellowship*, and that we must seek further for a full comprehension of its meaning.

The passage most nearly parallel with Acts 2:42 is 1 John 1:3: *"The things which we have seen and heard declare we unto you* [the apostles' doctrine], *that ye also may have fellowship with us; and truly our fellowship is with the Father and with his Son Jesus Christ. And these things write we unto you, that your joy may be full."*

In the light of the classical and spiritual import of this term, we are constrained to regard the church of God as a grand partnership, in which God and man come into most intimate relations. In this firm there are *divine* partners—the Father, the Son and the Holy Spirit; and these three agree in one. There are also *human* partners. All who are baptized into the name of the Father, the Son and the Holy Spirit enter into partnership with God and with each other, for certain clearly defined purposes.

In brief, these objects are: (1) To redeem a world of perishing sinners from ignorance, sin and death; (2) to educate such as are saved for the dignities and felicities of immortality. To lift men of all nations and all generations from death to life, from sin to holiness, from vileness and shame to glory and honor, and make the heirs of wrath and ruin the inheritors of heaven's immortal honors and delights—this is the mighty enterprise which God has set on foot, to which Father, Son and Holy Spirit give their united treasures of wisdom, love and power, and in which they invite the co-operation of all who have hearts to love and hands to toil.

We stand in the presence of this stupendous scheme, awed into reverence and adoration, and seem to hear the voice of God sounding in our ears: "Take off thy shoes from thy feet, for the ground whereon thou standest is holy ground." To us it is idle to ask for other evidence of the divine origin of the gospel. Any one familiar with the workings of his own heart, or the history of the human race, knows the inevitable tendency to ever-increasing selfishness. The history of our race is a history of grasping selfishness. Self, kindred, sect, country—these exhaust the love and sympathy of the human heart; and ever the free play of these is disturbed within these narrow circles by selfish antagonisms. But *philanthropy*—were does that dwell? Who loves *the race?* What school of uninspired ethics ever taught this sublime virtue? Even after enjoying the light of Christ's teachings for eighteen hundred years, the world and the church are controlled by narrow selfishness; the great lessons of philanthropy are not half comprehended; the earth is drunk with blood; the groans of the oppressed issue even from under the altar; the narrow and

The Fellowship

virulent spirit of sect is the highest inspiration of most religious movements; and

> "Man's inhumanity to man
> Makes countless thousands mourn."

When we see through what slow and painful processes men are enabled to grasp the conception which the gospel furnishes of the love of man as man, and how utterly unworthy are our best conceptions of what is due to our fellow-creatures, who can believe that the selfish heart of man ever gave birth to such a scheme of benevolence as the New Testament unfolds? "Who can bring a clean thing out of an unclean? Not one." Talk not of miracles and prophecies. The grandest of all miracles is the sinless Sufferer dying to redeem the race that scorned Him; and all the tongues and harps of prophets are hushed into dead silence before that matchless oracle, *"God so loved the world, that he gave his only begotten Son, that whosoever believeth on him might not perish, but have eternal life."* Philosophy is dumb; the worthiest religions are abashed; the glories of the grandest empires fade into nothingness; sages, poets, statesmen, heroes—even the purest and best of them—are nothing, and less than nothing, and altogether vanity, when this founder of the everlasting age reveals His wonderful counsel, and projects this divine scheme of the universal brotherhood of man under the Fatherhood of God.

New Testament Christianity

Into this grand partnership all true believers enter. In it they stand on one common platform as brethren in the Lord. All the selfish and wicked distinctions prevailing in human society are lost. There is neither Jew nor Greek, neither male nor female, neither bond nor free, but all are one in Christ Jesus. Redeemed from a common ruin by a common ransom, and made heirs of a common inheritance, they meet on the common level of Christian brotherhood—the rich rejoicing that he is made low, the poor that he is exalted, and all that they are the sons and daughters of the Lord Almighty. No ecclesiastical dignitaries are allowed to take the place of the Lord and be called master. "All ye are brethren." All are priests to God; all constitute God's clergy or heritage (1 Pet. 5:3). The least in the kingdom is, by virtue of his redemption and sanctification in Christ Jesus, greater than the greatest official dignitaries (Matt. 11:11). Nay, it is more to be a member of this grand copartnery than to be the brightest and highest angel in heaven; for the latter are *all* ministering servants of the former (Heb. 1:14), and in their highest ministries they are honored with no such mission as belongs to the members of this fellowship.

Let it now be said—and this brings us into the very heart of our subject—*that every one coming into this partnership brings with him all his capital, and invests it all in the common stock for the benefit of the firm.*

The Fellowship

The highest, deepest, vastest treasures of divine wisdom, love, power, holiness, justice, truth, mercy, compassion and condescension are invested in this scheme. The ineffable glories and riches of Father, Son and Holy Spirit are embarked in it. "The unsearchable riches of Christ," "the depths of the riches of the wisdom and knowledge of God," and the "deep things" of the Spirit, are all funded for the benefit of this enterprise. The universe is laid under tribute; the wealth of the ages belongs to it.

Every convert brings into the common treasury all that he owns. In this fellowship "no man lives to himself." It is written over the door of entrance, "Ye are not your own." It is a mistake to suppose that having "all things common" was peculiar to the church in Jerusalem. That particular form of bestowal and distribution evidently grew out of peculiar circumstances; but in *principle* and in *essence* the religion is the same; and, although a change in circumstances may work a change in the *incidents* of giving, the duty of bringing our all and laying it down at the apostles' feet, to be appropriated under apostolic authority, is the same now as then—*and the Ananiases and Sapphiras who keep back part of the price will yet be carried out dead, as liars against the Spirit of God.*

We are aware that these are "hard sayings," and that many will ask, "Who, then, can be

New Testament Christianity

saved?" We can only reply, "With men these things are impossible, but with God all things are possible." It is time that all who are "at ease in Zion" had a "woe" sounded in their ears that may startle them from their false security. It is time to strip off the delusive idea that any acceptance of doctrine, or any formal observance of ordinances, can avail to save a soul that refuses entire consecration of all its powers to the great aims of the church of God. It is especially due to the integrity of the gospel and the purity of the church that the narrow and mean selfishness which gives to God its tithings of mint and anise and cummin, and reserves for the lusts of the flesh, the lust of the eye, and the pride of life, its wealth of devotion, service and money, should be branded as an accursed thing, and banished without the camp.

As individual stewards of God, we have a control of our means which others have not, and have a right to employ our resources, under a sense of our personal accountability to the Master; but as *partners* in this great scheme, we owe to the firm our *just share* of toil and of money, and of whatever we possess that the partnership needs. We speak not of money only nor chiefly, *but of whatever we possess that the common cause requires.* "Freely ye have received, freely give." "For we, being many, are one body in Christ, and every *one members one of another.*"

The Fellowship

We have said that the ordinary bases of human distinction are ignored in this brotherhood. There is no aristocracy of wealth, nor of intellect, nor of blood. All these are perishable; *but the heart may grow forever.* Goodness is immortal. Love is more than all knowledge, all eloquence, all power. This brotherhood, therefore, is based on *character*—on the possession of the love of God in the heart; for "he that loveth is born of God and knoweth God."

There is, however, a variety of gifts, and there must be wisdom and economy in their appropriation. While, then, all the members of this fellowship stand on a common platform of dignity as children of God, it does not follow that there shall be no official distinctions—no division of labor. God has wisely distributed His gifts so that every one shall have need of His brethren, and all His brethren shall have need of Him. This mutual dependence makes society indispensable, and saves us from lawless invasions of the rights of others. But as equal partners in a mercantile firm, possessing different gifts, will make such a division of labor as will enable every one to work most successfully for the benefit of all—one acting as bookkeeper, another as salesman, another attending to the purchases, another to collections, etc.—so, here, wisdom demands that the variety of gifts shall be classified, and their possessors assigned to such departments of service as will render them most useful to the interests of the partnership. To illustrate:

1. Here is one on whom is bestowed the "gift of tongues." He is an orator. He brings his treasures of eloquence and lays them down at the feet of the apostles. Now, he is under no more obligations to preach the gospel than any other member of the church, except as his gift lies in that direction. It is the business of the partnership to preach the gospel, but the law of the apostles—the directors of this enterprise—is: "As every one has received the gift, so let him minister." "But," this brother says, "I have a family to support; the duty to provide for them is imperative; I can not preach only subordinately to their maintenance." But other members of the partnership come forward and say: "You can preach better than we; can make money better than you. You attend to our preaching—we will see to your money-making. You preach—we will make money; *and we will share.* We will be partners in your preaching, and you shall be a partner in our money-making." *This is "fellowship."* The preaching and the money-making are alike *in the firm.*

2. Here is one gifted to *rule*—a rare gift. It is all-important that it be made available for the general good; and if the general interests require that his whole time be given to this work, then the partnership must see that while he attends to

The Fellowship

their interests, they attend to his. So of teachers, ministers, etc. If the partnership demands all their time, or a considerable portion of it, they must be maintained by the partnership. And then righteousness requires that, in the service of the partnership, *they religiously render service equivalent to that which they receive from it.* If there must be an end to the selfishness and penuriousness of church-members, *there must also be an end to the indolence of preachers.* The round of easy visits at favorite resorts—the daily snooze—the tours of idle gossip—the week-long loungings, fishings and recreations—must give place to hard study and hard work for those who are working for him; and, we opine, there will be less complaint of poorly paid preachers when they earn a fair title to compensation by incessant toil, such as other callings demand in order to success.

3. Praying, singing, exhorting—gifts in these directions are not equally distributed. A wise division of labor in these departments is essential to the complete edification of the church. It should be understood that none is at liberty to withhold the talents which could be employed for the general good, but that, under the direction of the competent authorities, every one shall bring in his capital into the fellowship.

4. Money-making is a gift. Some men are evidently sent into this world on purpose to make money; and, in spite of pulpit homilies and dia-

tribes to the contrary, we hold that those whose gifts from God fit them for successful business life, may "buy and sell and get gain" as religiously as they can pray or sing, and as much "to the glory of God." In no paths of life are there better opportunities to glorify God than in the daily walks of business life, in perpetual contact with men, and amid phases of life and revelations of heart that show the surest avenues to the judgment and conscience, for men's salvation. The error is not in making money, nor so much in bending one's energies to the task—for "whatever is worth doing is worth doing well"; but it is in *failing to bring the gift into the partnership.* These money-makers must learn to continue stedfastly in the "fellowship"; and if they refuse to do so, they ought, after due admonition and patient effort to save them, to be dismissed from the firm. The man of wealth is under as sacred an obligation to bring his money into the partnership as is the orator to bring his gifts of speech, or the musician his gifts of song, or the ruler his ability to govern. Nor, if we have a multiplicity of gifts, can the appropriation of any one of them be accepted in lieu of the others. If we combine wealth and the ability to rule, or the ability to preach, we can not make the bestowal of the gift of preaching a reason for withholding the gift of money, any more than the eyes can insist on rendering precisely equal service with the nose, or the

The Fellowship

hands with the feet. Every member of the body is under obligations to render all the service it can for the general weal; and, whether that be much or little, all the other members are partakers of its benefits. The *principle* is still true which is expressed in the Old Testament: *"They that gathered much had nothing over; and they that gathered little had no lack."*

5. There are many other gifts which we will not take space to enumerate here, which a wise supervision of the interests, wants and capacities of the church will call into exercise. It may be safely laid down as a principle that no member of the partnership should remain unemployed.

This gives to the eldership in our churches a much more responsible task than is generally allowed to them, or than they are willing to accept. An *overseer,* in this partnership, should learn of the various gifts at his disposal. He should be a good judge of men—capable of seeing at a glance the places to be filled, and the persons best qualified to fill them. He should be able to train them for their work, and to go before them in it.

> "And as a bird each fond endearment tries
> To tempt its new-fledged offspring to the skies,
> He tries each art, reproves each dull delay,
> Allures to brighter worlds, *and leads the way."*

When we come to understand the *working* character of the church, the selection of overseers and guides will be a much graver task than at present, and the work of an overseer will be found to demand the highest and rarest qualifications, and daily and hourly attention. Moreover, the insubordination now so prevalent will be condemned as dishonorable and injurious to the general interest, and it will be required that when the appointed rulers direct any one to a given work, it shall be accepted, unless there are satisfactory reasons for declining the task. Let the reader turn to Romans 12 and 1 Corinthians 12 and give them careful attention, and he can not fail to be convinced that the ideal church presented to us in the New Testament is that of a community bound by common ties in a spiritual communism, to the prosperity of which every member is bound to communicate to the full extent of his or her ability; and that its variety of ministries is under a suitable headship. This is the "fellowship" of the Scriptures. The doorkeeper and the ruler—the orator and the janitor—are *partners* in a mutual work.

But while we pass by numerous ministries which a wise oversight will provide for, there are some strangely neglected services to which we feel bound to call special attention.

Why is it that Christian women find so little employment in the service of the church? Not only is their position inferior, but it is largely useless. They do, indeed, make a little work for themselves in a Dorcas society; they are sometimes dignified as deaconesses—it being understood that the sum of their duties is to prepare female candidates for baptism; and if a festival is called for to coax money out of unwilling hands for the purchase of a church carpet, or a new stove-pipe, the culinary skill of the sisters is invoked right earnestly. But except in occasional service of this kind, the sum of woman's duty in the church is to listen reverently, and, with a hymn-book before her, to sing by note. We can not forbear asking, Why this persistent refusal to enlist the warm devotions and generous sympathies and earnest activities of woman in this high service? She is more religious than man. She has greater powers of endurance in patient toil and suffering. There is abundant work which can best be done under the promptings of womanly instincts, and by the gentleness of womanly ministrations. Does not the apostle say, *"There is neither male nor female"?* Let it be granted that there are duties from which her sex and her peculiar organization debar her. Are there not duties enough left for which she is admirably adapted?

Her loving ministries in behalf of the despised Nazarene are among the most touching illustrations of faith and devotion in the Gospel narratives; her stedfast adherence to the Man of sorrows is marred by no cowardice, disgraced by no treachery.

New Testament Christianity

> "Not she with traitorous kiss her Saviour stung,
> Not she denied Him with unholy tongue;
> She, when apostles shrank, could dangers brave—
> Last at the cross, and earliest at the grave."

In the primitive church she shared the labors and honors of the partnership. The women with the men continued, "with one accord," in prayer and supplication till the hour of Pentecostal solemnity and triumph. The promised Spirit came to the *daughters* as well as to *sons*—to the *maidens* equally with the *young men*. Dorcas, Lydia, the daughters of Philip, Phœbe, Priscilla, Euodias and Syntyche are specimens of the active ministers of the church who, in various capacities, were "fellow-workers" with the apostles and brethren. Let us mention some kinds of active service in which godly women might find useful employment.

1. In our cities and large towns there are thousands and tens of thousands of neglected people who never attend church, and whose moral condition would be an offense even to heathenism. They can only be reached by personal visitations, by benevolent attentions, by schools and religious meetings conducted in their midst. There are also thousands of outcasts, driven to a life of shame by the heartlessness of society and the wrongs of offenders who go unwhipped of justice. They are encompassed with the horrors of utter hopelessness, and sink into the depths of crime under the irresistible pressure of a false public sentiment. We

The Fellowship

can not burden this paper with the startling statistics which are now before us—a fearful dishonor to any Christian land.

Now, our ministers and elders and leading men excuse themselves, on the score of pressing engagements, from any labors in these directions; and, generally, we are inclined to regard the excuse as just. But here are intelligent and godly women, who have to toil for daily bread, to whom this would be a welcome work. A very moderate compensation would enlist them at once. They would glide like angels of mercy through these dark scenes of woe and despair, and in the name of Jesus open the prison doors of captive souls, bind up broken hearts, and make known to them that sit in darkness the light of life. Why are they not employed? Who can tell? With the large wealth of intelligence and sympathy and strength that lies idle in our churches, is it possible to go before God free from the blood of these perishing souls?

2. There are much-needed ministries to be established among the homeless sick and dying. Homes, hospitals, asylums, refuges, are needed for the victims of misfortunes. It is the work of the church. It is woman's work. The state may attempt to accomplish it, and we may attempt to stifle our consciences by the reflection that we have paid our taxes; but there is a work for the church which the state can not do—spiritual ends

New Testament Christianity

to be sought which can be reached through no state machinery, and a *sympathetic* labor to be accomplished which no state system can command. Women like Elizabeth Fry, Dorothea Dix, Florence Nightingale, and the nameless host of worthies who, during our late war, were present on battlefield, in the march, in the ambulance, and in every hospital, abundantly and gloriously illustrate the capacity, bravery, endurance and administrative ability of woman in such work. The growing power of the Roman Catholic Church in this country is asserted over the best class of converts by the gentle and loving ministries of her sisterhoods. It is more invincible than logic. You argue in vain in the presence of toilsome, patient and gentle ministries that touch every heart and bring tears to every eye. It hides a multitude of sins. Unless Protestants awake to the demands of the times, and furnish at least equal proofs of needed benevolence, they will be shorn of their power. The power of the primitive church was largely in her divine charities; the church of to-day must not be wanting in this particular, or learning, eloquence, wealth and respectability will not be sufficient to save her from disgrace.

3. The mission work, at home and abroad, opens many channels of usefulness for woman. Where the heaviest amount of labor is private rather than public—and this is the case in almost all new missionary fields—woman can be the ready

The Fellowship

and efficient helper of man. In our own land, among the freedmen, there is employment for thousands of patient, gentle, pious women; and the church has them and ought to send them.

We pretend not to have exhausted, in our statement, the opportunities for profitable employment for Christian women; but we have said enough to show that there *are* such opportunities, and that it is a great folly, if not a great sin, on the part of the church, to shut out so much of her worthiest force from participation in the "fellowship" of labor and of reward.

If we have said but little of *money* as belonging to the fellowship, it is not because we deem it unimportant, but rather because that phase of the subject has been faithfully sketched by other pens, while those phases which have engaged our attention have been largely overlooked. We take occasion to say, however, that in money, as in all other elements of power, there must be *partnership*. It is but a partial restoration of the "ancient order of things" which leaves this unaccomplished. While we are not convinced that there is any divine law prescribing a uniform method of raising money, we are quite sure that, as a general rule, the method prescribed by Paul to the Corinthians and Galatians is the cheapest, easiest, justest and most effective of all known expedients: "On the first day of every week let *every one* lay by him in store, *as God hath prospered him.*" This will always give money in hand, will save all expensive agencies, will keep churches out of debt, and enable them to appropriate to their various benevolent enterprises a fair proportion of means. He who shall educate the churches to faithfulness in this particular will render to the cause of God a service of incalculable value.

Before closing we must offer a few suggestions touching another and most important phase of this subject—fellowship with God and with Christ.

There are many Christian lives that partake more of the bondage of the law than of the liberty of the gospel. They lack sunshine. They are consciously far away from "the fellowship of the Spirit." They are unblessed with any divine manifestations, uncomforted with any "earnest of the inheritance." It is all tame and hard drudgery. They sigh for the light of God's countenance, and sigh in vain. Tell them to read the Scriptures, and they will confuse you with assertions of its utter fruitlessness in their own experience. Urge them to pray, and they will tell you that all their prayers have failed to produce one rift in the clouds that hang in thick darkness over them.

These are cases which need to be treated in the light of these teachings concerning fellowship. A man may live in the church, and share

> "Her sweet communion, solemn vows,
> Her hymns of love and praise,"

The Fellowship

and still fail of joyful fellowship *with his brethren.* Why? Because he is not a *partner* with them in their toils and anxieties. He sings, but he does not work; he prays, but he does not pay; he communes in the Supper, but he does not commune in the sacrifices and toils and cares of the house of God. Consequently, "there is a great gulf" between him and them; while they are rejoicing over the fruits of their labors, and happy in projecting new toils, his barren heart pines in desolation. He lives in the midst of love without enjoying it. *He must come on to the same plane of labor and suffering with them* if he would enjoy their fellowship. And if such a failure shuts one out from the fellowship of *his brethren,* is it strange that it should shut him out from *the fellowship of God?* Not at all. Prayer is indispensable to this fellowship; so is Bible knowledge; but these are not all. A man can not pray himself into fellowship with the *suffering* Christ; he must suffer with Him. He can not read himself into fellowship with the *loving* Christ; he must give himself to similar labors of love, and in such experiences as that life gives him he will be able to interpret the heart of Christ and enter into its sympathies. There will be no lack of influx of heavenly light and peace when we place our souls in a position to receive it. But religion is not mere sentiment, nor a mere creed, nor a ritual; *it is a life.* He who would know its treasures must partake of its life. "If a man love me, *he will keep my sayings;* and he shall be loved of my Father, and I will love him, and we will come unto him and make our abode with him." "Behold, I stand at the door and knock. If any man *hear my voice,* and *open the door,* I will come in and sup with him, and he with me." But the voice of Jesus calls us to share His labors and His sorrows; and if we "open the door," it is to bid Him welcome to take us and guide us into His own paths of self-abnegation and self-sacrifice. It is only in some Gethsemane that we can understand the tempests that swept over His soul, or know the sweet peace that succeeded; only when the world has altogether forsaken us that we can see the strong angel of God at our side; only through the cross that we can reach the crown. The poor woman who cast her living into the treasury of the Lord could have better interpreted the sayings and doings of Jesus, and have approached into a more immediate intimacy with Him, than the most learned and acute of selfish, carnal, ease-loving Pharisees or Sadducees in the land. It is thus that His counsels are hidden from the wise and prudent, and revealed unto babes.

It can not but be evident, in the light of the considerations we have submitted, that our churches have by no means fully entered into "the fellowship." We have resources enough to fulfill our mission, but they fail of appropriation. *There is no genuine partnership* of labor and of expendi-

The Fellowship

ture. The mass of our membership exhaust their piety in church-going, sermon-listening, and the payment of such trifling sums as must be paid to maintain a respectable standing. The genuine workers are few; so are the voluntary contributors. There is no consecration of *all* to Christ—no laying down of all our treasures at the apostles' feet. The result is leanness, barrenness, impotency. We are smitten with mildew and blasting—the locusts and caterpillars eat up our substance. We receive as we give. We give little to God, and we receive little in return. We are shut out from the highest *joys* of spiritual fellowship, because we shut ourselves out from its highest *duties*. We are looking for happiness in a wrong direction. We seek it in selfishness, in ease, in the world's voluptuousness; it is found in giving, in toiling, in suffering, in condescension, in compassion, in self-denial for others' good.

The abode of happiness is in Bethlehem, in Gethsemane, at Calvary, and in the eternal home of love and joy to which *these only* lead. We can only know the "power of Christ's resurrection" after we have known "the fellowship of his sufferings," and have been made "conformable to his death." The beatitudes of the Sermon on the Mount distill not in the souls that riot in abundance and revel in selfish enjoyments. Heaven's immortal fellowships belong only to a brotherhood of heroic and patient sufferers, who have "come

New Testament Christianity

up out of great tribulation, and washed their robes and made them white in the blood of the Lamb.''

Man of sorrows! divine Sufferer! toiling Son of God! teach us to be willing to know the fellowship of Thy labors and Thy sorrows, and to give our little all to Thee, who gavest all for us. Then shall we have fellowship with each other; then will Thy blood cleanse us from all sin; then shall we have unclouded views of Thy glory, and rise to the possession of the everlasting fellowship of heavenly rest and joy.

THE NAME "CHRISTIAN"

ELIJAH GOODWIN

"And the disciples were called Christians first in Antioch."—Acts 11: 26.

HAVING spoken, in this series of discourses, on the new church in contrast with the old Jewish kingdom, and having considered that church under the figure of the human body, of which Christ is the head, and having pointed out some of the leading features or distinguishing characteristics of the church of Christ, as a sect that was everywhere spoken against—in doing which, we have laid down some plain rules by which the true church may always be known—we propose now to speak expressly of the name "Christian," as the great family name of this religious association. This title was merely referred to in the preceding sermon, but we now propose to make it the subject of a separate discourse.

Without stating any particular order to be observed in this lecture, we proceed to observe:

1. That the term "Christian" is derived from the term "Christ." The term "Christ" is translated from the Greek word *kristos*, which means

"anointed." *O Kristos:* the Christ the anointed One. Seeing, then, that the term "Christian" is derived from the term "Christ," which means "anointed," may not all who wear this name Scripturally, or who are Scripturally entitled to it, be regarded as the anointed people of God? Under the old covenant, all the priests were anointed with holy oil. Under the new covenant, all the covenanted people of God are regarded as priests. Peter says: "You are a royal priesthood, to offer up spiritual sacrifices acceptable to God by Jesus Christ" (1 Pet. 2:5). Then, are not these spiritual priests anointed? Their name "Christian" indicates that they are. To this holy anointing the apostle John refers when he says: "Ye have an unction [*Krisma,* that with which any one is anointed, an anointing], and ye know all things" (1 John 2:20). (See also v. 27.)

Now, there was a very great sacredness attached to anointing, under the Old Testament dispensation. I remember, on one occasion, when Saul was seeking the life of King David, having heard that "David had hid himself in the hill of Hachilah, which is before Jeshimon," that he marched his army of "three thousand chosen men" into the wilderness of Zeph, and pitched his tent "in the hill of Hachilah, which is before Jeshimon." Wearied with the march, he and his army lay down to rest, leaving Abner, his captain, to keep guard; but he also fell into a deep sleep.

The Name "Christian"

David, seeing their position and condition, from the hill, took Abishai, and went even unto Saul. There he lay, wrapped up in profound sleep, and there lay his entire army in the same condition. "Then Abishai said to David, God hath delivered thine enemy into thy hand this day: therefore let me smite him, I pray thee, with the spear even to the earth at once. And David said to Abishai, Destroy him not: for who can stretch forth his hand against the Lord's anointed, and be guiltless?" (1 Sam. 26:8, 9). They took Saul's spear, and the cruse of water from his head, and left him to enjoy his sleep. Thus, notwithstanding Saul was anointed with a direct warrant from God, and though he had been pursuing David for a long time, fully resolved upon his death, yet even when David had him completely in his power, he would not touch him, just because he had been anointed. Addressing Saul afterward, he said: "The Lord delivered thee into my hand to-day, but I would not stretch forth my hand against the Lord's anointed" (1 Sam. 26:23).

The chapter contains a very important lesson, which all would do well to study; but I have merely referred to it to show how sacred this anointing was regarded. Hence God said: "Touch not mine anointed, and do my prophets no harm" (1 Chron. 16:22). Then, if Christians are God's anointed ones, as their name teaches, oh, how sacred are they in His sight! If His ancient people, who were only a type of Christians, were to Him as dear as the apple of His eye, what must be His tender care for those who are His according to the stipulations of the new and better covenant? Who would not be a Christian, in view of this glorious fact?

2. This name is a name of distinction, intended to distinguish those who wear it from all other people. Indeed, this is the only use we have for names. We use proper names for the purpose of distinguishing one person or thing from another person or thing. Doubtless this is the reason why the Lord, in the beginning, permitted our father Adam to give names to all the cattle, and fowls of the air, and beasts of the field. This was done, so that in all coming time every kind of living creature might be distinguished by name.

Well, the same is true in reference to organized societies. Whether the society be literary, political or religious, it must have a name, so it may be known when it is spoken to or spoken of. Now, when this new man, or church, was set up, there were very many religious sects and parties in the world, and each of these had its respective name; hence it was necessary that this church should also have its name. It is also worthy of remark that ancient names usually expressed some quality or circumstances connected with the persons or things to which they were applied. Adam means

The Name "Christian"

earthly, red; Moses, taken out of the water; Herod, the glory of the skin; Pharisees, separatists, etc. How natural, then, that this new church should be called "Christian," which would not only distinguish it from all other parties then in existence, or that ever should come into being, but that, by this significant title, the purity of their hearts and lives might be expressed, and they pointed out as the anointed children of God.

3. The term "Christian" is intended to point out those who bear it as the property of Christ. It implies that they are not their own, but that they belong to Christ, being bought with His precious blood. Peter, in giving directions to the elders, says they should not discharge their duties "for filthy lucre, but of the ready mind; neither as being lords over God's heritage, but being examples to the flock" (1 Pet. 5:3). In this Scripture, the church is called the heritage of God. The term which is here rendered "heritage" is *kleeros*, which occurs thirteen times in the New Testament. It is translated in the Common Version, "lot" eight times, "part" twice, "inheritance" twice, and "heritage" once; namely, in the Scripture just quoted. This word literally means "a lot." Dr. McKnight, in his note upon this verse, says "the word *kleeros* properly signifies 'a lot.' But because the land of Canaan was divided among the Israelites by lot, the word came to signify 'an heritage.' Wherefore, believers being

God's people, or portion, the different churches, or congregations for worship, are called here God's heritage. In process of time, the name *kleeros* (clergy) was appropriated to the ministers of the gospel, because, being considered as the successors of the Levitical priests, they were regarded as God's lot, or portion.''

Yes, Christian reader, that is the way this term became the exclusive title of preachers. At the beginning, it was not so. The Lord's people is His portion, over whom these elders were not to act as lords; for the apostle says: "Not as being lords over God's heritage"—God's lot, or clergy. Every true and faithful disciple of Christ belongs to the clergy; and hence it is a very presumptuous procedure for any class of men to appropriate this title exclusively to themselves. But I know no one name, ever used as the name of an organized body of people, that points out those to whom it is applied as the people of God, with so little circumlocution as the name "Christian."

But I fear that all who bear this name do not always consider this truth as they should. Do you, Christian reader, when you call yourself a Christian—or when you speak of yourself as belonging to the Christian congregation—appreciate the fact that you are not your own, that you are the property of the Lord, and, therefore, that you ought to "glorify him in your body and spirit, which are his"?

The Name "Christian"

4. The name "Christian" is a catholic name, intended to swallow up all other ecclesiastical titles. As we have seen, there were many religious parties when Christ came into our world, and each party had its respective religious cognomen; but the church which Jesus built was intended to embrace the good of all parties, hence this new, catholic body should be called by a truly catholic name, which would apply alike to the members of this new body, or church, wherever found. Such is the name "Christian."

When a Jew was baptized into this body, he left his former name on the other side of the baptismal wave, and arose on the Lord's side of the line that separated them that serve the Lord from them that serve him not, bearing the simple name "Christian." When a Gentile obeyed the gospel, he left his old name behind, and was now known as a "Christian." This great family title swallowed up all others, and designated the people of God without any accompanying, qualifying terms.

Antioch, too, seems to have been the most fitting place to first bestow that name, this being the first Christian congregation which was composed of persons from both nations. In Jerusalem, and the regions round about, there were congregations of disciples of Christ formed exclusively of believing Jews. In Samaria, many of the Samaritans "believed Philip, preaching the things concerning the name of Jesus Christ, and were baptized." At the house of Cornelius, many of the Gentiles embraced the truth, and became the disciples of Christ. Still, they kept up a kind of division between Jew and Gentile. But in Antioch these two were made visibly one. Here was a congregation formed of members from both nations, and hence it was right, it was appropriate, to give the great family name at this place; and therefore *"the disciples were called Christians first in Antioch."*

5. My fifth proposition in reference to the important name is that it is a patronymic name. I mean by this, that it is intended to refer to the founder of the church and the author of our holy religion. A patronymic name simply means "a name of men or women, derived from that of their parents or ancestors" (Webster). But the names of states, kingdoms, cities, societies or churches, derived from the founders of these organisms, are also patronymics. Pennsylvania is a patronymic name, and refers to William Penn, the honest old Quaker from whom the State was named; Washington, when applied to the capital of the United States, is a patronymic name, referring to that celebrated chieftain who is so justly styled the "Father of His Country." So, the name "Lutheran" is a patronymic name, derived from the great reformer, Martin Luther, who is regarded as the founder of that religious denomination that is called by that name. Wesleyan is another name of the same sort.

The Name "Christian"

So, the name "Christian" is a patronymic name, derived from Christ, the builder of the church (see Matt. 16:18), and the author of the religion of the New Testament. All such names have a commemorative influence. As long as towns and cities are called "Washington," the name of that great man will never be forgotten; as long as there is a religious denomination called "Lutherans," so long will the name of that mighty reformer be handed down to posterity. Should all the records of the sayings and doings of Martin Luther be buried in oblivion, yet would his name be repeated and remembered every time the name of that church is called; and those who wear the name would still talk to each other and to their children of the deeds of the reformer, and thus he would still be remembered by his followers.

So, the name "Christian" carries the name "Christ" in its own bosom, and as long as there is a people on earth called by that name, the author and finisher of the Christians' system of faith can never be forgotten.

This can not be said of any other *church name* known to me. The name "Episcopalian" would remind one of bishops; the name "Presbyterian" would remind one of aged persons, or elders, as officials in the church; the name "Methodist" would suggest the idea of a body of persons who work by method; but not one of these ever directs the thoughts to Christ, the Son of the living God.

New Testament Christianity

And even the Scriptural names—brethren, saints, disciples—without some adjunct, would not do it. These are Scriptural terms, and no disciple of Christ should be ashamed to wear them; but still, the pronunciation of them does not so directly lift the thoughts to Christ, as the simple appellative "Christian." No wonder that the apostle should say: "If any man suffer as a Christian, let him not be ashamed, but let him glorify God on this account" (1 Pet. 4:16).

6. This name "Christian" seems to have been given by divine authority. This is my sixth proposition in reference to this consecrated name.

This seems to be reasonable. If Christ built the church; if He gave its constitution and laws and ordinances; if He is the head of the church—is it not reasonable that He should name it?

I will here introduce some remarks of the very learned Dr. A. Clark, upon this subject. As he was a minister of the Methodist Episcopal Church, he can not be supposed to have any sectarian or traditionary partialities for this name. In his notes upon Acts 11:26 he says: "The word *chreematisai*, in our common text, which we translate 'were called,' signifies, in the New Testament, to appoint, warn or nominate by *divine* direction. In this sense, the word is used in Matt. 2:12; Luke 2:26, and in Acts 10:22. If, therefore, the name was given by divine appointment, it is most likely that Paul and Barnabas were directed to

The Name "Christian"

give it, and that, therefore, the name 'Christian' is from God, as well as that grace and holiness which are essentially required and implied in the character. Before this time, the Jewish converts were simply called, among themselves, *disciples*— *i. e.*, scholars—*believers, saints, the church,* or *assembly;* and by their enemies, *Nazarenes, Galileans, the men of this way,* or *sect;* and perhaps by other names which are not come down to us. They considered themselves as *one family*, and hence the appellation of 'brethren' was frequent among them. It was the design of God to make all who believed of *one heart* and *one soul*, that they might consider Him as their Father, and live and love like children of the same household. A *Christian*, therefore, is the highest character which any human being can bear upon earth; and to receive it from God, as these seem to have done, how glorious the title!"

Again, the Doctor says in his general remarks at the end of the chapter: "It appears that 'Christian' was the first *general* appellation of the followers of the blessed Lord, and there is presumptive evidence, as we have seen, that this appellative came by *divine appointment*. How very few of those who profess this religion are satisfied with this title. That very church that arrogates *all* to itself has totally abandoned this title, and its members call themselves *Roman Catholic,* which is absurd; because the *adjective* and *substantive* include *opposite* ideas; *catholic* signifies *universal,* and *Roman* signifies *belonging to Rome.* If it be merely *Roman,* it can not be *catholic;* if it be catholic, it can not be confined to Rome; but it is not catholic or universal, in any sense of the word, for it contains but a small part of the people who profess Christianity. The term 'Protestant' has more common sense in it, but not much more piety. Almost all sects and parties proceed in the same line; but 'Christian' is a title seldom heard of, and the spirit and practice of Christianity but rarely occur. When all return to the spirit of the gospel, they will probably resume the appellative of 'Christian.'"

I have introduced this long quotation from Dr. Clark, for three purposes:

(1) To show, to the reader of this discourse, the reasons which the Doctor had for thinking that the name "Christian" was given by divine authority, and thus to place this great and good man in favor of the proposition now under consideration.

(2) To present his views of the cause which led to an abandonment of this *name* as a church name, and the adoption of other, sectarian and unauthorized titles. He says: "When all return to the spirit of the gospel, they will probably resume the appellative 'Christian.'" This shows that this name was dispensed with by a departure from the spirit of the gospel. This is the unvarnished truth in the case. The Doctor's criticism on the

The Name "Christian"

name "Roman Catholic" is very just *and true* and forcible; but, with the same skill and learning which he employed, many other church names might be shown to be as inconsistent. There is the name "Protestant Episcopal Church." The Doctor admits that the name "Protestant" has not much more piety in it than the name "Roman Catholic." But take the entire name, and what does it mean? "Protestant" means "one of the party who adhered to Luther, at the Reformation in 1529, and protested against a decree of Emperor Charles V. and the Diet of Spires; and appealed to a general council" (Webster). Episcopal is translated from *episkopos,* which means overseer; church is from *ekklesia,* which means assembly, congregation. Then, *Protestant Episcopal Church* would mean a congregation of overseers protesting against a decree of Charles V. *Methodist Episcopal Church* would mean a congregation of overseers, all acting by method. *Baptist Church* means a congregation of baptizers. How much more does either of the above examples accord with truth and consistency than the name "Roman Catholic"?

(3) But my third object in introducing the Doctor's testimony was to show his views of the use that will likely be made of the name "Christian" *"when all return to the spirit of the gospel."* From what he says, he must have believed in a time to come when all true believers in Christ will return to the spirit of the gospel; and

that when that time comes, all these party names will be laid aside, and the followers of the blessed Saviour will be simply called "Christians." And oh, who does not long to see such a time? Then, as at the beginning, if any man shall say, "I am a Christian," all will know his religious position. It will not have to be asked, "What church do you belong to?" The name "Christian" will show.

It may not be improper to notice the three passages of Scripture referred to by Dr. Clark, to illustrate or confirm the meaning which he has attached to the Greek word *kreematizo*. These are Matt. 2:12; Luke 2:26; Acts 10:22. In the first, the name of God is not found in the original; the whole phrase "warned of God" is translated from the simple word *kreematizo*. The same is true in reference to Acts 10:22. The word is rendered "revealed" in Luke 2:26, and the Holy Spirit is named as the agent by whom the revelation is made; but an admonition made by the Holy Spirit is of the same divine authority as if made by the heavenly Father Himself. These examples show very clearly that the king's translators understood this term *kreematizo* to signify, as Greenfield has defined it, "in the New Testament, to impart a divine warning or admonition; give instructions or directions under the guidance of inspiration."

This word occurs nine times in the New Testament, and is translated, in the Common Version,

The Name "Christian"

"warned of" (or "from") "God," four times; "revealed," once; "called," twice; "that spake," once, and "admonished," once. In all these occurrences of the word, there are but two that admit of any doubt as to the fact that the warning, revealing or speaking came by divine authority. These are Rom. 7:3 and Acts 11:26. In Rom. 7:3, "She *shall be called* an adulteress," surely means more than that she shall be so styled by her enemies, or by the people; it signifies that she shall be so called *by the will of God.* So I think in our text it means that the disciples *were called Christians* by the divine authority which Paul and Barnabas received from God.

In further proof of the proposition that the name "Christian" is of divine origin, we will compare Amos 9:12 with Acts 15:16, 17. The former reads thus: "At that day, I will raise up the tabernacle of David that is fallen down, and close up the breaches thereof, and I will raise up his ruins, and I will build it as in the days of old, that they may possess the remnant of Edom, and of all the heathen which are called by my name." The latter reads: "After this, I will return, and will build again the tabernacle of David, which is fallen down; and I will build again the ruins thereof, and will set it up; that the residue of men might seek after the Lord, and all the Gentiles upon whom my name is called, saith the Lord, who doeth all these things."

New Testament Christianity

1. My first remark upon these Scriptures is that whatever is done, or is to be done, in fulfillment of them, is the work of the Lord, for it is here declared that *"the Lord doeth all these things."*

2. The apostles understood Amos 9:12 to apply to the Christian church in the gospel dispensation. At the time the apostle James made this quotation, the apostles and elders of the church at Jerusalem were sitting in solemn council, deliberating on one of the most important questions that had ever disturbed the church of God. The question was: May the Gentiles become Christians, and be saved, without being circumcised—without becoming Jews by proselytism? In order to prove that the Gentiles may be saved without being circumcised, and keeping the law of Moses, James quotes Amos 9:12. "The heathen," in Amos, and "the Gentiles," in Acts, mean the same people.

Now, if James had not understood the prophecy of Amos to apply to the church of Christ in the gospel day, he could not have used this Scripture in defense of his position. And had the other apostles believed that this prophecy had a literal meaning, and is to be fulfilled at some far-distant day, they surely would have made their objection to James' application of it. But we hear of no such objection, hence we must conclude that they were all of one mind upon this subject.

3. We see that, according to this prophecy, the Lord's people were to be called by His name, in

The Name "Christian"

the gospel dispensation. *"To be called by my name,"* as in Amos, and *"upon whom my name is called,"* as in Acts, mean the same thing.

Now, I ask, How is it that the Lord's people were to be called by His name? Are they so called now? Or have they ever been? What is meant by being called by His name?

In answer to this question, and in further illustration of the position now assumed, I will here introduce a quotation from the learned and pious B. W. Stone, who now rests in paradise:

"The Greek verb *epikaleomai* is both in the passive and middle voice, and signifies both passive and active. In the New Testament, when its passive voice occurs, it uniformly signifies 'surnamed,' or 'called'—when its middle voice occurs, it as uniformly signifies 'to invoke,' 'call upon,' or 'appeal to.'

"I will bring to view the texts in the New Testament where the passive of this verb is used, and commonly translated 'surnamed.' Matt. 10:3: 'And Lebbeus, whose *surname* was Thaddeus.' Luke 20:3: 'Then entered Satan into Judas, *surnamed* Iscariot.' Acts 1:23: 'And they appointed two, Joses called Barsabas, who was *surnamed* Justus.' Acts 4:26: 'And Joses, who by the apostles was *surnamed* Barnabas.' Acts 10:5: 'And now send men to Joppa, and call for one Simon, whose *surname* is Peter.' The same phrase occurs in the eighteenth and thirty-second verses, and also in chap. 11:13. Acts 12:12: 'He came to the house of Mary, the mother of John, whose *surname* was Mark.' The same occurs in the twenty-fifth verse. Acts 15:22: 'Judas, *surnamed* Barsabas.' James says (2:7): 'Do they not blaspheme that worthy name by which ye are called?' or *surnamed*, for it is the same word.'' Undoubtedly this name blasphemed was *Christ*, or *Christians*. Now, reader, notice. ''The prophet Amos says (9:12): 'And of all the heathen which are called by my name.' James quotes this passage in Acts 15:17, thus: 'And all the Gentiles upon whom my name is called.' This demonstrably proves that the phrase *to be called by my name* is the same as *upon whom my name is called.*

''This phraseology is of frequent occurrence in the Old Testament, and signifies there surnames attached to their proper names. Israel was one of those names; for in this name is *El*, the Hebrew name for God. This was the name given by the Lord to Jacob, and by this name were all his children called—the children of Israel. Thus, the phrase, 'the Gentiles who are called by thy name,' or, 'on whom thy name is called,' is the same as that 'by which ye are called,' or *surnamed*, which all must agree to be Christian, after Christ.''— *Chr. Mess.*, Vol XIV., pp. 161, 162.

Then, to be called by the Lord's name, according to Amos 9:12, is to be called ''Christian.'' To make this matter more plain, read Dan. 9:19:

The Name "Christian"

"O Lord, hear; O Lord, forgive; O Lord, hearken and do; defer not, for thine own sake, O my God, for thy city and thy people are called by thy name." Now, on what other principle was this true, except the one that was named above? *El,* one of the Hebrew names for God, is incorporated in the word "Israel": hence, whenever the name "Israel" was pronounced, the name of God was pronounced. When God gave Jacob this name, he placed His own name upon him. Well, then, might the prophet say: *"Thy people are called by thy name."*

So, the name of Christ is embosomed in the name "Christian"; and hence, whenever that name is pronounced, the name of Christ is spoken. Surely the apostle had reference to this fact when he said: "If you be reproached for the name of Christ, happy are you" (1 Pet. 4:14). According to this same apostle, to suffer as a *Christian,* and to suffer for the name of Christ, is the same thing. He says if you are reproached for the name of Christ, you are happy. "But let none of you suffer as a murderer, or a thief, or as an evil-doer, or as a busybody in other men's matters; yet, if any man suffer as a *Christian,* let him not be ashamed." Thus are the phrases *"for the name of Christ,"* and *"as a Christian,"* used interchangeably, as both meaning the same thing.

The same fact is referred to by the apostle when he says: "Do not rich men oppress you, and draw you before the judgment-seat? Do they not blaspheme that worthy name by the which you are called?" (Jas. 2:6, 7). This worthy name was surely the name of Christ or Christian, by which they were called. How appropriate, then, was the response of the king, when he had heard the argument of Paul in favor of Christianity: "Almost thou persuadest me to be a Christian" (Acts 26:28). The king was almost persuaded to receive the Christian faith, adopt the Christian's course of life, and take upon him that worthy name by which the disciples of Christ were called. But, alas! he was only *almost* persuaded. And how many go this far, and yet die in their sins!

The prophet Isaiah, fired with the spirit of inspiration, looked forward to the gospel day, and said: "You shall leave your name for a curse unto my chosen, for the Lord shall slay thee, and call his servants by another name." And again: "Thou shalt be called by a new name which the mouth of the Lord shall name" (Isa. 65:15; 62:2). Now, I ask, what is this new name? Dr. Clark says this new name is "Christian." If he is correct, then the name "Christian" is given by the mouth of the Lord.

If this new name is not "Christian," then this prophecy has never been fulfilled; for this is the only *new name* by which the people of God were called in the New Testament. They are called saints because of the purity of their hearts and

The Name "Christian"

lives, but this is an Old Testament name. They were called brethren, but this is no new name. David said: "Behold, how good and how pleasant it is for *brethren* to dwell together in unity" (Ps. 133:1). They were called disciples, but this name was known to the Old Testament saints, and was also applied to students of the different schools of philosophy. Indeed, I remember no new name by which the followers of the Lord were called, save the name "Christian." It was a *new name*, emphatically; a name unknown to Jew or Gentile until Paul and Barnabas had assembled with the church at Antioch a whole year, and had taught much people. Then it was, while these divinely authorized teachers were fully instructing the people in the holy will of God, that the disciples were called Christians *first*. Then was fulfilled the word of the Lord, which saith: *"You shall be called by a new name, which the mouth of the Lord shall name."*

I will now proceed to answer some objections to making this the name of the church, and to considering it a name of divine origin.

1. It may be objected that if it can be proven that this name came by divine direction, as the surname, or family name, of the Lord's people, then we should discontinue every other New Testament name. But I can not see why this should be so. The Lord changed the name of Jacob to Israel, but he was often called Jacob after that, and even

his descendants were called Jacob, as a national title. "The Lord's portion is his people; Jacob is the lot of his inheritance" (Deut. 32:9), was said near three hundred years after Jacob's name was changed to Israel by divine authority. Why, then, may not the followers of Christ answer to any name that was acknowledged by the disciples of Christ in the days of the apostles, and still regard the name "Christian" as the great family name which the mouth of the Lord hath named? Paul addressed the members of the church as saints, the servants of God, the beloved brethren, and yet he said: "I bow my knees to the Father of our Lord Jesus Christ, of whom the whole family in heaven and earth is named" (Eph. 3:14, 15). This must mean that the family was named "Christian" after Christ.

2. But it is said, by those who wish to justify themselves in wearing other and unscriptural names, that the name "Christian" was given to the disciples of Christ by their enemies, as a name of reproach.

Now, I can not see any reason for such a conclusion. They were called by some names by their enemies out of contempt, but we never read of any apostle or disciple acknowledging these names. Can you suppose, dear reader, that if the apostle Peter had known that this name came from the enemies of the cause of Christ, he would have left it on record for the comfort of the Lord's

The Name "Christian"

people to the end of time? "If any man suffer as a Christian, let him not be ashamed, but let him glorify God on that behalf," or account. Why did he not say, If any man suffer as a Nazarene? Because he would not give countenance to a name which had been hurled at him and his brethren out of contempt.

When King Agrippa said to Paul, "Almost thou persuadest me to be a Christian," would the apostle have given countenance to that name, as he did, had he known that it originated in the dark, black hearts of the children of the wicked one? Suppose some of our brethren should be preaching to a congregation, and, while urging the holy claims of Christianity upon his audience, one should arise and say, "Well, sir, you have almost persuaded me to be a Campbellite," would he be likely to reply: "I would to God that you, and all who hear me to-day, were not only almost, but altogether, such as I am"? By no means. If he thought the man sincere, but ignorant of the right way of the Lord, he would be likely to say: "My dear friend, I am not trying to make Campbellites; I only desire for you to become a Christian."

There is a sect of Methodists in England who, on account of their religious exercises, are called Ranters. Now, suppose, at the close of a sermon delivered by one of the preachers of that party, some one should speak out in the crowd, and say,

New Testament Christianity

"Almost thou persuadest me to be a Ranter," what do you think the preacher would say? Surely, he would not acknowledge the name "Ranter" on such a solemn occasion as this. No, nor would Paul, standing before the king's court, not knowing but he was making his last public address on the subject of salvation through the blood of Christ, with legal chains upon his emaciated person, and all the sanctions of his apostolic office resting upon his conscience, have even appeared to sanction a name which had been hurled at the church of God by the bitter opposers of the blessed Jesus. But he did acknowledge the name "Christian," by saying: "Would to God that not only thou, but also all that hear me this day, were both almost, and altogether such as I am, except these bonds" (Acts 26:29).

3. But this name is objected to, as a church name, because it is too exclusive. For a church to call itself the *Christian Church,* they say, seems to imply that none other are Christians; it is appropriating a name, which of right belongs to all the people of God, to one individual party of the disciples of Christ.

But, if there is anything wrong in this, I ask, At whose door does the sin lie? At the door of these who are endeavoring to return to the *old paths*—that are laboring to bring the church of God to apostolic ground in all things? or does it lie at the door of those who have departed from the primitive order of things, and have assumed human names by which to distinguish themselves? Surely if there is any sin in the case, those who have taken names which God has not authorized must account to the Judge of the living and the dead for that sin.

It must be admitted by all that there was a time when this name was not too exclusive. It was not too exclusive when Peter said: "If any man suffer as a Christian, let him not be ashamed, but let him glorify God on that account." And had the church remained pure, or, according to Dr. Clark, had she not departed from the spirit of the gospel, this name would not be too exclusive now.

I am willing to admit that it would be wrong for a body of people, organized upon a constitution, or confession of faith, of human origin, and governed by laws of their own enacting, to call themselves the *Christian Church*. They may—nay, they should—adopt a name corresponding with the nature of their organism; but I doubt the propriety of their claiming to be the church of Christ, after they have thus organized.

When we repudiate all unscriptural titles, and adopt the names by which the first followers of Christ were called, we do it from principle. Beholding the awful ravages which sectarianism has made upon our holy religion—the army of the Lord's hosts being thus weakened—while the

New Testament Christianity

prince of darkness is mustering his combined forces against the Lord, and against His anointed, saying, "Let us break their bonds asunder, and cast their cords from us;" and while infidels and skeptics were laughing at the division among the Lord's people—we began to inquire for the cause. It was soon discovered that party spirit had originated party creeds, and party organizations upon those creeds had given birth to party names, and that these things were standing directly in the way of the success of the gospel and the salvation of sinners.

We therefore resolved to clear ourselves of the responsibility of resting upon those who caused or kept up this state of things. But how was this to be done? Shall we form a more liberal creed than any now in existence, and try to bring all to that? We could not hope to do that. But should we bring many of the more liberal-minded to unite with us on such a creed, we would only have made one more sect, and those who remained upon their old party platforms would justly charge us with presumption, for asking them to unite with us, while they had just as good a right to make a creed, and originate a party, as we had. And then we feared to meet the awful question in the last day: *"Who hath required this at your hands?"* We therefore resolved to take our stand on the Bible alone—determined to reject everything in Christianity for which we could find no precept

The Name "Christian"

or precedent in the teaching of the apostles of the Lamb.

Now, no one will say that this was wrong; for to say so would be to say that the church of Christ, under the immediate inspection, direction and supervision of the holy apostles, commenced its career in error!

Then, if the principle upon which we set out was right, what could we do but adopt Scriptural names? When we adopt the name "Christian" as the family name of God's people, we mean no disrespect for any body of people on earth; we do not do it for the purpose of exalting ourselves, or abasing others; we are driven to it by the holy principles which we have adopted. We do it, therefore, from principle, and to exalt Him by whom are all things, and for whom are all things.

4. It is sometimes urged, as an objection to this name, that it is too assuming; it is taking too high ground. But, I ask, was it taking too high ground for the disciples to be called Christians first at Antioch? If it was not too assuming then, it ought not to be so considered now.

5. But it is objected that the church is not worthy of so sacred a title. I once heard of a good old Baptist brother saying, when the subject of changing the name "Baptist" for the name "Christian" was under discussion: "I am opposed to the change. Now, that I am a Baptist, I know; but whether I am a Christian admits of serious

New Testament Christianity

doubts—and hence I am opposed to taking that name as a church title." And I fear that many who profess to have taken the Scriptures of divine truth as their only directory in all things pertaining to Christianity sometimes feel the same embarrassment. How often they seem to blush, and hesitate, when asked what church they belong to. Some will say Reformers, or something else, rather than come square out and say, "I profess to be a Christian—I am a member of the church of God."

But, suppose we admit that none of the ecclesiastical organizations are worthy of this name, and that we, after all our efforts to restore primitive Christianity to the church, or to restore the church to primitive Christianity, have not yet arrived to a point in Scriptural order and Scriptural holiness that would justify us in taking this sacred name, what shall we then do? Shall we remain where we are, and take to ourselves some name more in accordance with our low state of morals? Or, would it not be better to hold on to the name, and try to bring the church up to a point in Christian perfection where she might consistently wear the name? This certainly would be the better course. Whenever a person professing Christianity says that he is not worthy of the name, I would advise him to do one of two things at once: either *reform* or *renounce*. Reform in spirit and manners until he could wear the name without blushing, or renounce the profession altogether. But, for the

The Name "Christian"

Lord's sake, and for his own soul's sake, I would advise the former.

But it may be said, after all, that names are small matters—that it makes no difference by what name we are called, so the heart is right—that, therefore, though we are right in wearing the name "Christian," still they are not wrong in adopting other names.

But, my dear reader, do you suppose that Christ has no regard for the name by which His people shall be called? If the Lord built the church, and gave it all its laws and ordinances, as clearly shown in the first discourse in this book—if He is the head of the church—if He loved the church, and gave Himself for it—if He sympathizes with the church so much as to regard an act done to the church as done to Himself, as shown in our second discourse—I say, if all these things are so, He must have a will in reference to the name by which His people shall be called. He watches over the church with a kind, but jealous, eye. He will not allow His glory to be given to another.

If it is an honor to a man to have towns, cities and organized societies called for him, is it not still more honor to have churches called for us? Should a portion of the members of the Lord's body organize themselves into a party, and take to themselves the name of some good and great man, would not this be giving to another person a portion of the glory that belongs to Christ? Can we do this, and be guiltless?

But I will leave this investigation with the reader, after propounding one question which I desire every one who may read this discourse to ponder well, in the light of sound reason and of revelation. Here it is:

Can anything be religiously right and Scripturally wrong, at the same time? Can any church name be religiously right when it is unauthorized by the word of God?

Remember, reader, the name of the church is a religious matter, and should be governed by the Holy Scriptures, as long as we hold the great truth that the Bible is higher in authority than the church.

I will now close this discourse with a few words of advice to those who stand upon the Bible, who wear the Christian name.

Dear brethren, you stand on holy ground. Our religious neighbors are correct when they say that we have taken high ground; that we have assumed an elevated position in the religious world. Oh, then, let us show by our daily walk and conversation that we are sincere. Let us give the enemy no reason to speak reproachfully of us, but let our behavior be such "that they who are of the contrary part may be ashamed, having no evil to say of us." Never be ashamed of the holy name by which you are called.

The Name "Christian"

It was spoken to the praise of the church at Philadelphia that they had not denied the Lord's name. (See Rev. 3:8.) Yes, notwithstanding the corruption of those times, and the persecutions to which the church was exposed—under which all the seven churches in Asia had erred, more or less, save this one congregation—the Lord said to this church: "Thou hast a little strength, *and hast kept my word, and hast not denied my name.*" They still kept the word of God as their rule of faith and practice, and therefore wore the name of Christ—the name "Christian"—and for this they received the approval of the great head of the church.

My brethren, if this name implies that we are the anointed of the Lord, anointed priests, to offer up spiritual sacrifices, holy and acceptable to God through our Lord Jesus Christ; if this name is intended to distinguish the people of God from all other persons; if this name is intended to point out those who wear it, as the Lord's property, the Lord's lot, the Lord's inheritance; if it is a catholic name, intended to bury and swallow up all party names in religion; if it is a patronymic name, referring to Christ, the author of our holy religion and the founder of the church; if the name "Christian" was given by divine authority, of which there is very strong evidence—I say, if all these things are so, what manner of persons ought we to be in all holy conversation?

New Testament Christianity

When Moses approached the burning bush—which burned, but was not consumed—the Lord said unto him: "Put off thy shoes, for the place whereon thou standest is holy ground" (Ex. 3:5). And do not we stand on holy ground? Most assuredly we do; and should we not, then, put off all unrighteousness, and all filthiness of flesh and spirit, and practice holiness in the fear of God?

Brethren, this reformation in which we are engaged has not done its work until the people of God who occupy Bible ground in theory have become so upright, so pious, so devout, so heavenly minded, that all who revere the Bible will be constrained to say, "These people are not only Christians in name, but they are Christians in deed and in truth." Brethren, with the proper effort, made according to the word of God, and with His divine assistance, this may be done.

May the great head of the church help us all to do His will, and make this discourse a blessing to all who may read it, is my sincere prayer. Amen.